Contents

Contents

Prosperity Attraction Made Easy: A Simple Way to Eliminate Doubts & Excuses

by Joe Vitale

Introduction

In most of the things I write and talk about today, you'll hear me mention the word *inspiration*. And there's a reason for this:

It's been the path that has led to my greatest fulfillment.

For example, as a result of learning to hear and follow Divine inspiration, I've been able to transform myself into the world's first self-help musician. I've also been able to begin to bring a sense of mastery and peace into the realm of health and wellness, and pursue what means the world to me – a healthier, more vibrant body.

But this chapter isn't about inspiration, really.

It's about getting whatever is in the way of inspiration *out of the way.*

You see, back when I was homeless and in poverty, struggling to survive, I wasn't listening to or for inspiration. Quite honestly, I wasn't particularly aware of it.

This doesn't mean the Divine wasn't giving it to me, just that I had so many doubts, fears, and limiting beliefs (which then became my excuses) that I wasn't available to hear, let alone follow, the subtlety of inspiration.

And it is subtle.

The voice of inspiration doesn't scream, it whispers.

There are many techniques and methods I've used over the years to rid myself of these limiting beliefs and fears that operate as counter-intentions. Sometimes people refer to them as blocks, but the word *block* just means a belief – and a belief is simply a thought.

Beliefs are thoughts you bought into and *kept repeating*, until that belief seemed like it was reality.

In this chapter, you'll have a chance to explore thoughts that get repeated over and over, as well as play with better ones – new ideas and realities you'd more readily and happily welcome into your life.

The effect of all this will be to become more aware of the thoughts that limit and bind you, thoughts that move you into inspiring directions. And the more you let the Divine know you're interested in being inspired, the more it will participate with you and deliver it. It's a two-way communication.

Ah, but there is a catch.

Every time you receive inspiration, you'll notice *more* niggling doubts come up. This is why it's so important to know how to work with yourself to release them.

Are you ready? Let's get started.

Awareness

"If inspiration is so readily available, where's mine?"

That's the million dollar question, isn't it?

Unfortunately, blocks keep inspiration from happening. Here's how it works: Inspiration comes from the Divine and blocks come from your unconscious belief system. They prevent inspiration into your awareness, into your consciousness.

So, in essence, you have a job – and it all begins by stopping the excuses, stopping the complaining, and focusing on what you have with gratitude. Then, from there, focus on what you would prefer to have.

It's a mind shift.

Sounds simple, right? (I said simple, not necessarily easy.)

Before you can focus on gratitude, though, you'll have to become aware of those limiting beliefs and their underlying fear. The thing about this is that people often don't even know they have fear because they're so used to living with it. They may have lived with it their entire life.

To them, it's "normal" to not have something – even if it's something they'd really like to have.

You know, the old "That's just the way it is" routine.

****

As an exercise, get a piece of paper and write down at the top of the page something you've wanted for a while but for some reason haven't manifested. Below that, draw a line down the middle. On the left side, write down any negative thing you can think of that could occur if you don't have this now or in the future. On the right side, write down any negative thing you can think of that could occur if you do have this.

****

The idea in this exercise is to simply notice that we have hidden counter intentions – fears – that hold us back. They're lurking everywhere, in both the worst of things *and* the best of things.

Pesky little devils…

Nothing like a Good Excuse

Where does fear come from?

It can come from the past, present, or future.

For example, a person may not trust their spouse because they were cheated on in a *past* relationship. People can get cold feet or anxiety when they're ready to take certain actions in the *present,* like launching a new product. Or people can worry about things in the *future* that haven't happened yet, like imagining people criticizing their book before they've even written and published it.

One way to recognize you have fear is to notice your "excuses." Excuses are the thing you say when you're explaining why you don't have something, or you're not being and doing something.

They can cover a pretty wide territory.

For example, a general excuse might be, "This isn't going to work out" or, "This isn't going to work out for me" or, "I don't deserve this" or, "This is too good to be true."

Or, they might sound more specific like, "I don't have the money, I don't have the time, I don't have the skills, I don't have the energy, I don't have the experience, I don't have the education."

Excuses are blocks, so whenever you want something but don't take action, it's because of one of these blocks. At an unconscious level, they're trying to keep you safe and comfortable. Whether you do something and it works out or doesn't work out can create uncomfortable thoughts and feelings – as you saw in the previous exercise.

****

In this exercise, write at the top of your paper the following: Health, Money, Career, Relationship. Then, in each category, write up at least one and up to three desires for that particular area.

For example, in the health category you might write,

I would like to lose 10 pounds.
I would like to eat more organic foods.
I would like to get better nutrition.

After you've completed that, write down any reason you feel you cannot accomplish that. For example, you might write,

I can't don't have the money to buy organic food.
Organic food is too expensive.
I don't have the money to buy vitamins.
I don't have the time (or money) to go to a gym.

****

Now look at your list. Did any of these excuses cross over into other categories?

For example, did you find yourself saying, "I don't have enough time for a relationship" and "I don't have enough time to go to a gym" and "I don't have enough time to make my own fresh and healthy meals?"

That's a clue.

The idea here is to become aware of common things you say to yourself as to why you don't have something (or can't have).

For the next week, pay attention to how often you repeat these excuses either to yourself or to someone else in a conversation — especially when you're out for a relaxed evening with a friend or spouse and just shooting the breeze. In these moments, when your guard is down, your unconscious will try to "slip one by."

I Want This, I Think

In my book, *The Attractor Factor*, I talk about the importance of knowing what you *don't* want. (In fact, it's the first step in the 5-step formula.)

Knowing what you don't want is highly useful information, and here's why: Most people have little or no idea what they actually want.

Don't believe me? Conduct a personal survey and ask 10 people, "If you could have anything you want tomorrow, but only one thing, what would it be?" Notice how many of them can, or can't, give you a quick and clear answer.

One of the easiest ways I know to figure out what you want is by starting with what you don't want and turning it into something you do want.

For example, "I am 50 pounds overweight and I don't want it" becomes "I am 50 pounds lighter and now weigh 150. I love my new weight." The focus is now on being 150 pounds, lighter, and loving it.

Now you'd think it would be simple and straightforward, I know. But I've found that because of our habitual patterns of language, what people don't want often stays at the forefront. In other words, at some level they're actually focusing on the negative (what they don't want) rather than the positive (what they do want).

****

In this exercise, write each of the following statements on a piece of paper. Then, as you go down the list, decide whether the statement reflects something you would want or you would not want. In other words, is it clear? Make a simple notation next to it.

As you do this, remember that people talk like this every day in conversation! (Okay, I did throw a few goofy ones in just to make sure you're awake…and to have a little fun…:-)

I won't be distracted by people's insults.
I'll decrease my anxiety of heights.
I can't stress over being fulfilled.
I can minimize my phobia of losing everything.
I can't be tormented by losing my hair.
I'll end my fear of losing friends.
I'll not worry about reading problems.
I can overcome my anxiety of teachers.
I can't be afraid by starting good habits.
I need to eliminate my phobia of losing money.

I need to not stress over being harassed.

I won't be troubled by hateful people.

I'll control my anxiety of being interviewed.

I can't worry over taxes.

I can remove my phobia of new technology.

I need to not be upset by dieting.

I can conquer my fear of getting a raise.

I'll not stress about losing weight.

I need to rid my anxiety of being inaccurate.

I can't be frightened by insensitivity.

I'll beat my phobia of being gossiped about.

I need to not worry about being hampered.

I won't be distracted by interruptions.

I can lessen my anxiety of the internet going down.

I can't stress over negative body language.

I need to avoid my phobia of being in a rumor.

I can't be tormented by being ignored.

I need to block my fear of intimidating people.

I'll not worry about being stared at.

I can't be afraid of being in the dark.

I need to not stress over the future.

I can stop my fear of being guilty.

I won't be troubled by negative emotions.

I need to restrict my anxiety of getting into arguments.

I can't worry over being hurt.

I'll defeat my phobia of the ocean.

I'll prevent my fear of investing money.

I'll not stress about being investigated.

I can lower my anxiety of being humiliated.

I can't be frightened by negative visualizations.

I need to abandon my phobia of the way I look.

I need to not worry about irresponsible people.

I need to terminate my fear of product warnings.

I won't be distracted by being homeless.

I'll decrease my anxiety of not being trust.

I can't stress over undiagnosed medical symptoms.

I can minimize my phobia of medical examinations.

I can't be tormented by being stoped.

I'll end my fear of the police.

I'll not worry about possible job cuts.

I can overcome my anxiety over feeling helpless.

I can't be afraid by different cultures.

I need to eliminate my phobia of the sun.

I need to not stress over not being talented enough.

I need to stop my fear of the ordinary.

I won't be troubled by selfish people.

I'll control my anxiety of keeping secrets.

I can't worry over being single.

I can remove my phobia of joint venturing.

I need to not be upset by skeletons in the closet.

I can conquer my fear of being insignificant.

I'll not stress about asking for help.

I need to rid my anxiety of hiring outsourcers.

I can't be frightened by the reality.

I'll beat my phobia of having huge wealth.

I need to not worry about using proper etiquette.

I'll stop my fear of being insufficient.

I won't be distracted by jealousy.

I can lessen my anxiety of being fair.

I can't stress over getting an ultimatum.

I need to avoid my phobia of being robbed.

I can't be tormented by getting justice.

I need to block my fear of not completing projects.

I'll limit my anxiety of being incorrect.

I can't be afraid of kissing.

I can get over my phobia of learning something new.

I need to not stress over threats.

I can stop my fear of being incompetent.

I won't be troubled by thinking for myself.

I need to restrict my anxiety of things not working.

I can't worry over not passing a test.

I'll defeat my phobia of being inefficient.

I'll prevent my fear of social conflicts.

I'll not stress about going on a vaccination.

I can lower my anxiety of inconveniences.

I can't be frightened by my nightmares.

I need to abandon my phobia of new traditions.

I need to not worry about being afraid.

I need to terminate my fear of a little physical discomfort.

I won't be distracted by being inadequate.

I'll decrease my anxiety of social gatherings.

I can't stress over reunions.

I can minimize my phobia of paying bills late.

I can't be tormented by being incapable.

I'll end my fear of smiling.

I'll not worry about being laughed at.

I can overcome my anxiety of asking questions.

I can't be afraid by riding on boats.

I need to eliminate my phobia of being inconstant.

I need to not stress over social media or networking.

I need to stop my fear of being scammed.

I won't be troubled by new laws.

I'll control my anxiety of getting laid off.

I can't worry over being rushed.

I can remove my phobia of receiving praise.

I need to not be upset by traffic violations.

I can conquer my fear of traveling.

I'll not stress about social situations.

I need to rid my anxiety of being made fun of.

I can't be frightened by riding on train.

I'll beat my phobia of showing emotions.

I need to not worry about potential lawsuits.

I'll stop my fear of being judged.

I won't be distracted by getting insulted.

I can lessen my anxiety of showing fear.

I can't stress over laying someone off.

I need to avoid my phobia of trees or forests.

I can't be tormented by trying new things.

I need to block my fear of different lifestyles.

I'll not worry about being uninsured.

I'll limit my anxiety of trusting people.

I can't be afraid of showing off.

I can bypass my phobia of learning something new.

I need to not stress over unfriendly people.

I can stop my fear of being manipulated.

I won't be troubled by new experiences.

I need to restrict my anxiety of showing true feelings.

I can't worry over being ripped off.

I'll defeat my phobia of showing weakness.

I'll not stress about learning a new language.

I can lower my anxiety of potential problems.

I can't be frightened by a recession.

I need to abandon my phobia of leaving a safe place.

I need to not worry about trying out weightlifting.

I need to terminate my fear of new clients.

I won't be distracted by new surroundings.

I'll decrease my anxiety of being labeled.

I can't stress over being isolated.

I can minimize my phobia of getting an award.

I can't be tormented by untidiness.

I'll end my fear of new ideas.

I'll not worry about letting go.

I can overcome my anxiety of new drugs.

I can't be afraid of moving.

I need to eliminate my phobia of using new software.

I need to not stress over an unromantic relationship.

I need to stop my fear of being late.

I won't be troubled by being put down.

I'll control my anxiety of having liabilities.

I can't worry over dinner conversations.

I can remove my phobia of being proud.

I can conquer my fear of getting audited.

I'll not stress about my limitations.

I need to rid my anxiety of being questioned.

I can't be frightened by answering the phone.

I'll beat my phobia of people's ridicule.

I need to not worry about my vehicle breaking down.

I'll stop my fear of visiting another country.

I won't be distracted by moving forward.

I can lessen my anxiety of working with chemicals.

I can't stress over my limiting beliefs.

I need to avoid my phobia of being overweight.

I can't be tormented by being victorious.

I need to block my fear of red tape.

I'll not worry about being rewarded.

I'll limit my anxiety of waiting for responses.

I can't be afraid of negative voices in head.

I can bypass my phobia of being a business owner.

I need to not stress over being away from home.

I can stop my fear of living out fantasies.

I won't be troubled by long waits.

I need to restrict my anxiety of working with computers.

I can't worry over long lines.

I'll defeat my phobia of working with machines.

I'll prevent my fear of being a coward.

I'll not stress about getting dirty.

I can lower my anxiety of loud noises.

I can't be frightened by being made an example of.

I need to abandon my phobia of being lonely.

I need to not worry about being too lucky.

I need to terminate my fear of my spouse leaving me.

I won't be distracted by wasting time.

I won't be troubled by being blamed.

I'll control my anxiety of being well known.

I can't worry over being neglected.

I can remove my phobia of promoting a product.

I'll stop my fear of exercising.

I'll not stress about living a healthy lifestyle.

I won't be distracted by production delays.

I need to rid my anxiety of poverty.

I can't be frightened by too much knowledge.

I'll beat my phobia of having a crises or tragedy.

I need to not worry about destiny and fate.

I can conquer my fear of being an entrepreneur.

I'll decrease my anxiety of possibly being assaulted.

I can't stress over being back stabbed.

I can minimize my phobia of border line illegalities.

I can't be tormented by missing an appointment.

I'll end my fear of wild animals.

I'll not worry about weather forecasts.

I can overcome my anxiety of weird vehicle noises.

I can't be afraid by lots of sales.

I need to eliminate my phobia of water.

I need to not stress over wishes not coming true.

I need to stop my fear of winning a competition.

I won't be troubled by going to rehab.

I'll control my anxiety of winning to0 much money.

I can't worry over misunderstandings.

I can remove my phobia of working as a team.

I can conquer my fear of writing a book.

I'll not stress about having disadvantages.

I need to rid my anxiety of worms.

I can't be frightened by work goals.

I'll beat my phobia of getting bullying.

I need to not worry about being inexperienced.

I'll give up my fear of being nude.

I won't be distracted by wrecking vehicle.

I can lessen my anxiety of bill collecting.

I can't stress over being betrayed.

I need to avoid my phobia of having an accident.

I can't be tormented by making wrong decisions.

I need to block my fear of possible natural disasters.

I'll not worry about getting beat out by younger people.

I'll limit my anxiety of writing someone off.

I can't be afraid of myths.

I can bypass my phobia of being abused.

I need to not stress over life coaches.

I can stop my fear of potential work strikes.

I won't be troubled by having low energy.

I need to restrict my anxiety of a blind date.

I can't worry over money.

I'll defeat my phobia of birds.

I need to not be upset by naysayers.

I'll prevent my fear of borrowing money.

I'll not stress about disagreements.

I can lower my anxiety of piling bills.

I can't be frightened by my boss.

I need to abandon my phobia of possible wars.

I need to not worry about rejection.

I need to terminate my fear of being productive.

I won't be distracted by breaking up.

I'll decrease my anxiety of neglecting responsibility.

I can't stress over boredom.

I can minimize my phobia of having business goals.

I can't be tormented by getting no attention.

I'll end my fear of a bad credit rating.

I'll not worry about trying to be perfect.

I can overcome my anxiety of being protected.

I can't be afraid by potential catastrophes.

I need to eliminate my phobia of cats.

I need to stop my fear of having a career.

I won't be troubled by my obsessions.

I'll control my anxiety of investing my savings.

I can't worry over meeting celebrities.

I can remove my phobia of cemeteries.

I'll not stress about my aging process.

I need to rid my anxiety of open spaces.

I can't be frightened by the obstacles of your goals.

I'll overcome my fear of success.

I'll not worry about high expectations.

I can't be afraid by my insecurities.

I need to eliminate my phobia of people's opinions.

I can lower my anxiety of falling in love.

I can end my anxiety of what people think.

I can remove my phobia of self-doubt.

I can conquer my fear of being used.

I need to stop my fear of being vulnerable.

I won't be troubled by having bad taste.

I'll control my anxiety of workplace competition.

I can't worry over having extra tasks.

I'll not stress about feeling unattractive.

I need to rid my anxiety of business competition.

I can't be frightened by face to face meetings.

I'll beat my phobia of making eye contact.

I need to not worry about failure.

I'll stop my fear of not achieving goals.

I won't be distracted by end of world prophecies.

I can't stress over being vandalized.

I need to avoid my phobia of amusement park rides.

I can't be tormented by self pressure.

I need to block my fear of making errors.

I'll not worry about having deadlines.

I'll limit my anxiety of having low confidence.

I can't be afraid of being unsupported.

I can lessen my anxiety of having a girlfriend.

I can stop my fear of dentists.

I need to not stress over having setbacks.

I won't be troubled by feeling unwanted.

I need to restrict my anxiety of separation.

I can't worry over flying.

I'll defeat my phobia of making friends.

I'll prevent my fear of having goals.

I'll not stress about managing employees.

I need to not stress over having bad credit.

I can't be frightened by being call in the office.

I need to abandon my phobia of my sensitivity.

I need to not worry about farewells.

I need to terminate my fear of being broke.

I won't be distracted by self sabotage.

I'll decrease my anxiety of having hardships.

I can't stress over family member's comments.

I can minimize my phobia of being unsecured.

I can't be tormented by having imperfections.

I'll end my fear of uncertainty.

I'll not worry about false statements.

I can overcome my anxiety of sex.

I can't be afraid of being unqualified.

****

There's just no end to the things we find to fret over, is there? As you can see, though, *it's all in how we say things.*

Sadly, you'd be surprised how many people repeat things like this to themselves all the time with no thought of what they're really saying.

Is it positive? Is it negative? Who knows – *but I guarantee you your unconscious knows which it is.*

You have to get conscious.

Over the next 30 days, pay attention to your language. How precise is it when you're talking to yourself and others? Are you speaking in the negative (reinforcing what you don't want) or in the positive (what you do want)?

Do you know?

Splitting Words

You've seen some of the mistakes we make – all the many words we use ineffectively in talking to ourselves or in describing what we want. Based on this, how could we expect the Universe to understand and deliver?

Learning how to formulate a clear and precise intention is an art and science, but it doesn't have to be hard.

So now you're going to declare your intention – and the way you do it is to take what you said you don't want and turn it 180 degrees around. "I want to be a healthy weight."

You want to state it in the positive and stay away from the word "overweight," for example, which can be loaded for people. You wouldn't say, "I am no longer overweight." Similarly, you don't want to say, "I want to get rid of my fat," because then you're still dealing with a negative statement.

You want to make a very clear statement about radiant health, happiness, freedom of movement, or whatever the phrase is. The intention needs to be something that resonates with you.

You can also add intentions together to make a longer sentence. For example, instead of saying, "I attract the perfect house" and stop there, you might want to make a complete intention that says, "I have attracted the perfect house that suits me wonderfully, is in the best neighborhood and school district, and convenient to my work."

You want to state your intention as completely as possible so that it gives you a sense of peace – even a smile – when you think about it.

****

In this exercise, pick 20 items from the previous chapter's list that you can relate to. Then, rewrite them into a more appropriate version of itself – you know, something you *do* want.

For example, "I can't worry over flying" could be changed to, "It's fun to fly and I enjoy it."

****

The point of this exercise is to take a poorly phrased idea – or intention – and give you some practice in clarity and effectiveness.

Act as if every word counts.

Actually, it does.

Clear Intention

Now that you've learned about the importance of language-ing and how to fine-tune it so that you're speaking in the positive and being clear, we're going to apply it more specifically to you.

The number one thing that holds people back from attracting money, happiness, success, relationships, and freedom is fear. Often, one of the best – and easiest – ways to conquer fear is to say daily affirmations silently or out loud.

The more you tell your brain something the more it will believe it. This type of mental repetition will reprogram yourself to reach your goals without being stopped by your fears.

Sometimes people ask me if they should listen to audio recordings to work with themselves, and I highly recommend this. I have my own recordings for myself like this. In fact, Pat O'Bryan and I created "clearing" audios – some subliminal and some audible – that have statements on them.

Is it useful?

Yes, they can help – but there's nothing more powerful than you doing it for yourself, either out loud, or internally, with a clearly defined focus and intention.

****

In this exercise, you'll need three pieces of paper. At the top of each one, write down a clearly defined personal intention. For example:

> *My body feels wonderful and I'm exercising every day.*
>
> *I am enjoying my children and spending plenty of time with them.*
>
> *I love to cook and make exciting, healthy meals for myself and my family.*

Now say the first intention three times out loud. Write down any thoughts, positive or negative, that come to you.

Do the same for the other two intentions. Over the next 30 days, continue focusing on your intentions in this way.

****

This exercise is designed to bring unconscious counter-intentions to the surface, as well as any inspirations that might pop up for you to take action on.

Do this daily and, before you know it, inspiration will far outweigh the "mumbo jumbo."

A Little Gratitude Goes a Long Way

As I said in the beginning, you have a job – stop the excuses, stop complaining, and focus on what you have now with gratitude. What you'll discover when you do this, when you remember to feel gratitude in each moment, is that *any doubts, fears, concerns, or worries disappear.*

This is the miracle state – and why gratitude is the space you want to be in as you focus on what you want.

The opposite of gratitude is a counter-intention – a limiting thought or belief that keeps you out of the flow of your good. If you've done the exercises in the book thus far, you've run into a few of these.

I think of gratitude as a kind of superpower, and the fastest way I know to transform your life no matter where you're at. It's like having your very own time warp.

****

For the next 30 days, keep a gratitude journal. It's a place for you to make lists and literally count your blessings. Gratitude Journals are a helpful process for your mind to actually "see" what's present and good in your life.

Set your journal up this way: On one side, write things you're grateful for that day. On the opposite page, write down *anything you give*. Giving is a way of *showing* gratitude.

On one page it comes in, on the other it goes out.

****

This exercise is designed to move you into a positive mindset by using a gratitude journal. Simultaneously recording your blessings and noting anything you give offers a valuable way to see how everything's changing over time.

You'll be amazed at how much you accomplish and feel grateful for, and I think you'll discover more and more miracles showing up unexpectedly.

Gratitude is like grease for the soul.

Conclusion

People often ask me how I accomplish so much and, the truth is, I have a secret.

I've found that whenever I want to do something new, once I've pulled away from the blocks and limitations and gotten a taste of success, things move faster.

In other words, there's nothing in me stalling. There's nothing in me saying, "You can't do this. You're not the right person for this." Or, "You don't have the time for this."

Those are all excuses.

When I first received the inspiration to become a musician, I didn't exactly have it all down. I still had to decide. I still had to choose it. I still had to declare to myself, "I am going to do this."

All along the process of taking action, I had my doubts

and excuses. At times, I said things like, "Wow, I don't know that I can actually do this. I don't know that I can pull this off."

But, by now, I'm used to this kind of thing.

Every time I want to grow or create something new, all the limiting beliefs have to have their say. The difference now is I know what to do about them.

I question them, release them, and keep stretching.

So what do *you* need to stretch for in your life?

Whether it's living a healthier lifestyle or pursuing a dream, it all gets down to facing those fears and eliminating excuses. By using your language clearly and efficiently, you can convert your fear to energy and get that dream created.

Make every word count.

Joe Vitale is President of Hypnotic Marketing, Inc., a marketing consulting firm. He has been called the "The Buddha of the Internet" for his combination of spirituality and marketing acumen. His professional clients include the Red Cross, PBS, Children's Memorial Hermann Hospital, and many other small and large businesses. His other books include The Attractor Factor, There's a Customer Born Every Minute, and Life's Missing Instruction Manual, all from Wiley. He is also one of the stars of the hit movie The Secret.

Visit Joe at mrfire.com.
Please take your time, browse and enjoy!

Your Divine Right - Prosperity and Abundance

by Roger Palmieri

"I came and gave you life so you may live it more abundantly"

John 10:10

"Wealth is a mind-set, not a time and place thing."

~Roger~

In order to transform your experience of wealth, so that you can now manifest wealth into every area of your life, you must recognize that you now are the source of your supply – which means there is abundance. There is truly an unlimited supply for all of us. You have it all already, so nothing is lacking.

Let's briefly explore the law of increase. Those who have – have more. Those that don't have – even lose that which they do have. When you become aware of what you have, you automatically reinforce that behavior. Remember and make a mental bookmark of the following statement:

"You always know what your intentions are by the results you produce."

Think of how many people you know of today that live their lives from a condition of scarcity. Not believing in themselves, they are always trying to get or keep others from getting what they have. Such a life is about fear. There is really nothing to lose. We have it all at our disposal.

To raise your level of consciousness about prosperity, you must truly believe that you have it all already. Acknowledge that abundance is already yours. If prosperity and abundance keep eluding you in life, then there are some unresolved barriers preventing prosperity from entering into your life. You have closed off, and that means you have made a decision sometime in your life having to do with supply; whether it be in the area of money, love, great health, great happiness or even opportunities.

Now we need to let go of the self-imposed limitations that we call separation. If you feel separated from money, love, health or abundance, now is the time to fully know that you are love and abundance.

You must be love and abundance because you cannot add to yourself by just thinking it. Use your actions to acknowledge the abundance you already have and always did have.

Look into your daily living experiences and see if you

have been affirming your self-talk cycle. The way you feel. The way you think. Look to see if you are acknowledging the abundance that is already yours. Or are you acknowledging a belief in scarcity? Notice a result that you have been producing in your life to get your answer. Our consciousness is cluttered with scarcity from behavioral conditioning. Our parents many times spoke only in terms of what we couldn't have; thereby creating an attitude that we now have as adults called scarcity.

Remember, you are the cause. You are responsible. The more you give – the more you get. Many people still hold on to beliefs of scarcity by their opinions; such as money is scarce, we're in a recession, or not everyone can have what they want.

The statement I am about to give you should be written down and placed somewhere that you can see it daily.

"Whatever you truly want – wants you"

This principle applies to every area of your life, such as friends, love, harmony and money. When you accept other people's beliefs that are not based on your own experiences, but based on their doubts and fears and limitations, those beliefs become yours.

Think for yourself and know the truth for yourself in your own life. Begin today to live from your imagination because we are doing it daily anyway. Most people are really living out of their past. You hear people say that they have thousands of new experiences every month or year. And if you look closely you will notice that they are simply having the same experience over and over.

The reason most people do not experience abundance in

living is because they base their future on today, which is a carryover from yesterday. Only those who know they have can give. All the others, who don't know they have, think they have to get.

Declare that abundance is what you want most in your life because abundance wants you. Admire what you have in your life. You are the source of everything you have. Have some – and get that inner appreciation. By making contributions you know what you have and your awareness of abundance begins to increase. Have the experience of being the way that you want. You create out of your imagination. Know that it is perfectly okay for you to have what you want – and what you want does not take away from someone else. And what someone else has does not take away from you.

The best way to start creating prosperity and abundance in your life is to write down what you want to give yourself. This is better known as journal keeping, and I learned this principle from a man you all know, Walt Disney.

When Disney wanted to create Disneyland he first started writing it down in his journal. His imagination went wild as he wrote down all of the things he wanted to have in his theme park. This successful man knew that in order to get what he wants, he first must give people what they want.

Although journal keeping may be time consuming, I strongly suggest that you commit to yourself by doing it. Make the time to write down specifically what you want to give yourself – and do it daily. This reinforces the belief you have about yourself and elevates your self-confidence and self-esteem on a daily basis.

Action Exercise To Get What You Want

An additional part of prosperity and abundance involves you creating a personal treasure map. So let's outline what a personal treasure map is all about. Making a treasure map is a very powerful tool, and it's a fun project to undertake.

A treasure map is an actual, physical picture of your desired reality. Its value lies in the fact that it creates an especially clear, sharp image, which you can then use to attract and focus energy into your dreams or goals. It works along the same principle as a blueprint for a building.

Supplies You Need

1.) Two (2) poster boards, approx. 24" x 36" – preferably white.

2.) Glue or scotch tape

3.) Magazines, travel brochures, etc.

4.) Scissors

5.) Pens and Markers

Items Needed for your Personal Treasure Map

1.) Five (5) pictures of yourself, 1 photo in the center and 1 photo in each corner

2.) Whatever your dreams, goals, rewards, etc., start cutting out pictures that symbolize your dreams and paste or tape them on your board. (These might include vacations, jewelry, cars, or anything else that you have dreamed about and talked yourself out of.)

3.) Put captions and dates (mm/yr) under each items – no longer than 2 years away.

4.) Incorporate yourself in the picture. For a very realistic effect, use a photograph of yourself. Show yourself being, doing and having your desired objective: traveling around the world, wearing your ideal clothing, proud author of a best-selling new book, making a million dollars, whatever it is that you would like it to be. Use this as a psychological trigger mechanism and incorporate it into your Big Dream/goal setting plans.

5.) Use lots of color in your treasure map to increase its psychological impact. Show the situation in its ideal, complete form as if it already exists. Remember, we are always dealing with the present. Visualize vividly the end results.

To stimulate your imagination here are a few of the infinite possibilities that exist with the implementation of the treasure map.

Health

Show yourself radiantly and perfectly healthy, active, beautiful, and participating in whatever activities would indicate perfect health to you.

Physical Condition

Show yourself with your perfect body. Cut a picture from a magazine that looks like you would in your perfect condition and paste a photo of your head on that body, feeling wonderful about yourself. Make personal statements that indicate how you are feeling. As an example, "I feel wonderful and I look fantastic now that I weigh my ideal weight of...", and fill in the pounds, "and I am in perfect physical health."

Self-Image and Beauty

Show yourself as you want to feel: beautiful, relaxed, enjoying life, warm and loving. Include words and symbols that represent these qualities to you.

Career

Show yourself doing what you really want to do, with interesting and agreeable people around, and you earning plenty of money. And be specific about the amount you intend to have and all other pertinent details. "Here I am driving my new..." and your desired automobile. "I love it and I have plenty of money to maintain it."

Family and Friends

Show members of your family and other important relationships with you communicating openly, harmoniously and successfully.

Any Other Area of Your Life

Show yourself in any situation and whatever you want it to be. With plenty of time and money to enjoy the experience as you visualize it; and so on.

Here are 5 profound prosperity affirmations for you. Write them down on 5, 3 x 5 cards and post them where you can see them daily and carry one on yourself. Also, add these affirmations to your Treasure Map.

1.) Large sums of money, big happy financial surprises and rich appropriate gifts now come to me in perfect ways and I use the gifts wisely.

2.) All affirmations of abundance and prosperity I tell myself are now truth, fact and reality in my life NOW.

3.) I am now living my vision of prosperity, health and total abundance.

4.) Everything I do and everyone I come into contact with prospers me now in my daily living experiences.

5.) I am filled with excellence, wealth, prosperity and I am magnificent!

Have fun and create your BIG DREAMS and goals successfully.

Summary of Prosperity and Abundance

- You are the source of your magnificent supply.

- The Law of Increase - You always know what your intentions are by the results you produce.

- To raise your level of consciousness about prosperity you must truly believe that you have it all already.

- You are the cause. You are responsible. The more you give – the more you get.

- The best way to start creating prosperity and abundance in your life is to write down what you want to give yourself. This is better known as journal keeping.

- Create your personal Treasure Map – an imperative exercise

- Use these compelling affirmations on a daily basis.

"May all of your dreams become reality and
all of your efforts
become magnificent achievements"

~Roger~

~ For more information ~

Contact Roger at
DREAMBIG@ThePalmieriGroup.com
and visit my website – ThePalmieriGroup.com

Roger Palmieri, Co-Founder, The Palmieri Group, is an internationally acclaimed speaker and trainer in the field of human behavior since 1978. He has spoken to more than one million people around the world as a keynote speaker for major conventions, company awards, management conferences and sales training meetings. In his provocative presentations on Sales and Management Performance as well as LifeStyle Entrepreneurship he shows people "how to" unlock the limitless potential you were born with.

Mr. Palmieri major concentration in psychology and philosophy studies with focused attention on behavior modification in career business development. Drawing on his extensive background of human behavior he shows people how to "remove effort and struggle" from the process of change through proven behavioral research and practical implementation.

ON HUMAN BEHAVIOR *... He radiates a super-charged, high energy presence that immediately engages people. Mr. Palmieri delivers messages that are meaningful, practical and coherent. Lacking from his presentations are the usual time-worn platitudes and masses of data and statistics that are quickly forgotten and have little meaning.*

ON COMMITMENT . . . *His passion for excellence is a testament to his commitment of "Quality Care." He creates a memorable learning experience that combines unique, perceptive insights laced with down-to-earth humor.*

ON KNOW HOW . . . *With more than thirty-five years of practical sales and management experience, he possesses a rare quality of taking complicated techniques and simplifies them into workable ideas that people can apply immediately to transform their current business activity beyond their own expectations. Because of his outstanding performance with sales and management people, he is a speaker listed in the WHO's WHO AMONG U.S. EXECUTIVES.*

ON INSPIRATION . . . *As a highly decorated U.S. Marine Corps combat veteran of the Viet Nam war, he talks about courage and perseverance and day-to-day heroism.* **He's a rare breed that can connect, not only with your intellect, but also with your heart and soul.**

Wealth from the Inside Out

by Chris and Marlow Felton

I t wasn't working. Nothing was. "Why are we working so hard and still feeling so stuck?" Chris and Marlow, experienced financial professionals, had all the training necessary to be wealthy. But they weren't wealthy. In fact, they were frustrated with their financial situation. It was consuming their thoughts and wearing on their relationship. "We were frustrated with each other," said Marlow. "We just felt there was no way out. We were working hard and thought working harder was somehow going to eventually get us ahead and fix our problems."

They did what many people do; they started to look for solutions a bit outside the box. Working harder wasn't helping their financial situation so maybe, they thought, they were missing something – some key or universal law. They sought direction through a variety of personal development programs and books - many of which came from the cast of The Secret, including Joe Vitale.

After reading the books, following the steps and practices, they still weren't getting ahead. Nothing had really changed, until one angry afternoon that changed everything. "When your husband asks you why you are married to him, you really have to stop and take a deep look inside," said Marlow. Yet it was at that pivotal moment when Chris and Marlow started to make the transition from debt and struggle to prosperity.

Delusion and Optimism Often Sleep in the Same Bed

For Chris, the "a ha" moment was to realize the problem wasn't external. Not only did he realize he was part of his problems, he also realized the delusion he'd been living with – the "if I just work harder" way of thinking – wasn't going to fix it. "I realized going from 70 hours a week to 90 wasn't going to solve it."

Incongruent Thoughts and Actions

Magical thinking wasn't going to solve it for them either. "In order for the Law of Attraction to work, you have to actually believe it will work. Too many people put a wish in a box and then go back to worrying about money. Or they spend it and repeat their money mantra and wait for it to come true. It doesn't come true if your thoughts and actions are incongruent," said Chris. So if working harder isn't the solution, and if you can't wish for more money and have it land in your lap, then what is the solution?

Your Internal Story Has to Shift

Chris and Marlow came to a point where they realized

they had to stop blaming one another and stop looking for external solutions. The solution was to look within. What you believe about yourself and about money must be explored and dealt with honestly and openly. Sometimes the most powerful questions are the ones we ask ourselves.

They started digging and looking at their beliefs about money, and how those beliefs influenced their actions. "My dad was so incredibly cheap," said Marlow. "It was embarrassing. So I taught myself 'don't be cheap, don't be cheap, don't be cheap'. Because I found my dad so embarrassing as a teenager, in my adult life, I became overly frivolous. After really thinking about this, and realizing 'yeah, that was super-embarrassing,' so what did that turn into? I discovered my overspending was an attempt to be the opposite. I got into deep credit card debt trying to prove I wasn't cheap." Sometimes our desire NOT to be something can be more powerful than our desire to be something.

Your mental approach to money has to change for your financial situation to change. Chris began looking at his spending as a project instead of a problem and he started to dig at the root of it. Together they began to shift internally.

From Debt and Arguing to Peace and Prosperity

Getting clear on your beliefs about money and your financial personality is the first step. The second step – and the one that takes time, diligence, and a continued awareness – is to begin taking action. It's not enough to write yourself a check for a million dollars and meditate on it every day. You have to start taking action toward achieving that million dollar check, and that doesn't mean working more hours. It means paying attention to your money, respecting it, and setting goals.

For couples, it's particularly challenging because there are two people involved. They both have to deal with their own unique programming. Honesty, communication, and acceptance are essential. Today Chris and Marlow work with couples to help them navigate the often tumultuous waters of financial prosperity. They coach their clients and share the following advice for individuals or couples going through a difficult financial time:

Give it time. You've had years of programming to get where you are today. Clarity and shifting your thoughts is possible, but it will take time. Whatever dominates your thinking really comes to pass, but you have to give yourself time.

Accept it. Accept where you are. You don't need to love it; you don't need to hate it. But you need to accept it. You are where you are. You're supposed to be there. Accept where you are. By taking responsibility for your role in creating your current situation, you can then be emotionally freer to move forward and create a new reality. You have to take it one small step at a time. There's real compounding momentum that happens. The whole "don't beat yourself up" concept is significant. People try to take on personal development while simultaneously hitting themselves over the head with a hammer. It never works.

Respect your money. People get into financial trouble because they don't respect their money. It's possible to have financial flow and abundance while also respecting your money and paying attention to what you're doing and how it's working for you.

Keep your head in the clouds and feet on the ground.
Have a relationship with your money, your financial goals,
your results, your savings and your net worth. Know your
cold hard numbers. Also allow yourself to think big. Do
write that million dollar check for yourself, visualize and
dream, but don't stop there. Decide how you want to achieve
that goal and start taking action today.

Get clear on your vision. Whether you're single or in a
relationship, you really have to get clear on what your vision
is first. If you know where you are going and what your
ideal life looks like as a couple, then you can work backwards and create your dream life together.

Get help. Both Chris and Marlow readily admit they
wouldn't have been able to achieve financial prosperity and
a happy marriage without assistance. They found mentors to
guide them. They know there are always things to work on,
and sometimes the programming runs so deep, it takes an
outside perspective to move forward.

You'll Never Know How Good You Are Until Money is Behind You

If worrying about money is dominating your thoughts,
it's impossible to be the best version of you. It also impacts
how you're able to contribute to the world. When you can
let go of this worry and know your financial goals are being
realized, you can find peace. Letting go of this worry will
create clarity of purpose and allow you to be open to infinite
possibilities you never noticed before. This peace is worth
whatever it takes to get there. It's not always easy to look
inside ourselves to uncover our programming, and it's even
more difficult to change our behaviors. The end result is
beyond your wildest dreams. It's worth everything.

Chris and Marlow Felton, the "Couples Money Experts" and authors of Couples Money, *have inspired thousands of couples across the country with their personal story and the insights they share in* Couples Money. *Chris and Marlow have 27 plus years combined experience in the financial services industry working with couples of all walks of life. They mentor and train over 180 financial professionals in their business across the country and are highly respected public speakers. They are recognized as leaders in the financial services industry and have presented for thousands of financial professionals all over the country.*

Chris and Marlow have a unique perspective on wealth, and share insights from their years of experience and personal development. They share their personal story of financial transformation, and how they got on the "same page". They take an introspective approach to creating wealth from the inside out, and share insights from numerous financially independent couples.

Chris and Marlow help couples have more productive conversations about money and prosper together. Visit www.couplesmoney.com to learn from their experience and achieve your goals for financial abundance.

The 6 Rung Ladder of Wealth

by Dan Lok

My students all want to have wealth. But when I ask what technique they are currently using to attain wealth, they have no idea.

When you wish to attain wealth, don't go after it directly.

Going for wealth paradoxically guarantees that wealth will elude you. Like the horizon, it continues to recede as you chase it. Wealth and happiness are the two goals that you cannot approach directly. Rather, you must direct your efforts elsewhere, and wealth and happiness come along afterwards for free. So where do you direct your efforts?

Use the 6 Rung Ladder of Wealth as your guide.

4 – Profitability

3 – Creativity

2 – Credibility

1 – Visibility

-1 – Invisibility

-2 – Instability

They Have to Know Who You Are

Setting aside the two rungs at the very bottom, which we'll talk about shortly, you can see that the first rung on the ladder is VISIBILITY.

Visibility means that people are aware of who you are. Instead of pursuing wealth, focus on pursuing visibility. Make yourself known. The more visibility you achieve, the closer you are to wealth.

Let me state this very strongly – as a general rule, everyone who has wealth first achieved visibility. The more visibility– which means the more you are seen and the more that people know of you – the faster you move towards wealth.

How do you increase visibility? Let me give you some examples from my own life.

I have one of the most popular business podcasts on iTunes, called Shoulders of Titans (ShouldersofTitans.com) and I give at least ONE interview a week on the radio or by podcast.

I have a YouTube channel with over 200+ videos on it (www.DanLokTV.com). As a professional speaker on business development, I address more than 50,000 people a year. I have shared the stage with leaders such as Richard Branson, Bob Proctor, Robert Kiyosaki and Jack Canfield.

I've written more than a dozen books, some of which are best-sellers. I am the founder of Vancouver Entrepreneurs Group, which is the fastest growing entrepreneurial community in my area, with over 1,400 members.

I am not telling you these things to impress you, I am telling you to impress upon you that's what I do to get visibility.

Now, just because they know you doesn't mean they like you or trust you. So let's move up the ladder and take a look at what's next.

Credibility Matters

People do business with people they know, like and trust – so the next level is CREDIBILITY. Once you've attained visibility, you must ensure you have credibility. That means that they don't just know of you, they also like, admire and respect you. They believe what you have to say is worth listening to.

For example, people respect you if you've been a guest on Oprah, or if you've written a book. People believe you to be trustworthy and credible if you've appeared on radio or television. People respect you if you've had a newspaper article written about you. People respect you; that's some kind of status.

Credibility also extends beyond what you say. You earn credibility in what you do as well. For example, people respect you if you've given money to charity or you donate your time to charity. People respect you if you've done something well, you carry yourself with confidence, you dress well or you speak well.

You need to notice how other people view you, and most people don't know that at all. They just dress however the heck they want to dress, and they don't really care what's going on. So if you don't care if you've got visibility and you don't care about credibility, then what you're really saying is you don't care if anyone knows who you are or, if they know who you are, you don't care if they like you.

Once you've achieved credibility and visibility, what's next? Looking up the ladder you can see that it's creativity.

Innovation and Inspiration - The Third Rung on the Ladder of Wealth

Then the next rung is CREATIVITY. And this means essentially that you need to be able to differentiate yourself from others. You can achieve a certain degree of financial success with visibility and credibility alone. However, if you want to truly attain wealth, the creativity is essential.

Let's say there are three furniture stores in a strip mall with a huge parking lot, and you own the middle furniture store. You come to work one morning and, to your shock, there's a giant banner across the front of the furniture store to the right of you that says "Semi-annual Sale!" And all that day, all the cars were parking in front of that store.

And then, to make things worse, you come in to work the next day and here's a giant banner across the furniture store on your left that says "Annual Clearance 90% Off!" Oh my God – that day all of the cars were parked in front of that store. But then the next morning both of them were horrified when they came in to work and saw the banner across the top of your store that said "Main Entrance."

That's the kind of creativity that I'm talking about. That's the kind of creativity you need. The ability and desire to position yourself apart from the rest. And finally, if you have visibility and you have credibility and you have creativity setting up your business model correctly, then you get profitability.

It's a ladder. You must take each rung one at a time, and in the proper order. Strangely, you don't have to next go up to the top rung of Wealth. Once you have visibility and credibility, you are already at the top rung of wealth. It's like a Free Pass.

We've already done four and we're at the top. Sounds like there are a couple of rungs missing. And you see, visibility is the ground floor rung. We are now going to go backwards and go negative.

The Bottom Two Rungs – Negative Wealth, But There's Tremendous Potential

It's important to point out that while these are the bottom two rungs and they may be your experience or situation right now, but it doesn't have to stay that way. You can climb the ladder. However, it's also important to be aware of where you are right now so that you can envision what's possible.

The first negative level is invisibility. That's what most people have. It's very sad. If you're a small business owner, then you are likely known by a handful of people in your employ. That's it. A handful. Maybe six, maybe a few dozen, but basically a small number of people.

So, most people have complete invisibility except for a few dozen people in their employ. Nobody else knows them. I'm not talking about family or friends. I'm talking about business. In business, most entrepreneurs have complete invisibility, and let me prove it to you. As soon as somebody loses their job, they suddenly realize how invisible they are because they have to create their resume. Well that's fine, but they have no idea who to send it to. Nobody knows them. They're starting from zero. They're starting from complete invisibility.

Not only do employees suddenly realize they have complete invisibility when they lose their jobs, but almost every businessperson has complete invisibility as well. It's evident when they lose a client and it hits them hard. They have to scramble for new clients, which is difficult because nobody knows who they are. It's stressful and no way to run a business or achieve wealth – scrambling for clients all the time isn't any way to achieve wealth. If you're invisible, you can't make money! You can't! If no one's ever heard of you, then they, by definition, can't give you money because they don't even know who you are!

But it can get worse…The worst rung of the ladder is instability. And instability is below invisibility. Financial instability is bankruptcy, going out of business, losing your job, being horribly in debt. Emotional instability is having an affair, losing your marriage, going insane, committing suicide.

So here's your job. Identify which level you're at right now, as embarrassing as it might be. It's okay because even if you're at the bottom of the ladder, the only place you can go is up.

And that is the whole point. If you want to improve your life and your income potential, you need to work on improving your position on the "6 Rung Ladder of Wealth." Take it one rung at a time and watch your wealth increase with each step.

So where are you on the ladder?

NOTE: If you don't know me, I'm Dan Lok. Husband, millionaire mentor, & serial entrepreneur...

If you're an entrepreneur, let's you and I connect at http://www.danlok.com

How I Discovered the Secret to Explode the Full Power of the Law of Attraction

by Robert Mc Donagh

ave you ever tried the Law of Attraction? You practice it and believe in it, but somehow something is not clicking for you? You're buying the books, you're buying the programs, you're buying the courses, you're attending the seminars... but it's still not happening fast enough, or perhaps not at all? And somehow deep down you know something's missing!?

Well, let me tell you my story. When I first heard of the Law of Attraction back in 2007, I was blown away after watching the movie The Secret. What I learned about it made a lot of sense, and it made me think about it how I attracted through the LOA a lot of crap throughout my life.

As far back as I can remember, up until very recently, my life has been one hard battle. No matter what I tried to achieve or gain, it did not come to me easily or effortlessly like it does for others. Most often, whatever that 'thing' I tried to succeed in just fell to pieces. Same old story, different YEAR!

Things changed the day I met my mentor Dan Lok. For those of you who don't know him, Dan is a very successful businessman, entrepreneur and bestselling author. And I have the privilege of been his mentee and apprentice since start of 2015.

One day, Dan and I were having this discussion, we got talking about the Law of Attraction, and I was sharing with Dan every aspect of my life; the struggles, the financial debt, the sleepless nights, basically everything. Our conversation went like this:

Rob: Dan, I'm 35 years old, I've got 5 kids and a wife to support, I hate my job, I've got no money, no direction in life, no support, nobody to guide me and no friends. You know I practice the LOA, but still everything I touch turns to shit. Where am I going wrong?

Dan replied: Rob, I know you're a good guy but that doesn't cut it by itself. Neither does having great intentions; that alone is not good enough for you to create massive wealth. Neither is practicing the Law of Attraction enough. Plain and simple. The LOA on its own, without action, is meaningless. You need to take action. You need to act on your inspirations.

Rob: What do you mean Dan? I'm taking action. I'm talking to you!

Dan: Rob, Just look at Joe Vitale himself; he teaches the LOA, but without having taken action, without the next step, he wouldn't be where he is today.

Rob: But I studied the LOA, took courses on the LOA, bought most of Joe's books on the LOA, along with others, and became a certified LOA practitioner (through Joe's course), but all of that brought me ZERO success. I've visualized my goals, I've done affirmations, and I have my vision board on my wall. So how come I'm still broke? Why does it work for Joe, for example, but not for me? And what do you mean by the 'next step?'

Dan: Good question. It's because you aren't implementing the Law of Effection, and all of that is meaningless without the other laws. When understood and implemented with positive action, it will change your life like night and day.

Rob: LAW OF EFFECTION, I shouted back like he was from another planet. 'What the hell is the Law of Effection,' I asked? (All that was going through my mind was 'now I have to learn another Law when I can't even get the LOA to work for me!?!')

Dan went on to explain: Law of Effection is serving people, how you can have an effect on people's lives positively. It means having a huge impact on people and giving value through useful and practical advice.

Rob: What do you mean? Please explain it to me.

Dan: It means asking how many lives you can positively effect. You can think positively until the cows come home, you can chant as you will, you can meditate, you can visualize, you can do affirmations all day (and those are all good), but if you are not impacting people, if you are not serving the world, if you are not getting your message out there, then you are not going to attract prosperity, wealth and abundance in to your life… period.

Rob: Oh I see. Then how…..

Dan: Look at what I have. I have more than enough money, I have the cars, I take vacations whenever I choose, I have my dream home, I eat healthy, I make a fortune and the list goes on. That's because of the Law of Effection in action. It's taking the Law of Attraction to a whole new level.

You see Rob, I can be the most negative person on the planet, but if I practice the Law of Effection, I'll surely still attract wealth, success and abundance in to my life. I might not even be happy, but I will still get those things.

Rob: Ok I get it now but *how* do I that? How do I practice the Law of Effection? Give me the steps.

Dan: Well first you need a Personal Media Platform.

Rob: What is that?

Dan: A media platform means podcasting, or setting up a blog or a website that is personal to you. It's yours, and it is your way to communicate with the public through the internet. It's something that you can build an audience with, something that can add value – a platform on which you can share your story and make money.

Rob: (The penny started to drop!) So in a nutshell, what you're saying is that I need to find a way to serve others, and to bring value to others through one of the platforms you just mentioned.

Dan: YES! It's the Law of Effection you need to practice. How many people's lives can you positively effect is the key to your success. How big of an audience do you have? How many people you can serve. These are the questions you need to be asking yourself and, more importantly, deciding upon a media platform. This is basically taking the LOA to a whole new level.

Rob: So you're telling me, that's what I've been doing wrong all these years? Trying to succeed on the LOA alone, without implementing the LOE? The missing secret so to speak?

Dan: Yes, and you know my story, my background. If it worked for me, it will surely work for you. It has to!! It's the LAW..!!

Rob: But surely, there's something missing. It can't be that simple. Don't I need to at least have a skill of some sort? Like you?

Dan: Now you're getting it Rob. You're correct. The only way to add value to the world is to first increase your value, to acquire a valuable skill.

Rob: Ok, Dan, any skills in particular?

Dan: Acquire a valuable skill and impact people's lives through a Personal Media Platform. Find a skill that is needed; one that will bring value to a lot of people and solve problems. Specifically, the skills of online marketing, running and hosting an effective Podcast, copywriting... how to create a valuable product, a course, an ebook, a marketing funnel, how to build a large audience and email list.

Rob: (All hyped up) Is that it? That's what I need to do?

Dan: Yes, mastering new skills through your personal media platform of your choice, this will ultimately set you financially free.

And that's how my conversation with my mentor went.

Since that moment back in February 2015, I've been practicing and taking the LOA to a whole new level by implementing the LOE just like my mentor Dan Lok told me.

Implementing the LOA without the LOE is the part that most people forget to do, hence the reason they never see results.

And that's how I found out that Personal Media Platform with the LOE in action is the key to great wealth. It's how all successful people achieve great wealth.

Just take a look at Dan Lok (www.danlok.com), or take a look at Joe Vitale (www.mrfire.com). They've impacted a lot of people through their own personal media platforms. All of the true wealthy people we know today create their wealth by adding value and impacting people.

And my own personal media platform is Podcasting. I use iTunes, I have a blog, I run a website, I'm on Facebook, Twitter, and I have a YouTube channel. Even this book itself is a form of media platform. My last No.1 bestseller book, The Midas Touch, is also a personal media platform.

I hope you find your own Personal Media Platform, something that works for you. And when you find it, I'm sure success will follow.

That's The Prosperity Factor.

Rob Mc Donagh is the bestselling author of The Midas Touch with Joe Vitale and Dan Lok. Rob is a husband, father of 5, and an internet marketer. Rob has been in the trenches, poor all of his life, and knows all too well what it is like to suffer and struggle.

Rob turned his life around and now runs a successful Podcast called The F.U. Money Show, which is designed to help people escape the rat race, fire their boss and live life on their own terms. You can visit Rob's popular website and check out his blog at www.fumoney.com, where you can get instant access to The Massive Passive Income Workshop - so you can take your life to the next level, learn profitable online business ideas you can start today, and more! You can also catch up with Rob on iTunes every Wednesday 2pm EST.

Wow

by Salvador Aragao (A T)

Wow, what a life… How grateful am I now? Very Grateful! Wasn't always like this though…

Where am I now? Sitting on deck of a 54m sail yacht, bathing in the sun after swimming in the warm waters of the Mediterranean. Let's go back a few years…

As a lot of people I've met, feelings of separateness led to years of drug abuse and everything that brings; isolation, despair, rejection, alienation and emptiness. It wasn't what I wanted for myself and after spending time in rehab I was happy to be moving forward.

I knew I was designed to go well through life, to achieve greatness, to live a meaningful life, abundantly and in peace!

I am still in the building process of my lifestyle; the yacht where I am now, it's not mine… yet!

The four years after rehab were a struggle… getting back into society, playing by the rules and trying to be a good citizen was a hard task. There were bills to pay, old and new ones, and I had no money. While working I was also studying to achieve a University degree. I thought that if I finished a degree of some sort I'd have my life sorted.

Most days I was depressed, and I would isolate myself to mountain tops, beaches or the usual forest spots for inspiration and meditation. While running away, I was actually connecting with nature, and this was a source of clean, pure energy, where life succeeded without effort, naturally growing, with a birth right to happiness. "Humans fit well with Nature, we just need to find a place and a rhythm and we can live in plenitude" I used to think. Then back to reality, with the running clocks and timetables and rules and obligations. I was getting exhausted.

Since young age that I had been dealing with feelings of rejection. This was actually what led to drug usage and low self-esteem. So... when it happened again, having to deal with rejection after coming out of rehab and trying to turn my life around was the end of the line for me, and my wish of death was very strong.

For the next hours, days and weeks I felt I had no purpose in being alive. As a symptom, I had a heart attack. The plug was pulled, and I literally couldn't breathe. I couldn't even move a finger. I immediately saw that I was in trouble. I fought it as hard as I could, trying to get up, and falling again and again until I realized that I was not in control and I was "going away". At that moment I realized how much I love Life, how blessed we are for having one, and that I wanted to keep living a life on Earth. I also realized we go somewhere after this, there is life after Earth, but I wasn't done yet!

Apparently, I saved myself using a Yoga technique where you breathe so little oxygen and reduce your heart beat to just once or twice per minute. It was in that moment I gained insights about the works of life and how to go through it.

I found myself in the clouds, looking at my body on the garage front door, with a feeling of abundance fulfillment and peace, but no pain. Here, I'm faced with an individual, also made of the same white energy I'm made of, we don't speak, everything is explained in thought and image, we know what we're talking about, we see the same thing, same images (relevant episodes of my life) and there are no doubts.

He shows me what I did wrong in my past life, what I did right, good or bad influences, and why, and now he tells me: "you're not staying here yet, it's not your time to come. You have to go back down to the physical world and you're going to do great, you're going to have fun, you're going to enjoy the good life, in peace, love, plenitude and abundance, and, with no struggle." I believed him.

I move away from him and slowly come down to my body. As soon as I'm back in my body, the heart pain kicks in again (the worst pain I've ever felt) but... I get a good breath of fresh air. I walk to the nearest house, and find my Grandmother who calls for an ambulance to take me to the hospital.

After my stay at the hospital I felt like a new person. I can feel people now, feel events, feel places and immediately, I know if they're good for me or not. I have new tools.

The key points of this experience were:

- Gratitude for being given time on Earth, grateful for being alive and well.

- The Knowledge of the power of thought associated with Strong Emotions and Desire.

- A great Sense of detachment from everything, people, places and things.

- We can do whatever we want with our lives, we Are Free. We can be whoever we wish to be.

- Our life is supposed to be lived in an abundant state of being, Plenitude, a bliss, in peace and not suffering or struggling.

- We have the power of thought and imagination to use in the creation of the life we want or wish, we just have to put action on it.

- Desire to find something you love doing in life and follow it!

- We must listen to our intuition as it's our best guidance.

- People that matter will come to us; we'll know for sure who to stick with and with who not to stick with.

When I left the Hospital, seeing the traffic on the streets, people's faces down, running all around, I immediately felt and said to myself: "this is not the way to live, I'm out of here!" And this time I knew nothing could stop me.

I did a course in life coaching, and discover the tools to move forward with my life. Around the same time, "The Secret" came out. As a result, I learn:

- Macrobiotic food: we are what we eat

- Yoga: breathing, centering, good self-assessment and self-confidence

- Surf: good overall feeling, healthy mind and body, connection with the Earth

- Studying the Secret / LOA: getting a clear mind and using the Ether

- Gardening: just for relaxing

- Practicing Coaching: setting goals, overcoming obstacles

In between these tools and exercises, there was a book that helped me change my perception of my body. It's from a Master, called Martin Broffman and it's called *Everything Can be Cured, the Body Mirror System*.

This book explains to you how master your "Chi" (energy, light, life source) and align your Chakras (energy centers) and your energy field around you. It teaches you how you free your body of any stress in the energy field.

With this you can achieve greatness regarding your body and soul.

So, here I was with a lot of information and a desire to finally get the life I wished for myself.

Since 3 years of age, I've always sailed on with the family. Spending time at sea on father's boat for the weekend or for the all summer was the most anticipated activity. I was at home on a boat, everything was easy for me, what to do, what to expect, where to go and how to get there. I rediscovered sailing as an adult, and realized that I had found my passion! I had found my desire and I had found my energy to pursue my dream! The fact that I had no money at the time was no issue anymore. I had a dream, and I had the energy to chase it!

Ok, here I get all the other key points working together and come up with this solution:

1. Making a plan. I did a plan for the life I wanted to achieve and when I wanted. I was specific to what I wanted in 1 year; 3 years; 5 years and 10 years.

2. Overcoming Obstacles. I got it from the Buddha that "If a problem has a solution, don't worry with it and if a problem has no solution, don't worry with it, it's already solved right?"

3. Putting action. This is applicable in two senses. Physical exercise – Healthy Body, Healthy Mind – and with Discipline of not quiting!

4. Take good care of yourself. Good food and rest are as essential as the working hours.

5. Getting involved with the right people and asking for help when needed. Chase your idols and get in touch.

6. Re-assessing the plan. As achievements where happening, re assess and re-shape your plan. Keeping it up to date and in tune with reality helps to clear the path.

7. Visualize every morning. How you want your day to unfold. Take the time to breathe in the love and gratitude of a wonderful positive day, including how to react to situations.

8. Kept on following the Masters of LOA and Coaching, I still use their guidance!

With this process I got to a point where after 5 years I went back to read my first written plan to find that everything had happened as planned. The jobs I had, where I lived, the money and the relationships. Health was at a peak and I had good people around me. Everything happened as I wished and wrote in that piece of paper! So I wrote more papers!

I can accomplish whatever I wish next... So... What comes next? What's my next Big Dream? Fortunately for me, my dream and passion walk hand in hand with my job, sailing beautiful amazing ships with amazing good people to fantastic places.

It's out there, it's real, it's energy and we work the energy with our thoughts and desires, all we need is the time, focus and the correct frame of mind!!

As Bob Proctor would say "I am So Happy and So Grateful right now, that I'm doing what I need to achieve my goals."

I'll let you know how this goal went!!

Keep dreaming!

Salvador is a sailor by nature and a professional seafarer. His passion of sailing across the oceans, exploring the most exotic beaches and corners of the world, has lead him to "paradise on Hearth" situations. He can guide you in your search for that peace and quiet, good vibe, nature filled place you've been looking for! It's your dream, and he'll help make it happen! You can reach Salvador at salvadorat@gmail. com, for the beginning of your next crusade!

Conscious Parenting: The Art Of Raising Your Child To Thrive

by Judy Banfield

"The words just came flying out of my mouth," Melinda said to me.

"There was Katie, just three years old, calling me to see her new drawing. When I went into her room, there was her drawing – all over the walls of her room.

"I just snapped and out came all these words I swore I'd never say: 'I can't believe you did this. What's the matter with you? How could you be so stupid? You are a bad, bad girl!'

"And then… I smacked her.

"Katie was shocked. She stared up at me wide eyed and disbelieving. Then she started wailing and ran into her closet and hid. She was afraid of me. It was the last thing I ever wanted to happen."

Melinda was crying as she told me the story. I have heard many such stories in my years and years of supporting parents.

"I vowed and promised myself that I would never, ever, ever strike my children, nor would I ever belittle them. But I did both in one instance" Melinda said.

Melinda was shocked at her own behavior. She was a loving parent who wanted to raise her daughter to feel good about herself, be strong, happy, motivated, caring and successful.

But on this day something snapped. Katie's drawing on the wall triggered something inside, and the words and the slap just exploded from her.

Melinda felt awful and ashamed of herself.

You might be thinking "What's the big deal? Her daughter misbehaved and she got the consequences. Now she knows not to draw on the wall again."

But as someone reading this type of book, I invite you to look a little deeper to understand what's really going on for Melinda.

And when I say look deeper, I mean deeper into yourself.

As a reader of this book, I'm going to say that you've probably embarked on a path of personal growth and development.

You are probably trying to rid yourself of all the limiting beliefs and counter-intentions that are blocking you from leading the life you want.

And where did you acquire those beliefs? You probably acquired the majority of them in your childhood home, from your parents or primary caregivers.

Every time you were told you were stupid, or bad, or that something was "the matter with you," you took that as truth and it became a deep belief embedded in your subconscious.

Every time your parents smacked or hit you, you were given the message that you deserved to be physically hurt by someone much bigger and stronger than you, and you accepted that as truth, and part of your belief system as well.

And those were the exact powerful messages that Melinda gave her daughter in the moment when she "snapped."

Her little girl had an intense emotional response. First she froze, then she wailed, then she fled to her closet for safety.

It turns out that the day she "snapped", Melinda's own mother was coming to visit, and all of her deeply held beliefs about herself sprung up from her subconscious. When her mother would see Katie's drawing on the wall, Melinda would feel completely inadequate. She'd feel "stupid" and "bad" and that something was "wrong with her" as a parent. She would probably get a verbal "smack" from her mother.

Melinda's fear of her mother's response triggered deep unconscious parenting behaviors she had learned as a child. They just burst to the surface.

Imagine growing up in a home where the kind of interaction Melinda had with Katie that day happens regularly, day in and day out.

That's how Melinda grew up.

Perhaps that's how you grew up as well.

It is, in fact, the way the majority of children are raised, in North America and in many cultures around the world.

Is it any surprise then that the most common limiting belief that adults have is "I'm not good enough"? And that the lack of self-love, and low self-esteem, are practically epidemic?

With so many of us walking around with deep emotional wounds, resentments, anger and self-loathing, is it any surprise there is so much mistrust, prejudice, poverty, violence, greed, and abuse of power in the world?

Imagine, just imagine, if you could change this.

I believe parenting can change the world for the better — one child at a time.

And you can be someone who makes that change happen.

As a parent, you have a profound impact on how children develop.

Every action, every reaction, every word, every experience you offer to your children, impacts their developing subconscious, and consequently their self-concept, their self-image, their beliefs about themselves and the world they live in.

Most of us unconsciously parent the way we were parented by our parents. Generation after generation we pass on dysfunctional patterns of behavior, and limiting, self-defeating beliefs.

Although we love our children and want the best for them, unless we bring our unconscious beliefs about ourselves and about parenting, into our awareness, we will burden our children with our own limitations. We will get "triggered" as Melinda did, and automatically say and do things we never thought we would.

We have to choose to parent consciously.

How do you do this?

1. Know yourself! Work with a coach, a therapist, or some kind of support group, explore your own belief systems, your own childhood and how you were parented. Get support to clear limiting beliefs and build your self-esteem.

2. Do real soul searching to decide what your long-term goals are for your children. Sometimes we are so anxious to get our children to behave, we lose sight of the impact of how we interact with them. What kind of people do you want them to be? How do you want them to feel about themselves? How do you want them to treat others?

3. Educate yourself about the normal course of child development. So much of parents' frustrations and hurtful responses are caused by parents having unreasonable expectations for the developmental level of their children. It's normal for babies to wake a lot at night. It's normal for two year olds to say "no."

4. Educate yourself about the research on different parenting techniques. Some common techniques are very damaging, while others are very supportive of healthy development.

5. Educate yourself about the importance of attachment and connection. The stronger the attachment between parents and children, the easier and more joyful it is to parent, and the better the outcomes for children.

Parenting is the hardest job in the world, and it is also the most important. You are shaping human beings. You are creating the future of the world.

Parenting is also one of the loneliest jobs. It actually does "take a village to raise a child", but most of us in North America are parenting in isolation and struggle to find our ways. It is important to find support from people who help you to feel good about yourself, and to discover your strengths and abilities.

Remember that there is no "right way" to parent. Every parent is different and every child is different, and no parent in the world is perfect!

Once you start on the path of self knowledge, you will find your own inner wisdom, learn to trust yourself and become a more confident, connected parent. Parenting will still be hard work, but it will bring much greater joy.

Judy Banfield is the founder and owner of Mountain Baby, the unique, award winning retail store for young children.

Known for her wealth of knowledge, experience, wisdom, compassion, her sense of humor, and her ability to inspire and empower new mothers and fathers, for 35 years she has worked to instill confidence in thousands of parents and caregivers of children.

Her achievements include, teaching young children, teaching at the college level, coordinating programs for new parents, facilitating postpartum depression groups, counseling breastfeeding mothers, authoring a popular parenting blog, writing newspaper parenting columns, appearing as a radio parenting commentator, and being a Lactation Consultant in a maternity clinic.

Judy is excited to have combined all this invaluable experience and now has a flourishing coaching practice for new parents and parents of young children!

She holds a Master's Degree In Early Childhood Education.

She is an Internationally Certified Lactation Consultant, An Achieve Today Certified Life Coach and is the proud mother two thriving grown children.

Deeply committed to the emotional and physical environment of our planet, Judy is here to make your life, your children's life and the world, happier and more loving.

She can be reached at judybanfield.com

The Secret to Increasing Your Self-Confidence

by Andrew Barber-Starkey

There are few things that are more important to a financial professional than confidence. The confidence to set the appointments, to close for a sale, ask for referrals or – as far as that goes – get what you want in any area of your life.

But how do you increase confidence? Is there a formula that will work every time, without fail, to leave you feeling stronger and better about yourself?

As it turns out, there IS a formula.

It was years ago but I will never forget that moment. I walked into the kitchen and my wife had the radio on and was listening to radio therapist Dr. Laura. On the line was a young woman who was crying and whimpering about how bad her life was with men and so on. Dr. Laura said to her, *"Young lady, what you need is more confidence."* The caller surprised me with her response. She said, "*I know. But how do I get more confidence?*"

Being a coach, I waited with great anticipation for Dr. Laura's response. Her simple answer? "I can tell you how to get more confidence in two words: *Impress yourself.*"

It took me a moment to realize that Dr. Laura had hit the nail on the head. You see, most of us spend our time, effort and money trying to impress other people. We believe that other people's approval will validate us and make us feel better about ourselves. But the truth is that confidence and self-esteem are an inside job. It is what YOU think of yourself that matters. In fact impressing other people sometimes undermines your self-confidence, because deep down it can make you feel like a fraud.

Your confidence increases each time you prove to yourself that YOU can trust yourself. Each time you impress yourself with an action you take, your self-image receives a boost. If you impress yourself repeatedly, your self-image will become stronger and you will reap the rewards both internally and externally.

How to Avoid the Pitfalls

Here are some ways you may inadvertently be diminishing your self-confidence:

1) Comparing yourself to others

If you are like most people, you look to see how you compare to others and judge yourself accordingly. The problem is that you will always see yourself as better than some people but not as good as others. You must learn to view others as not better or less than you but simply as different.

2) Judging yourself by other people's opinions

One way to feel great about yourself is to be true to yourself instead of being concerned with what others think you should do. When you listen to and follow your own inner guidance, your confidence increases. Grammy-winning music producer Quincy Jones had it right when he said, *"Not one drop of my self-worth depends on your opinion of me."*

3) Defining your self-worth by your performance

Many people, men in particular, have been programmed since childhood to base their self-worth on their ability, productivity and accomplishments. Impress yourself with who you are, not how much you do.

4) Focusing on failures rather than successes

You have undoubtedly had far more successes than failures. Instead of replaying what didn't work over and over, develop the habit of noticing your progress and successes. This simple shift in attention can literally change your life.

5) Being a perfectionist

Perfectionists have unrealistic expectations of themselves. Nothing is ever good enough. Perfectionists are hard on others but even harder on themselves. When they fail to achieve their own unreasonable expectations they beat themselves up mercilessly. This undermines their self-confidence creating a downward spiral that leads to inaction and failure.

How to Build Confidence

Free yourself from the above traps and you will be in a better position to impress yourself. Here are some tips and practices that will help:

1) Take action

When you take action you will almost always be more impressed with yourself than if you don't take action. Procrastination, over-analyzing and rationalization usually cause you to be self-critical.

2) Be decisive

Practice making decisions quickly rather than putting them off. Act boldly; take the initiative when opportunities arise.

3) Set goals based on actions instead of results

Most people set goals based what they want to achieve. However in many cases, especially in sales, getting the results you want is not within your control. The only thing you can control is the actions you take. So state your goals in terms of the activities you will do and let the results take care of themselves. That way no matter what the outcome you can win.

4) Keep your agreements with yourself and others

Making a commitment to another person and failing to keep it is a bad thing to do because you lose their trust and damage your reputation with yourself, too. But breaking agreements with yourself is far more damaging because it erodes your self-trust. When you think about it, self-trust and self-confidence are the same thing. Every time you follow through on a commitment you make to your-self, your confidence increases.

5) Be on time

When you are late, how do you feel about yourself? Certainly not impressed. So stop it! In fact try arriving 10 minutes early for all meetings and appointments; it will change your life!

The Ultimate Confidence Building Question

Here is a powerful question you can use in virtually any situation that will help you increase your confidence. Simply ask yourself, "How can I handle this situation in a way that causes me to be impressed with myself?" Listen to the answer inside yourself and follow through with it. Do this and over time our confidence will skyrocket.

I know this works because I have done it myself. In fact, I was so impressed with this concept that I bought the website, ImpressYourself.com.

No matter how successful you are today, if you want to achieve bigger goals it is essential that you increase your confidence. True success is being able to look at yourself in the mirror and feel proud of who you are. The more you impress yourself, the prouder you will feel!

Andrew Barber-Starkey has been coaching business owners full time since 1993 and has empowered over 6000 financial professionals, entrepreneurs and small business owners to greatly increase their income while enjoying a better quality of life. He was personal coach to multi-millionaire speaker/ trainer T. Harv Eker. In 1999 Andrew received the designation of Master Certified Coach from the International Coach Federation,

their highest award. He specializes in creating breakthrough strategies for his clients. His group coaching program, the ProCoach Success System, provides a simple structure that enables business owners and financial professionals to significantly and effortlessly increase their productivity and results. For more information visit www. ImpressYourself.com or email info@ ImpressYourself.com

Magnetic Joy

by Leonie Blackwell

The University lecturer asks, "How many people placed happiness as their number one goal?"

In the large class of fifty aspiring student counselors, forty-nine people raised their hands. All eyes turned to the only person in the room with both hands still resting on their desk. I was the youngest member of this class, and I could see in their eyes the mixed looks of confusion and confidence of maturity that I didn't know what they knew.

The lecturer turned and asked me, "Why don't you want happiness to be the most important aspect of your life?"

I replied, "Because happiness is a choice. I can be happy in any situation and at any time. I don't need to work towards being happy; I can just choose to be happy."

Needless to say, my older classmates tried in vain to convince me that not only was I wrong, but I was just plain naive!

Fast forward twenty-five years and what I've learned is that happiness is a cognitive process – we really do choose to be happy, but the dynamics of life have shifted. Now the focus is on feeling emotions that magnetize our lives and with it our happiness.

Happiness isn't a magnet to prosperity.

Let me say it again, 'Happiness is a cognitive process, it is something you think.'

While what you think matters, just consider these thoughts about happiness – 'I wish I could be happy;' 'I'm striving to be happy and when everything works out that's when I'll be happy;' and 'I can choose to be happy in any situation or at any time.'

There are beliefs that will support you to achieve happiness right now, and thoughts that will block your happiness. There is no doubt that choosing productive life-affirming thoughts, ideas, and attitudes improves your overall life experience; but thoughts alone aren't enough. You need emotion to add vibrancy to your thoughts.

Joy is the magnet. Joy is heartfelt. You can't choose to be joyous. For joy to be authentic and real it has to spring naturally from within. It can't be faked. When you are completely present and grateful in the moment, joy exudes from every cell in your body.

People want to be around someone who is authentically, heartfelt, and consciously present in joy.

Joy is the key to prosperity.

Joy is wealth.

When we come from a place of joy we can have more of everything we want in our lives, because that heartfelt place of gratitude and presence creates a magnetic energy. Joy creates more, and that is what prosperity is – the creation of more. The possibility of more. The experience of more. The expansion of wherever you are to wherever you are going.

The bonus of joy is – that it's such a beautiful emotion. You have so much fun being in the process of your unfolding journey that fears, struggles, and limitations will be dissolved naturally. No matter whether you are expanding the depth of connection in your relationships, the vitality of your health, financial wealth, business success, or personal growth, joy makes the journey more enjoyable.

There's nothing more attractive than a person fully expressing their joy. We all notice it, and so does the universe. When we are filled with joy our prosperity shines. We appear richer, more beautiful, and wealthy in the secret elixir of life.

Like all emotions, joy that isn't channeled, grounded, and effectively managed can be a magnet for distractions, unwanted attention, and unhealthy temptations. Everyone and everything will want to be a part of your magic. It's your job to filter the wheat from the chaff.

Better still, implementing simple grounding exercises into your daily routines will decrease distractions. Become aware of your energetic body, and each time you feel like the energy is sitting in your head set your intent to be grounded by simply saying, "I set my intent to be grounded."

When you are eating your breakfast, lunch, and dinner – focus on eating. Don't watch the television, read a book, or do the housework at the same time. This will help improve the digestion of the food, making you feel fuller, and therefore decreasing overeating. The more you do this, the more you are practicing to give your full attention to the tasks you are focusing on in other aspects of your life too.

Hydrating your body is vital for life. Drinking water is grounding. Make a commitment to your goal for prosperity by drinking at least eight glasses of water each day.

Physically moving your body keeps the energy circulating, which supports being grounded. This doesn't require you to become a marathon runner, but stretching, walking in nature, and simply moving all parts of your body every hour – even if it's just for a minute – keeps you grounded.

Your thoughts can sometimes be the toughest barrier to overcome because you have evidence to prove why your reality is the way it is. Emotional Freedom Technique involves tapping on meridian points to transform negative thoughts and feelings, but it also enhances positive beliefs. When your thoughts make you feel stressed, you become ungrounded. Using this process you will transmute the unproductive 'charge' in your interactions into grounded acceptance of what is.

As you feel physically well and shift your cognitive thoughts, emotional joy naturally elevates your mood, attitude, and approach to life. Aligning your body, mind, and emotions facilitates a natural progression in expressing your life purpose.

The flow brings more joy as you observe your unfolding. Prosperity becomes your natural state of being and attracts in your ideal mate, business success, financial wealth, vibrant health, rich and nurturing love, a broad and supportive network of friends. Enhanced personal growth is simply what you do. It's not even in question. Now you have the opportunity to step into the limitless expanse of opportunity and be more and more.

I have recorded a video clip just for you. If you are ready for more joy this Resolution and Empowerment Tapping Script – Joyful Life – will be perfect for you.

Leonie Blackwell, author of Making Sense of the Insensible and The Book of Inner Secrets, has the natural gift of hearing the deeper motivating needs and fears driving our relationships with ourselves and others. She has been running her naturopathic business since 1994, providing a service to more than 2,500 clients and teaching hundreds through her accredited practitioner courses and innovative personal development workshops. Leonie writes a weekly blog exploring our human reality with  *compassion and joy providing practical solutions to empower and enhance our lives. Her website is: www.leonieblackwell.com*

My Story

by Murielle Bocquin

Your potential at birth is Love and Abundance.

G rowing up, I was one of those very active, athletic people who believed that "when you don't move, you're dead" and who, since childhood, considered a naptime as a punishment.

My name is Murielle Bocquin. I was born in Annecy and lived in Rumilly, a town of 10,000 in the French Alps. As a child, I was shy and reserved. However, I had a globe of the world in my head and I loved walking for hours in the countryside neighboring my grandparent's farm. Miraculously, at the age of eight, I survived a 50-foot fall. I was a child of divorced parents by the age of 10. I completed my studies at 19 and devoted myself to a 20-year military career. I changed professions in 2009, pursuing a career in the French civil service for two years. Then....

In September 2011, I left for a three-year stay in South America, in French Guyana. There, I spent my time jogging, swimming and playing squash, I took flying lessons in an ultralight aircraft, I got my motorcycle license, and I had a job that required me to spend full days on difficult terrain as a Guyanese land technician. I took on all of this without allowing my body or my energy level to recover. I didn't consider one important characteristic of this part of the world: the equatorial climate – until the day when my body told me that it had endured enough. I was dressed in my athletic gear, ready to go jogging, and my body told me: "STOP, I can't go. I can't do it any more!" Because I had ignored the ever-present searing heat and the high humidity, I experienced the worst thing that could happen to me: to no longer have the physical strength to continue.

I didn't even have time to get a knee on the ground, let alone two, and I found myself sprawled out on the floor of my apartment. Less than 5 minutes later, something happened to me that was trivial, yet incredible. Somewhere, deep within myself, I cried out: "There, now I'm relaxed!" It was a first for me. For my entire life, I had never considered my own well-being. I was too occupied being active or in motion. Never before had I taken the time to feel relaxed.

I didn't realize at that time that this newfound awareness of my well-being, through relaxing my body and mind, would change my life. It took a whole new direction. It would now be guided by my well-being and I would take responsibility for my own personal development. It was a 180° turnaround!

What Changed

This revelation was followed by a frenzy of reading so I could learn more about relaxation, sports relaxation therapy, personal development and its various aspects; like success, the Law of Attraction, meditation, visualization, living in the present moment, and spirituality, as well as coaching and self-awareness tools like Neuro-linguistic Programming (NLP), Transactional Analysis (TA) and the Process Communication Model (PCM).

My free time in the mornings, evenings and weekends became time for learning, when I derived great satisfaction from improving myself, progressing and gaining access to "treasures" that were previously out of reach. I was fascinated and I discovered the amazing experience of watching myself change as a human being.

I improved my relationships with others, as well as my communication with and understanding of others. My life flowed more freely. The time I spent in my workplace changed. I learned to manage my time, and especially to better manage myself in time. I discovered the magic of the present moment. I overcame the psychological barriers that had previously limited me. I transformed limiting beliefs into supporting beliefs. I changed my identity – the one initially created by my environment and by others – by creating a new one for myself. I became a new person, and this new person is my true self. I experienced well-being every day and I resolved to be more human-oriented.

By turning to others, I took another step forward in 2014. I unleashed my creativity thanks to Julia Cameron and her book *The Artists' Way Every Day: A Year of Creative Living*. For my part, I decided to be creative in my own life. I created a YouTube channel and a blog (www.fullpowerpotentiel.fr) where I share my knowledge and expertise. I show that we can start a project from scratch without any knowledge of the respective field. All that is required in the beginning is a thought, followed by taking action; a small step. I undertook previously unthinkable challenges like riding a 650lb, 1300cc motorcycle. For the record, I weigh 100 pounds!

In 2015, I went to the next level by attending seminars and learning as much as I could. I chose the best individuals as my mentors, as I didn't want to waste time; I wanted to be successful and efficient. These included David Laroche and his *Académie de la Réussite* (Academy of Success), Lionel Donneley (Coaching Business), Anthony Robbins (UPW and Business Mastery, the RPM method), Sophie Bizeul, a coach with Anthony Robbins team, Martin Latulippe *(Académie Zéro Limite)*, Olivier Roland *(Blogueur Pro)* (Pro Blogger), Nathalie Cariou *(Education financière: Liberté & Richesse)* (Financial Education: Freedom and Wealth), Laurent Chenot *(Liberté 3G)*, Roger Lannoy *(Les clés de l'Abondance)* (The Keys to Abundance), Romain Delacretaz *(Liberté Financière Absolue)* (Total Financial Freedom), Joe Vitale (Wealth Trigger), Janette "Karuna" Bernissan *(MGK – Méthode de Guérison Karmique)* (Karmic Healing Method), Paul Wagner (Reiki) and Anthoni Dass (Achievers Self Actualisation - ASA). Learning is the best investment you can make in yourself.

In London in March 2015, Anthony Robbins changed my life. By walking across burning embers on the first evening of his Unleash Your Power Within (UPW) seminar, I overcame my greatest fear: financial insecurity. I then made two decisions. I decided to resign from my job and to leave the wage-labor system. And I decided to move abroad, initially to Morocco.

I tendered my resignation in April 2015. It was effective four months later. My move abroad intuitively evolved into an eight-month trip around our beautiful planet Earth. Why, I do not know.

My decision to leave the wage-labor system was crucial for me. Drawing from the realizations I had experienced over three years, my personal development transformed into releasing my human potential. The wage-labor system became a box in which I was too confined to be able to grow. I also needed to change my environment. Travelling opened doors for me in the spiritual dimension of my evolution.

I left the wage-labor system, in which we exchange our time for money, for what I call entrepreneurial freedom. I <u>am</u> an entrepreneur – not in the sense of creating an *actual* company or a business, but one within the mind. I have always been an entrepreneur, but I wasn't able to remember that fact, as I had been locked in the wage-labor system since childhood, during my formal education and lastly during my 25-year professional career as an employee. I remembered that I was an entrepreneur when I created a blog and a YouTube channel from scratch, and I was able to remember this thanks to David Laroche's seminar "The First Level of Confidence" in January 2015. When it was over, I continued my creative momentum by writing and publishing my first book online, *Lettre à ma fille Jennifer* (Letter to My Daughter Jennifer).

Then, I went to Anthony Robbins' Business Mastery conference in Las Vegas. I left there with two words: Risk Taker. I realized that inside of me, and as incredible as it sounds to me, I am an "investor" in my soul. It's this path that I now choose to express my creativity.

A human being's personal evolution is a road paved with realizations. When I watch my niece and my nephew playing a video game, I see them start a game, learn new skills when they encounter new situations or challenges, then go to the next level, and so on until the end of the game. I see them appreciate their progress in the game. I see them congratulating each other and celebrating when they advance to the next level. I see them beginning a new level, where they discover a new environment and adapt to it by using previously acquired skills more easily, while experimenting with new ones. I see them moving ahead and enjoying their path. I see them enjoying the present moment. I also see them sharing the skills they have acquired with others. I see them naturally playing in a network, expressing themselves beyond all borders. I see them leaving their comfort zones.

The best gift you can give yourself is to self-invest. Buy a personal development book and read it instead of watching television. Then buy another, read it and feed your brain with new, useful information. Personal development books are goldmines and they contain wonderful treasures. Then invest in yourself by surrounding yourself with mentors and inspiring people from whom you will learn an enormous amount in a short period of time. Your mentors are like "shortcuts" that will help you save time – your most valuable asset. Invest in yourself as if you were a company on the stock market.

For those of you with ambitious projects who want to make money, get your financial education, and then learn how to think like a millionaire. Spiritual work in abundance, and love, will help you break down the final barriers anchored deep within your being, for therein lies your full potential: Love and Abundance.

Whatever dream you want to achieve, and regardless of the path you choose to get there, spiritual work on yourself awaits you. It will be an outward journey to Love and Abundance, ever-present deep within you. Make them gush out of you like a fountain. Your best mentors for this are babies, as they are born with Love and Abundance. Are you a parent or planning to become one? Observe your baby and sustain the human being's greatest strength within it. Make sure your child reaches adulthood with the best assets to achieve their full potential and live a fulfilling life.

To learn more about me, you can visit my blog www.fullpowerpotentiel.fr

Namasté.

With Love, Abundance and Prosperity.

Murielle Bocquin

Murielle Bocquin spent 20 years in French Army and 5 years in civil service as a computer engineer. She changed her lifestyle in September 2015 by quitting the wage-labor system and travelling as a citizen of the world. Awarded "Firewalker" by Anthony Robbins, she is certified Master Coach at the "Institut de Coaching International" of Geneva and she coaches in Universal Creation Process. Her first French book "Lettre à ma fille Jennifer" is available on Amazon. Visit her blog www. fullpowerpotentiel.fr and feel free to contact her at contact@whenyouneedask.com.

One Moment In Time

by Kathleen Boucher

D o you believe that you are born with an ingrained set of personality traits? After all, have you not heard one or two of your relations mention "He has his father's hard-headedness" or "She has her mother's people skills"? And have you noticed someone forever giving you free advice, whether it's good or not? It is up to you to decide what you want to believe, as what you believe is very powerful. What you believe to be true, you attract.

Let's say you hear someone who you think very highly of saying, "I expect you to fail at French. No one in our family has ever been good at French." Would you be hurt and surprised by this statement? How does this person know you are going to fail, merely because other people in your family did so? How preposterous! And yet, do you believe them?

If so, take this moment in time and think back to something that made you feel on top of the world; when you felt unstoppable. Was it the first time you rode your bicycle by yourself, the first time you tied your shoes, the first meal you cooked, your first kiss, that incredibly difficult exam you passed, or passing your driving test? Whatever it may be, bask in the joy of this one moment in time. Hold on to this feeling. Now, tag this feeling onto you passing your French exam. Create a picture in your mind of the feel of your desk, the quality of the air you breathe, the feel of your clothes, the smell of the soap you used to shower with and the sense of utter joy you feel having passed your French exam or course. Joy and power flows through you! From this moment forward commit to never letting anyone steal your dreams or goals. Be mindful of what you believe.

Let me share with you how one statement affected my life and how I carried around this limiting belief for years. Then I'll explain how I solved this problem.

When I was ten years old my weekly allowance was ten cents. Yes, stop laughing, it was ten cents. For ten cents I could purchase one candy apple and one chocolate bar. I will let you do the math. And no, I am not *that* old.

I received the ten cents every Monday, at which point I would gallop down to the corner store and buy my candy apple. I say gallop because I had polio at the age of five; this meant I did not run per se, but gallop, which is running lop-sided! Can you see this in your mind? If so, I hope you are smiling. I want you to see a ten-year-old girl galloping to the corner store five blocks away with ten cents clutched in her hand… smiling the entire way. It was the highlight of my week. One day my mother said to me as she gave me the ten cents, "You are never going to have money as you always spend it!" I felt awful and devastated that for the rest of my life I would never have money. My entire world deflated. You see, I believed my mother with my entire heart and soul. She was the grown-up and she knew things I did not.

The sad thing is that I carried this limiting belief around with me up until last year. Why did it take me so long to get rid of this limiting belief? Well, I had to realize that I had a limiting belief *before* I could take action to change it. Here is one way my limiting belief manifested itself.

Let me backtrack. Before I tell you specifically the way it manifested, I need to say that I've written two award-winning children's books. They are called *A Simple Idea to Empower Kids: Based on the Power of Love, Choice and Belief* and *A Simple Idea to Empower Kids: Teen's Edition.* Both books have the same texts but different covers and illustrations geared towards kids aged 6-8 and for pre-teens and teens, respectively. How did the books win awards? If you want to win awards, you enter contests and hope for the best. There are no guarantees, but if you don't enter you cannot win. I hired a publicist to advise me.

Now it's time to tell you my limiting belief. Picture this. I have a stack of my books and I am selling them to family, friends, and colleagues. Each time I ask for money in payment for the books I feel extremely ill. I feel so ill that I would rather give the books away for free. How insane is that? After some soul searching I realized that the statement my mother innocently made when I was ten years old – "You are never going to have money as you always spend it!" – is something I have been validating my entire life. You see, up until a year ago I was terrible at saving money!

So, how did I solve this problem? I joined Achieve Today

and worked with a wonderful coach by the name of Jerry Mutz. He guided me with open-ended questions to seek the answers to help me get rid of my limiting beliefs. Every successful person has a coach. This is one of the reasons they are successful. If you are looking for ways to reach your dreams then the best advice I can give you is to get a coach who will assist you in finding the answers you seek. After all, are you not worth it? Are you a carbon copy of someone else? Or do you wish to leave your mark on the world and a legacy for generations to come? Yes! You are unstoppable! Believe me, if I can do it then so can you!

Kathleen Boucher is a registered nurse and an award winning author of two children's books. Her mission is to inspire and motivate kids to follow their dreams. Boucher is passionate about writing and empowering kids. http://greatkids.me/ She lives in Ontario, Canada with her husband, and two children.

The Prosperity Factor: Meditative Alchemy – Healing from Within

by Lydia R. Brodie

The power of choice is to decide whether or not to listen to your body's inner wisdom. The body manifests your reality; your universe. The body reflects everything you have manifested up to this moment with your underlying emotions, thoughts, beliefs and actions. This chapter attracted you, because of your body's specific message of self-healing.

The next step is revealed as you go within and discover meditative alchemy. Our bodies, minds and spirits alchemize energy from cosmic prosperity. It is our Divine right. This flourishing energy arrives when we allow and receive healing. Channeling the energy arriving through our bodies for an inner healing begins to regenerate each and every cell within – cells that are always sending out, receiving and attracting more prosperity. The inner power to heal comes from the alchemy of the breath and the willingness to transform what the heart desires into prosperity; whatever form that takes in our lives.

The cells in our body are the storehouses for the key to prosperity, health and abundance. The energy fires along these cells in a negative or positive stimulus, like a train track. Energy can click down the negative track of fear, or the positive track of love. The mind is incapable of thinking negative and positive thoughts at the same time; it's either fear-based thoughts or love-based thoughts.

You create what you believe and attract similar thoughts, people, events, and desires into your life, depending upon which track is cycling over and over in your mind. To detach from the track, or switch tracks, conscious thought needs to show up using the breath to release the negative energy and emotions. By drawing this positive breath energy into us, consciously or unconsciously, the flow of energy through our vital systems is alchemized. For example, a miscommunication can manifest itself as a sore throat, which is the bridge between the heart and the mind. In swallowing unspoken words, the body needs to release, speak or accept it to return to harmony and balance.

To arrive at this natural harmonious state, the perspective or track needs to shift in a state of stillness. The easiest way to arrive at stillness is through relaxation or mediation, but reaching a meditative state does not require sitting on a mountain chanting OM; it requires sitting still, being present and breathing out the tensions in the body and mind. Breath links all the systems of the body together in one harmonious symphony of flow in order to achieve balance. When not in balance, chronic stress may lead to the manifestation of ill-ness or pain, as well as warning flags of minor or major dis-ease in the body; such as, constant struggles, emotional upheaval, infection, inflammation, feeling lost, lonely, isolated, bored, or a disconnection with the true self.

Through a meditative and relaxed state, any loss or dis-ease in the body is alchemized into a state of health, prosperity and balance; such as lack to prosperity; limitations to infinite possibilities or simply fear into love. Being mindful eases tension from the body, the mind relaxes, flows through the emotions, and a feeling of positivity is achieved. Some call it "Bliss" or being "In-the-zone."

Through stillness, you mindfully learn from the infinite wisdom of the body and what is encoded there. It is our very own, private Akashic records unlocking in order to heal from within. When trusting our body's inner wisdom, the prosperity of life unravels layer by layer, revealing our true Divine Self. This shows up in optimal wellness, being physically fit, balanced emotions, abundant finances or health, dynamic relationships, self-acceptance/respect, love, and a career or job with purpose and meaning – motivated and enthusiastic to start each day.

When natural healing gets blocked or stuck, only awareness of the breath brings the flow of energy back to the body. This applies to the emotional and mental energy fields in the body, where the dark circles of energy are slowing down the circulation or flow to restore healing and wellness. With the use of the breath, alchemy transmutes these dark energy circles of tension, stress, anxiety, disharmony, and fear encoded in our cells into harmonious PEACE, LOVE, and LIGHT circles of balanced positive energy. Most people breathe very shallowly and rarely take a full breath to cleanse the body. By using the breath to flush out the toxins, toxic thoughts and emotional tension, nothing is encoded in the body and dis-ease alchemizes into complete well-being or health.

An Exercise in Meditative Alchemy (in nature):

Keeping your spine erect, shoulders back and down, feet firmly planted on the floor, palms up resting comfortably on the knees or thighs, sitting still for a moment, close your eyes, tune in and bring the awareness to your breath. Now, at this moment, to illuminate where you need to focus, send a few breaths to your navel. Let the breath rise up from your grounded feet to the top of your head, cascading like a waterfall over any dark areas or messages/pain manifesting in the body. Shift the next few breaths to the throat, your communication center, where you say or swallow words that may need to be spoken. Shift the breath from the top of the head sweeping down the body to your toes, and now focus on the throat. On the next inhalation, send a ball of white gold light energy to the throat and stay there; keep sending the breath and waiting for the energy to shift. Visualize the white gold cascading waterfall sweeping gently throughout your body, rinsing away the dark spots or darkness transmuting into crystalline white gold energy of pure love – bliss.

Bring the awareness back to any perception of stuckness;

send the breath there once again, sweeping white gold healing energy created, until you feel the shift in energy. Gently allow any emotions to float to the surface. Observe. Don't judge, censor, edit, or criticize the emotions or feelings; be a witness. Let the knowledge come to be recognized by the conscious mind and received, then release it. Let it go.

Breathe through the emotions and feelings, sending the energy to wherever it needs to flow to restore balance, peace, love and light. If it will not release, center on this one negative energy; instantly think of 5 things you are grateful for this negativity showing up right here. List them without thinking. Now gently alchemize the energy throughout the body. Breathe normally. Gently open your eyes. Say to yourself:

> I see me.
>
> I hear me.
>
> I appreciate me.
>
> I forgive me.
>
> I love me.
>
> Thank you! Thank you! Thank you!

Gradually return to regular breathing, and have a sip or glass of water to continue to flush out any residual, unnecessary energy or emotions from the body.

Now is a great time to journal to heal the experience; free-flow writing of one to three pages will lock-in this feeling into your consciousness. Pause, and feel gratitude for this moment; bask in the flow of positive energy just created. By locking in this positive feeling, it literally changes the neu-ro-pathways in the brain to flow in a positive prosperous track by switching off of the negative destructive pathway. Harmony and balance is restored within our body's systems.

Trust in the body's infinite wisdom to know exactly what is needed right here, right now. This alchemizes to attract the good things in life and flow with positive energy. By harmonizing a dynamic balance within the body, the mind relearns how to self-regulate thoughts and emotions to the positive love-track. From this moment onward, the body and mind connection remembers the harmonious centering and works to maintain this new position of balance. Harmony and healing within the body resets any negative messages attempting to switch the tracks. If the negative track switches back, stop or pause, breathe, and state five things to be grateful for this one negative thing – every single time this happens – to instantly switch back to the positive track of life. Eventually, the new habitual positive track is reinforced and becomes the new thought pattern or belief.

"It's now okay to choose health, well-being, abundance and prosperity radiating in positive alchemized energy flowing easily in my body, mind, soul and spirit. I accept myself as I AM. I AM AWESOME! And so it is! It is done."

Lydia Brodie has been a storyteller from the early age of five, with an innate healing gift of reading the body's infinite wisdom. This allows her to teach others how to shift through the body's complex energy centers and unlock the hidden code that lies within. Since 2000, she has been certified in Meridian Energy Healing, specializing in Guided Healing Meditation and Self-Healing.

Lydia is a consultant for businesses and individuals, promoting intuitive healing, meditation, mindfulness, journaling to heal workshops, and guided imagery for self-healing. Lydia holds a B.Comm. in Marketing from the University of Alberta, and one day hopes to complete her Masters in Counseling. She also has 20 years of media experience as well as numerous specialized certifications, including, meridian energy healing, coaching, writing, editing, guided imagery, and stress reduction. Some of her programs include: author of the self-help healing book "The Stream of Life," children's books, blogs on Healing Alchemy, and podcasts on topics such as meditative alchemy (healing from within), stress management, relaxation, and journaling to heal.

Desiring to inject more fun and adventure into the mundane weekly routine, Lydia enjoys solo artist dates to nurture creativity and inspiration.

She can be reached through her website www.Writer4Life.com or on Twitter @writer4lyf3.

Gratitude and Big Dreams, The Foundation of Prosperity

by Yvonne Chan

Like many other children, I had a dream as a child. I wanted to be an actress – an actress of the Cantonese Opera in Hong Kong. I never had the chance to watch the plays on the stage, but I watched a lot of Cantonese Opera movies on TV. The costumes were very attractive. Even when I was very sleepy, once I heard the opera music, I would awaken and watch the show.

I was lucky that my college was the first school to have Cantonese Opera available as an extra-curricular activity. Two maestros were invited to teach the art. I joined the Opera group for two years and learned some basic singing and performing skills, before I graduated from the secondary school in 1981. I wished to be a professional actress.

However, ever since the late 1960's, other types of TV series and western movies have attracted young people, while Cantonese Opera has been considered entertainments for oldies. As such, my parents commented that Cantonese Opera was a declining industry, and education was the only mean to get a good job and survive. Continuing my studies became my only choice.

Accounting was my major, and I graduated from the Hong Kong Polytechnic in 1987. Climbing the career ladder was my daily focus. I was subsequently qualified as a Certified Public Accountant, Certified Information System Auditor, and Certified Information Security Professional. I also earned my MBA. I have changed jobs many times, and have had the chance to travel to many different countries.

In 2000 I joined an IT development company. I was responsible for information security of the company in order to achieve the BS7799 certificate. In 2001, we became the first Internet project management company to attain this certificate in Hong Kong. It seemed that I had a big achievement in my career. However, at the same time, I found that I had muscle tissue problems after some Paida treatments. I developed two cysts in my back, near the infraspinatus muscle, overnight.

I also found that there were many knots inside my right arm. Though I was not trained with any massage skills, my left hand would naturally massage my right arm. I could "see" my knots in my mind. My fingers felt very tired after massaging my arm. One day, after the treatment and on the way back home at noon time, I thought as I paid the masseur and I felt so tired doing the massage, perhaps I should just be a good patient, meditate more and stop massaging myself. Within minutes, I found rashes on both of my inner arms. I was so worried that I called the masseur. I told him I had rashes and asked for reasons why this might be happening. He was busy and promised to call me back after work. Around 11pm he called and asked "What had you thought?" I was surprised, and then just said thanks and bye. Once I resumed massaging my right hand, the rashes went away. Instantly, I knew that I must be the one to take care of myself and could not rely on others.

Thereafter I learned aromatherapy, Swedish massage, ear candling and Bach flower remedies. I also read a lot of health and natural remedies information. The more I was exposed to this knowledge and these experiences, the more I thought health was the key in life, while career was just a means for achieving a better standard of living. I wanted to change my life so that I could work on something that I had a real interest in.

Shortly afterwards, I sent an email to a music production company asking whether I might buy their healing and relaxation CDs in bulk. I got a reply from the supplier that their company would be hosting a health products exhibition booth in the coming week, and she asked me to meet her at the venue. We met and had an enjoyable conversation. A few days later, the supplier called me and said that there was another similar but smaller exhibition coming up, and she suggested that I set up a booth. She would leave me all remaining CDs for the next exhibition. I would only have to pay her after I sold the products or returned the products to her upon their next visit. I went to my meditation class right after this conversation. During my meditation, a very detailed plan came out. Friends, colleagues and even my masseur came to help at the booth. I sold essential oils, candle diffusers, Bach flower remedies and music CDs for this first business.

I thought about trying to save some money and start a real business, say in five years' time. One day, my IT boss asked me to see him. It was a day in February of 2003, the year of the SARS outbreak in Hong Kong. I knew there must be something serious going on. I took few drops of the Bach Flower Rescue Remedy before meeting him. He said that my salary was too high and was considering laying me off. I replied calmly that I was fine leaving without any complaint. Instead I thought this development was simply my dream being heard.

I started making handmade soap with essential oils and intended to learn more about aromatherapy. However, aromatherapy was very new to Hong Kong at that time. Most people thought that essential oils were only used for massage. I was pressured by my parents because they felt that their daughter was giving up a professional career and becoming a massage girl. My dad reminded me that I still had a mortgage to pay.

To survive, I was forced to look for jobs. I found a part time professional job. I thought that I might then spend a half day in the office and a half day on my own business. But I was totally wrong. "Part time" meant that I would be only paid when I had a job. Anyway, I joined the company and worked for their clients. Sarbanes Oxley Act (SOX) 404 was passed in the U.S. and all exchange-listed companies had to implement internal control systems. With my experiences, I could easily handle these projects, and helped the clients to modify their procedures to meet the new legal requirements. Afterwards, I also worked on other projects like system implementation and Shared Service Center setups. I have travelled around the Asian countries for almost six years. During these years, I did a lot of research on natural health remedies and spiritual practices.

When I was working in Singapore, for example, I found that I lived in a place surrounded by a yoga studio, a book store selling books on various New Age topics, and a bakery wholesale store where I could find ingredients and molds for my soap. I bought a lot of books, including *Power of Subconscious Mind,* and books on forgiveness, aura, hypnosis etc. I still kept massaging my right arm. I started seeing some scenes of my childhood during the meditations which explained some of my odd behaviors and worries. Subsequently, I noted that this was similar to some of the hypnosis skills that certain professionals use to treat their clients.

During my business trip in Beijing, I travelled back to Hong Kong to attend some classes during the weekends. I have learned various alternate treatments, such as Bowen Therapy, Jin Shin Jyutsu, Dorn Method, power of water etc. I gave treatments to my family members and friends. Colleagues at client companies heard about my story and enjoyed asking me health advice, instead of talking about work-related issues.

I finally came back to work in Hong Kong in 2009. One day I bought a magazine of a maestro and found that he taught opera singing class. I joined the class and had my first singing performance with live music in 2010. Part of my first dream came true.

I am still passionate about the art of Cantonese Opera. It is too late to learn the skill to perform on stage. I wondered what I may do to promote the art. In 2009, Cantonese Opera was designated as an Intangible Cultural Heritage item. However, as I mentioned above, it was considered to be a declining industry and very few people joined the field in the last 30 to 40 years. Hence many skills were lost as older actors passed way. I remembered there were many Cantonese Opera movies produced in 1950-60s. Though many people complained it took only few days to create those movies and they were therefore of poor quality. Fortunately, their skills were recorded in those movies.

There were some websites focusing on these operas, but they mainly talked about the idols themselves. I decided that I wanted to develop a website focusing on the art itself, and the history of the art form. If possible, some specific skills would be introduced to the website's audience. This is a wish, but I don't know where and how to start. Fortunately, last year a friend told me that there was social group already set up comprising 20 members of the opera group of our alma mater. We already planned to have a 42nd year anniversary performance, to be held next year. I am assigned as the organizer of this performance!

To prepare for the website, I did some research. I found that some of the popular and famous movies were directed by my grandfather. In the old days, only male actors were allowed to perform on the stage. Only occasionally would female troupes be included. It was only in 1933, that a performance by a mixture of male and female artists was first allowed in Hong Kong. My grandma was one of three main female characters. So now, successful development of this opera website has become a mission rather than just an interest.

After resuming my opera dreams, I started making bar soap again last year. While I don't like cooking the oils for long hours to produce the liquid soap, I found a cold press method from the Internet. I successfully made the liquid soap on my very first try.

I made friends with a lady when we were watching a road show on the street. As we were talking, she commented that if I wanted to work on the alternate health or spiritual practices, then I needed to have knowledge of ho'oponopono. Together with the concept of the power of water and ho'oponopono, I made some great soaps, and my friends liked them.

Recently I have had some sickness and need to have surgery; I was diagnosed with hyperthyroidism and could not have an operation. After discharge, I sought out Bowen Therapy treatment. I had great improvements within just a few treatments. I will definitely resume the Bowen therapy practice. I think this is time for me to walk my dream again.

In the past, I felt upset that I was not doing what I liked. I felt frustrated that I had to choose between being an accounting professional and starting alternate health practices. However, when I look back, I now realize that I learned a lot from all of my experiences. I have never complained about my sickness as it only guided me to take care of my own health, and develop my abilities to take care of others. I feel abundant when I learned to be grateful and keep dreaming.

Yvonne Chan is a CPA with the Hong Kong Institute of Certified Public Accountants. She's a member of the The Chartered Association of Certified Accountants, a Certified Information Systems Security Professional, Certified Information Systems Auditor, and a member of the Information Systems Audit and Control Association. Yvonne also has a diploma in Nutrition and is a Bowen Therapy Practitioner. You can connect with Yvonne at her website http://livinghandsmadesoap.com and http://canton-opera-reading-spot.com

Limitless Love

by Devadas Chelvam

Everyone is looking for love; children in their parents and siblings, adults in their partners and friends. However, hardly anyone is satisfied with the love they experience. Actually, we need not look outside us for love, since limitless love is our very nature.

The sage who has captured the hearts of many millions in this age is Ammachi. She worships all the thousands gathered in various venues to see her, as "embodiments of pure love and supreme consciousness." It is truly marvelous to hear from a sage, that we are limitless love and pure awareness, playing temporarily in a bodily form.

We need to find the truth of our own being and experience genuine freedom. If we are sincere and earnest about finding the truth, we can realize that we are infinite awareness. That means we are one with everyone and everything, and are essentially peace, love and joy.

We pretend that we know ourselves and others, when actually we do not know. Forgetting the ever present beauty and wonder of life, we indulge in harsh and hard judgments about ourselves and others, as we are conditioned to do so from early childhood. To stop this constant pretension and see our innate innocence and beauty, we have to give up our false identifications.

True identity has to be present and permanent. Our body is constantly changing. Bodily cells die and disappear; new cells are formed continually. Essentially we are not the body, and hence not young or old, male or female, sick or healthy. Those attributes belong to the body we are currently using, and not at all to our essential being. Our name, education and profession also mean merely looking at the surface, and not at the central reality.

Personality, with its good and bad habits, keeps changing. Both the past history and the story we tell ourselves when we want to know who we are clearly miss the mark. Personality and personal history do not point to our essential nature. Race and religion have very little to do with our real identity.

We are not Americans, Africans, Asians or Europeans. None of us is exclusively Christian, Muslim, Hindu or Buddhist. We do not belong to any country. All the countries, religions and languages belong to us, since they are floating in our limitless awareness.

As seminary students in Sri Lanka, we were happily spending our vacation in Hatton with its beautiful hills, waterfalls and rivers. There I read the book *Existence and Existent* by the French philosopher Etienne Gilson. It moved me deeply and I was feeling high for days.

One moonlit night, after dinner, I walked up a hill alone,

thinking about what I had read. While I stood enjoying the beauty of the moon shining on the hills, it occurred to me that the hills, the moon and my thoughts were real due to existence – which is the essence of God. It plunged me into such depths of ineffable happiness that I was jumping up and down for joy.

Somewhat similar was the experience of reading the amazingly powerful book by Eckhart Tolle titled *The Power of Now*. The author writes about the wonderful process of his own awakening to the splendor of Reality. He stresses the importance of going beyond thoughts, being in the Now, and thus escaping the prison of the past and the illusion of a future.

Eckhart Tolle was teaching at Cambridge University in England as a graduate student. He had suffered from severe suicidal depression from childhood in Germany. One night he was in such despair at Cambridge that he decided to commit suicide. While thinking again and again that he must kill himself, Eckhart suddenly realized that there were two selves in him, and only one could be his true self.

It was such a shock that his mind stopped, all the thoughts disappeared and he was drawn into a vortex of energy. He felt an intense fear, and heard an inner voice tell him: "resist nothing." Then the fear too disappeared, as he plunged into a void inside him. He does not remember what happened afterwards.

He woke up to hear the sweet melody of a bird chirping outside, and opened his eyes to see the light of dawn filtering through the curtain. He felt that there was "infinitely more to light than we realize. That soft luminosity filtering through the curtain was love itself."[1]

Eckhart Tolle described his experience further: "Everything was fresh and pristine, as if it had just come into existence. I picked up things, a pencil, an empty bottle marveling at the beauty and aliveness of it all. That day I walked around the city in utter amazement at the miracle of life on earth, as if I had just been born into this world."[2]

Eckhart Tolle's false and suffering self had vanished altogether. He spent almost two years sitting around in park benches in a "state of the most intense joy." People approached him, wanting for themselves the palpable peace that he seemed to emanate. Answering their questions, he became eventually a spiritual teacher.

The Power of Now provides some powerful techniques to find inner peace and realize our true Self. As our thoughts and feelings veil the peace and joy within us, witnessing them without any judgment (if judging happens, see it as another thought) allows us to see the silent space underneath the thoughts. As we continue to witness, which means accepting and surrendering to what is, the silent space deepens, and we feel the peace and joy.

Another technique is to feel the life energy within our body. Stretch the right hand in front, feel the energy in your palm; then, feeling the energy, go up the arm to the shoulder, neck, and on to the left side. Continue to feel the energy in the face, head, chest, stomach, abdomen, thighs, knees, calves and the feet. As we continue to be aware of the

---

1   *The Power of Now* by Eckhart Tolle, New World Library, Novato, CA, 2004, p. 4
2   Ibid, pp. 4-5

life within the body, we can feel the same energy spreading around our body to connect with plants and other things near us.

It is a common human tendency to identify people with their acts, especially when the acts are seriously wrong. Such identification spells immaturity. There are sins, but no sinners. There are crimes, but no criminals. The Masters do not identify us with our evil acts, since they know that we are essentially perfect. We are truly one at heart, yet forgetful of our true nature, act in ways that are hurtful to us and to others. Hence the need for an effective healing method!

Ho'oponopono is an ancient healing technique from Hawaii that cleans our memory or consciousness of any negativity, such as fear, anger, hatred, shame and guilt. It is a matter of using four phrases: 1. I am sorry 2. Please forgive me 3. Thank you 4. I love you.

Think of any person you resent even slightly, and keep saying the phrases. The words may be addressed to the person concerned by name, while you remember that you are speaking to the true divine Self within us all. Then you know that you are forgiven and feel grateful that your heart is healing. The external results are secondary. Say the words again and again, until the healing or cleaning is complete.

There are many reasons for anger. When we are angry, we feel superior. This sense of superiority is needed to compensate for the sense of inferiority that comes from our subconscious mind, which carries the memory of the numerous ways we have been put down by others from early childhood.

Digging a little deeper into ourselves, we can see that we do live with some sense of shame and guilt. Thus we cultivate the habit of being hard on ourselves. Then it becomes quite easy to be hard on others. Human life seems to be a constant struggle between inferiority and superiority complexes.

As things around me and my body continually change, the consciousness in me that witnesses the changing phenomena remains the same. When we calmly witness our thoughts and feelings, that witnessing consciousness can be seen as pure awareness.

Awareness knows no distinction or extinction, and is eternal. It seems to give reality to everything and everyone. No form is real apart from awareness, though awareness itself has no form. All this can be known intuitively, if we take the time to look deeply into ourselves.

The more we identify with our unchanging awareness, the more we would be able to accept ourselves and others as we are, with our strengths and weaknesses. Then we can be peaceful enough to feel unconditional love and compassionate kindness towards ourselves and others. There would be no need for apology or forgiveness. It would be a simple matter of right understanding.

Ammachi and Her devotees greet each other with the words: "Namah Shivaya." These Sanskrit words mean worshipping the other person as a manifestation of Supreme Consciousness and Limitless Love. Human contact is always a holy encounter, if we only know the truth about ourselves.

As we are essentially awareness, we have no beginning or end. Masters say that we are eternal and one with everyone.

Thus we are truly limitless love and endless joy. We get super-ficial glimpses of our essential nature now and then, espe-cially when we pray or meditate deeply, engage in selfless service, and are receptively in the presence of great Masters.

A devout Catholic priest first, then a materialistic unbeliever, now he ardently supports all the spiritual paths of mankind. Devadas Chelvam's profound personal experience that transformed him was utterly unexpected.

Ten years had elapsed since his father passed away. At a fifth floor apartment in mid-Manhattan, after dinner, Devadas spent the night intently observing his thoughts and feelings, without giving into the usual distractions.

*Towards the morning he was rather calm and alert, when he quite clearly felt the presence of his father, internally heard him say: "I love you" again and again and felt the vibrations of love in and around his body, as if he were swimming in a sea of love. He became aware that what he experienced went beyond the senses, was truly spiritual, and **much more real** than his body or the things around him.*

This started him on a journey of earnestly exploring various spiritual paths to encounter some saints and sages along the way. It resulted in a book titled: 'Limitless Love, Truly We Are That' website: limitlesslove.net or dchelvam.com

Empowerment

by Victoria Clark

For me, empowerment is a lifelong learning process that allows me to blossom further into my own power. I started with so little, I could barely speak. I felt disconnected, raw, vulnerable and suicidal. I became mentally ill, homeless, and just knew my life could not "work." As I triumphed over my "victimhood" mentality, I became more "in my power," conscious, and purposeful than I ever thought possible. You see, what I learned is that a victim mentality is a direct opposite of being conscious and feeling in control of your life. Why? As a victim I could not take any responsibility for my life. I was a leaf in the wind. My goal here is to share a little of what I've learned so that you too can become the CEO of your life.

When we think of the word "empowerment" it is often a vague sense of "being in your power." But what does that really mean. I like the Oxford Dictionary definition: "to make someone stronger, more confident especially in controlling their life." It is up to us to define the specifics of who our true essence really is. What makes us stronger, confident and in control?

There is one major principal with many corollaries. We'll talk about that principal and just a few of its corollaries. That principal is taking full responsibility for your life; it's about conscious choice-making. We are making choices constantly about what to do or how to feel. We often are familiar with goal setting in terms of career or financial areas of our lives. This same goal setting and decision making is also the way to gain control in EVERY aspect of your life, including how you feel. It is a choice.

You see, in order for us to be empowered we must know what specifically that is for us. We can't reach a goal that is not clearly defined. So this is the first corollary to that principal. Define the goal. So what would you and your life be like if you felt completely empowered? What would you have, do or be? What do you feel, see, hear, and smell? What does empowerment taste like? What is your physiology (posture, breathing pattern, tone of voice, muscle tension) like? Use all your senses to describe this you; your true essence.

What are the internal messages you tell yourself; your beliefs about you, your life and the world in general? Relating this principal to our beliefs and the meaning we give to each experience of our life is the first corollary. If we tell ourselves we have failed, that would be a disempowering interpretation of events. However, if we took the same event and declared it a "learning and growth experience" then there is no negativity, no failure – and therefore we are empowering ourselves. It is the same experience, but we just framed it differently. It is just information.

I used to be really negative toward myself. I'd beat myself up mentally constantly. As I started becoming aware and wanting to make changes, I'd beat myself up for beating myself up. It was a battle, but I realized it was actually simple (although not easy at first). If it made me feel good about myself, then it was empowering; if not, I chose to use it as information. "Is there any truth to this thought?" Maybe I was thinking that I was lousy and worthless. So the information was a disempowering thought. When I asked myself "What is going on that I say this?" I could decipher that I had just had a conflict with someone and did not handle it well. Ok, so that has a shred of truth. I can now choose to learn better conflict resolution skills. When I started thinking in this way, my life turned around. Did I still have "issues?" Of course. We are all continually growing. However I framed it so that no matter what, I felt empowered. The more I practiced this process, the easier and more effective it became. Mind you, I always acknowledge any feelings that come up rather than suppressing them. I am not advocating suppression. What I AM saying is that after you acknowledge what comes up you get to choose your interpretation and therefore how it all makes you feel. It is quite empowering to realize we are in control.

The next corollary is to take action that corresponds with your definition. Small steps are perfect for this. Keep the big picture in mind, but don't overwhelm yourself with steps that are too big. Taking small actions consistently keeps you in the game and creates more effectiveness and success.

With each experience we get to evaluate it to discover if we are producing outcomes that are moving us closer – or further – away from our stated goal. If it is moving us away, perfect – we now have that information so that we can redirect and choose a different course of action. It's just information. That is all it is. No failure; it doesn't exist if you think in these terms. The third corollary then is to evaluate and redirect if necessary. Like the Captain of a ship, we constantly steer our ship in the direction of our choosing.

When I was going through my darkness, I often asked myself why this was happening. I knew I "created" it. I knew about responsibility. What I didn't realize at first was that in my darkness I went back into victimhood. I was being triggered from past trauma. Asking "why" is rarely a good thing. So I started to ask myself "What meaning can I create? What can I do? What is the purpose?" I started again looking at the bigger picture and knew that I could make a bigger difference in the lives of others with this new experience and the growth and learning I received from it.

There is one missing piece that is also REALLY important. Success begets success. So CELEBRATE every little success. It is just as important as taking consistent action steps. Yell out "YES!!!" Make it a really joyous occasion every day. Always remember your goal and set aside time at least once a day to breathe it in using ALL your senses and awareness of what you will have, do or be when you are in your most empowered you; your True essence. Be it now! You can do it! I believe in you! Create your life anyway you choose.

Victoria first started studying psychology and human development in her teens. As she grew older, the focus expanded into consciousness, neuroscience, motivation and empowerment, as well as body-mind principals. As a Life Coach, she specializes in empowerment in all aspects of living. She incorporates and synthesizes what she has learned to create unique programs and plans for each group and individual. Her clients create the life they really want, become their own CEO of their life and bask in their brilliance. Victoria has an effective, straightforward approach that brings

> **YOU** into focus.
>
> **Y**our
>
> **O**ptimal living and
>
> **U**nlimited possibilities

> Meet Victoria and sign up for a FREE e-newsletter at:
> LivingInVisionLifeCoaching.com

The Art of Feeling Good

by Stéphanie de Tourris

MY JOURNEY

REVELATION

One night, in my living room, as I was having an argument with the father of my daughter, I realized that no matter what my wrongs were, I deserved so much better than this anger, this frustration, this sadness, this heaviness. I realized that this was not what I wanted. It was actually the opposite of what I had contemplated for my life, and definitely not how life should be lived.

I realized that I was very far from happy, and for the first time I fully recognized that life was too short not to be enjoyed to the fullest.

INSPIRATION

A couple of months later, teaching my class after the Christmas holidays, I looked at the kids and around the room, and I suddenly thought: "What the ... am I doing here?" Although I was somehow familiar with the feeling, this time the words were much more powerful than ever before. Right after that day, I listened to different talks on education and creativity, which inspired me and made me realize that what I had chosen once wasn't making me happy anymore, and that I was definitely out of place.

FEELING GOOD

What I was actually looking for at the time was a book which could help me regain my self-confidence. I bought *The Artist's Way* by Julia Cameron, and everything began shifting. I started writing pages everyday and began finding time for myself. I would find time to do things that made me feel good. And the more I was doing those things and feeling good about myself, the more I was willing to do that all the time. That's what life was all about: feeling good, enjoying, having fun! And as I was writing and revealing who I really was, I realized that the choices I had made a few years earlier did not correspond to who I was now.

WRITING and MAKING SPACE

I discovered the magic of writing. Whatever I wrote left me much more space during the day. Once I had written something down, it wasn't bothering me so much. I also realized that writing led to action. You can actually think about the same thing over and over, for hours, days, months, and even years sometimes, without ever acting. But once you become conscious of something on paper, it's as if you can't escape it; it's there. Things become clear.

MEMORIES

I began remembering things from when I was a kid. I remembered the games I played, what I liked doing, what I seemed to be good at, the books I read – books which, when I come to think of it now, may have shaped my life more than I had previously been able to imagine.

DUSTING OFF DISCOURSES & FINDING YOUR OWN VOICE

I started spotting the various voices that had had a deep impact on me: my parents, my teachers, my family, my friends, the news, the media, etc. And as I was remembering my own thoughts as a child and was clarifying the discourses around me, I think what I was doing was rediscovering my own voice.

READING

I started reading books and stories that inspired me; that filled me with enthusiasm – books about epiphanies, about people following their dreams, about change. And I started listening only to whatever felt good within. As I gained confidence, the other voices around were not as significant anymore because what I felt and what I did felt right and coincided exactly with who I was.

YOU CAN HAVE IT ALL

I came across a book in which I discovered several major life-changing facts, including how the mind works and some of the laws regulating the universe. I discovered how I could achieve anything I wanted in my life, that I could have it all, and that the only limits we come across are the ones we create in our minds.

SELF-ESTEEM

Most people I was listening to and reading about were mentioning the need for self-love. Self-love? I started digging into that! I started contemplating all the positive things I had achieved in my life, and then I started writing some positive affirmations about myself.

I think you kind of have to fall in love with yourself. Discover who you really are and love yourself. Only then will you start feeling really free to be who you are, and no longer need other people's recognition.

FEARS & DOUBTS

It is far easier to face fears and doubts once you've analyzed and realized where your present beliefs sprang from, because your outside reality is nothing but the manifestation of your conscious and unconscious beliefs about life and about yourself. Only then can you really begin to follow your intuition – which is very likely to take you exactly where you want to go. You also have to become clear about your destination. But don't listen to other people's advice or try to reason too much too soon. Listen to your own voice. Trust yourself.

OBSTACLES

I had never really understood before why obstacles were perceived as the best way to grow. It always sounded weird to me to hear that you had to suffer and be miserable at some point to grow. I think I get it now. You don't have to suffer unbearably, because it all depends on how you view things. You can feel sad or unsettled or angry, of course, but you don't have to feel miserable once you realize you're being taught something. Having this understanding helps you navigate your way.

The more you let go of your ego and listen to your own true self, the fewer obstacles you'll meet on the way and the more harmonious your life will be. There are times when it just all flows.

SAME ACTION SAME RESULTS

Once you feel prompted to do something, what happens is that, at one point or another, you will have to act differently or do something you've never done before. Because if you follow the same line or the same advice you've always followed, then you'll keep on getting the same results. This simply takes you where you've already been and where you are.

"You have been down there Neo, you know that road, you know exactly where it ends. And I know that's not where you want to be." Trinity, in *The Matrix*

JUMPING OUT OF YOUR COMFORT ZONE

You will *have to* leave your comfort zone and take a risk

that you've never taken before. And it seems to me that one way to overcome the fear or the doubt is to ask yourself: "If I go back to where I was and do not take this step, will I be happy and satisfied?" If you can feel deep within that the answer is no, then there is a good chance that you need to take this step... and trust life!

CONCLUSION - My tips

- Refuse what other people offer you as evidence of a reality that doesn't feel right to you

- Spot and dust off outer discourses

- Remember when you were a kid

- Listen to your own voice

- Start following what feels good and see where it takes you

- Read books and listen to inspiring people

- Consider the best

- Follow your intuition

- See the magic

- Re-watch *The Matrix* !!! ;)

---

*Stéphanie de Nas de Tourris was born in 1977 near Paris. She now lives in Southern France, in Marseille where she organizes workshops and events. She also sings in a band, "**Bruno**", and is preparing an album for next year. She has lived in Paris, Ivory Coast, Aix-en-Provence, Toulouse, Arkansas* and Massachusetts. She became an English teacher in 2000 and taught for fourteen years. After quitting her job last year, she co-founded " Les Allumettes - Bonheur Makers" with two friends. The three of them organize events called "Happy Breaks," for people to disconnect from their daily lives and learn about themselves and about life through activities linked to wellness and happiness.

She has started a coaching program for herself that has helped her to see more clearly and move forward, and plans to become a certified coach as well.

Stéphanie's will is to transmit what she's learning about life, inspire people and help them be happy by being the best possible version of themselves. She ultimately wants to offer a new vision for a new world.

Her message is that we all have an inner guide, our own voice, which we need to listen to in order to live meaningful and fulfilling lives.

Follow Stéphanie on Facebook at www.facebook.com/lesallumettes, and visit www.fullbliss.fr

Mindset, A Human Condition

by Sylvie Drapeau

In today's world, we are aware that our mindset or attitude defines the difference between making us or breaking us. Have you been looking for a way out of your job where you work hard all week and can barely afford to pay the bills? Do you look online to find opportunities so you can quit your job and follow your dream in life? Day after day, you hope to find the solution. The more you work at your present job, the more you are fed up. It's not what you want; it's not your passion. In fact, you do this job to make a living, to have a roof over your head and eat.

You think: "Well, I am young. I'll find a better job soon," but time passes, and kids arrive. Now your profound desire to find your dream job is less accessible because the kids come first, and you start thinking:

"I want my kids to have a better life than mine. I want them to succeed and be able to work in their dream job. It's too late for me now, so I'll keep this job. At least I have a job in today's economic world. I am lucky I have a job. Why am I complaining?

"The kids don't get everything they want but hey, I didn't get everything I wanted while growing up. I should be happy I have a job! If they can't make it to university or have their dreams jobs, it's not the end of the world. It's my life and it's not too bad. What else can I do? How can I change my life now? It's too late, too hard. Yeah, I am a fool thinking that I could increase my income and improve my life now."

What do you see in those paragraphs? Do you recognize yourself or a friend of yours? Do you agree with the internal dialogue? Do you have a similar internal dialogue? How often do you have internal dialogue which sounds like that? Do you see how the individual is trying to stimulate him- or herself to get the courage to change their life, but quickly becomes discouraged? Even when thinking of their kids, the person ends up giving up, accepting the fact that the kids may not achieve their dream jobs. They're destined to have the same kind of life as their parent.

That right there is mindset; it's attitude. You can decide to have an uplifting attitude or a down shifting attitude. It all depends of your internal dialogue. Now, why on earth do most humans choose a down shifting attitude instead of an uplifting attitude? Yes, we do it; 95% of the time we choose to have a discouraging internal dialogue, because we were raised like that. Our parents were raised like that; our grandparents were raised like that, too. We keep repeating the same mistakes again and again. You may ask, what is an internal dialogue, Sylvie?

An internal dialogue is simply us talking to us. Okay, here is a little exercise: go to a quiet place, where nobody and nothing can disturb you. Now just be quiet for two minutes. What did you notice? You probably began to think of something, you began to hear your thoughts. They were taking a specific direction and if you stayed quiet longer you would have begun an internal dialogue on a specific matter, or you would have begun to see images of action you need to do.

Our mind never stops thinking of what future actions we need to take, or produce an internal dialogue on a specific matter, and then we choose to uplift or down shift. The only time we succeed at shutting it off is in meditation; a good meditation can bring you to the quiet zone, where thoughts are sleeping. Your mind focuses on your breathing, on a mantra, or a specific set of sounds or set of images.

We mostly down shift our internal dialogue because of our education, our social environment, and how we were raised. Today, adults can change their attitude and reverse the process to achieve a 95% uplifting mindset, but what about the kids? Do we keep on teaching them the same old way or do we choose to give them the tools at a young age to develop 95% uplifting internal dialogues, because they have it as well? This is a human condition and it is the key condition which can make a huge difference in the way our kids become adults and what they do with their lives.

The most beautiful legacy we can give our kids is to teach them from birth. We should teach our babies, toddlers, kids, teenagers, young men and women how to use their minds properly, so they can achieve the highest potential and live a passionate fulfilled life. The 21st century shows us how kids are aggressive, bullying, low achieving, don't pursue their dreams, and have a very low self-esteem.

Kids' minds have been brainwashed with the old-fashioned, false concept that humans are made for limited lives. We got it all wrong; we have been doing it for centuries. Only a few privileged kids are able to receive different educations. They have been taught how to meditate every day and how our brains and attitudes can create anything. They have been taught how important and valuable they are in this world, that their life is precious, and they can make a difference.

I was an educator in public school and in my classes, I have used personal development methods to help kids improve and change their attitude with success. During my Master's Degree studies, I researched how those methods enhance kids' performance, attitudes, and abilities while improving on their self-esteem, the key to success.

Education, Knowledge, and Personal Development are the solution for every problem. I am a big believer in the Power of the Mind and am convinced that we need to integrate self-growth into OUR EDUCATIONAL SYSTEMS and foster the use of those same concepts by Parents. We need to use personal development to empower our minds and empower our lives in order to achieve our highest potential as humans, and that is done by introducing self-growth techniques to parents and educators.

Teach our teachers, parents, and kids how to improve learning abilities and discover their passion to enhance self-esteem at a young age. In fact, the younger a soul learns to identify their learning abilities with the help of their parents or guardians, as well as their teachers, the sooner they can improve their abilities to ultimately use all their unique potentials and develop who they are and give back to the world.

We all have the abilities to become Successful in anything we want to do. Empowering Your Mind by discovering the power of your Mind is essential. I offer guidance to help kids and adults Achieve Whatever They Want. www.sylviedrapeau.com

---

About the Author Sylvie Drapeau

Bachelor's Degree in French Literature, Bachelor's Degree in Education, with a Specialization in Teaching French as a Second Language, Master's Degree in Educational Technology. I created learning courses offline and online for kids of different ethnic backgrounds and age groups. I have worked in a team to create the high school exams of the Minister of Education in Quebec, Canada. I coached students to increase their learning abilities and overall average grade point, from 60% to 85–90%. I guided kids to discover their learning process to facilitated learning with effective strategies while enhancing their self-esteem. In class and in private, I have been teaching simple personal development techniques to kids and teenagers to use daily, helping them in the discovery of their true valor.

I have walked around the world, hitchhiking and backpacking for 20 years while homeschooling my son. I have taught in Guatemala, Israel, Egypt, USA, and Canada. I have coached parents and kids in Guatemala and Israel to use self-growth technique to enhance their family life, learning abilities and discover their passion and boost their self-esteem.

I am an avant-gardist and dynamic entrepreneur and teacher. I dedicate my life to learning how the human mind works, and how our learning process works, so we can enhance our lives. Life is a work in progress, based on what we learn and are willing to learn and do, to awaken our most precious gift and natural talents. Each newborn is unique and so precious, let's begin to give them tools to awaken their unique essence of life. www.sylviedrapeau.com

Get Out Of The Mud! – Raise Your Awareness and Be Able to Move Past One Layer of Illusion

by Andreas Djurberg

"The real voyage of discovery consists not in seeking new landscapes but in having new eyes."

- Marcel Proust

"Man can learn nothing unless he proceeds from the known to the unknown."

"What we already know is a great hindrance in discovering the unknown."

- Claude Bernard

I could probably write a whole book about what I'm going to share with you now, but since I can only write one chapter I will share a few perspectives that will hopefully add value to your life.

The chapter is about the importance of choosing your relationships, and how either your mental drama or other people's mental drama are often what's keeping you stuck where you don't want to be in life. As a result, you hopefully will be able to live a more authentic life. It will help you to no longer be sucked into destructive, pointless drama, and to be able to choose more freely what you want to do in life; to be able to focus on what is important.

To live a happy abundant life, you can't afford to surround yourself with people who consciously or unconsciously don't want you to succeed, and who consequently try to keep you as far away from success as possible. Life is short, and it can be quite brutal, so you are going to need all the help you can get in this world to succeed and stay positive.

Some people feel that they are stuck in life and that it seems impossible break free from the life circumstances they are in. This often has to do with the fact that they are addicted to drama; that is, the social dynamics with regard to roles and contexts of their life.

The drama they are part of is familiar, and lets them stay inside their comfort zone, and no matter how bad they feel at least they know what is going to happen. Many people are not even aware that these dramas are simply games they play in their heads; they think these dramas are reality.

Living on drama level, also known as "soap opera level," can be a prison, and there are many ways it can lure you in. So even if you are committed to change, it can be hard if you don't know all the different factors inside yourself that keep you stuck – and because of that ignorance you will be deceived time and time again.

You can be stuck the in soap opera of your mind, which means that you are captured in the assigned roles you have in the different contexts in your life. And if you would like to change something in your life, then that might mean changing a role, which in turn means rocking the boat of the social dynamics in the context you are in.

If you really want a change because you want something else, but the people in the soap opera of your life don't accept that you want change, then what can you do?

You can try to talk to them, but if the other people are addicted to their own roles and need drama in order to maintain status quo, then talking might not work. If it doesn't, then you will need to try something else. This is a vital point to even be able to start the journey; it is the foundation for progress.

How do you know if someone does not accept your change or progress?

They keep interacting with you as if nothing has changed and nothing is going to change. For example, if your parent has developed an addiction to the role of a parent, they will keep treating you as a child until they either get help or until you fully understand and accept that you will never be free until you let them go.

As long as they identify themselves as being your parent, rather than realizing that parenting is merely a role to play for the purpose of raising a child (and that they'll need to let go of this role at some point), then they will view you as if you are forever a child. Consequently, they will try to reinforce this pattern as long as they live and will therefore relate to you accordingly. And just like a person who is addicted to alcohol, a person addicted to drama does not want to understand, they are not going to understand. That's what addiction is about; staying in denial and getting the stimuli they need – in this case treating someone as a child in order to feel in control.

It is the neediness that drives the denial. Since they don't understand the distinction that the reality is they will always be a parent, even if they let go of the parent role, they cannot risk letting go of this role because that would mean losing the illusion of control. As a result, they'd be forced out of the comfort zone of the drama they are so accustomed to, or actually think is reality. In other words, that would mean change and having to face the fear of the uncertainty of who they would become.

It could be anyone that includes you in their comfort zone in the form of soap opera, and forever tries to preserve that social dynamic or role play. It could be an old friend, a partner, a coach, a teacher, a boss, just about any role that implies something at the drama level. And if you decide to change, then that means you are rocking the boat.

Cut The Strings That Are Holding You Back And Remove Those Who Drain You Of Energy From Your Life

"Keep away from people who try to belittle your ambitions. Small people always do that, but the really great make you feel that you, too, can become great."

- Mark Twain

I used to have some people in my life that would drain me of energy, but I have let them all go, and my life is since much better. I no longer surround myself with people who have the habit of reinforcing unsupportive drama-level thinking in me. You could say that I raised my standard of who I would accept to socialize with, with regard to the result I was aiming for in my life. In order to do that, you need to know who you are and what you will never accept from anyone. If you don't know who you are then you could accept just about anything.

If you are serious about where you are going then you need to be highly aware of this pattern. Whenever you feel that someone is trying to pull you down or include you in a drama that is not in alignment with where you intend to go, you have to be one hundred percent clear that the quality of your mental, emotional and financial life is more important than other people's approval. You need to immediately decide to have nothing to do with that person again and feel good about that decision – because you know you are right.

They might say things to lure you back in, by trying to persuade you, using role play, that you should play your role in a predictable way. And at the drama level you have a tough battle if you accept that another person's title carries a significant amount of authority, or if you need to be loyal to family or friends. Most of the time they are not out to hurt you, they just want to preserve status quo or establish the role they want in relation to you in the first place, and the status quo is threatened by you if you are trying to change.

Promise yourself right now that you will never ever be part of a group, or be in a relationship with someone, that does not want you to succeed. Life is too short, just refuse to do it.

In order to be able to let go of people that are determined to keep you stuck, you can't have dependencies to them. It is vital that you stand on your own two feet to be able to let go of these types of people; otherwise you are going to be stuck in the mud of the drama level indefinitely.

If you are not strong enough, because you feel that you can't handle certain situations alone, or for any other reason you are not able to say no to a life you are no longer interested in, then you need to do whatever it takes to handle that problem with the highest priority. This could mean educating yourself, learning a new skill, confronting some fear; whatever it is, you need to handle it for the sake of your own future and well being.

At the same time, you need to remove yourself from the person or group that keeps reinforcing the old pattern in you. You can't relate to people in the old way any more if you are going to change or raise your quality of life, so if you keep surrounding yourself with the same old people then you will be stuck.

You also need to create clarity of what exactly you want, and stay faithful to that vision. Otherwise the circle of madness will repeat itself over and over, i.e., you will be pulled back into your old subconscious patterns again.

The most detrimental thing with regard to drama role playing is the relationship involving a person needing something from another person who instinctively senses that dependency, and gets a high from the power that the dependency creates. If the person in power does not possess the ability to do the right thing (which, of course, is to not exploit those dependencies), then the scene is set for a drama of abuse of power, where the person of power may try to cling to that power forever, if given the chance.

In my life, for example, I had a teacher from grade 4-6 (age 10-12) who was suffering from narcissistic personality disorder with psychopathic traits – just like all cult leaders throughout history have suffered from. This person chose me, for whatever reason, to see if it was possible to make me crack, and put me through three years of psychological abuse. It was so bad that even on summer holidays I was physically ill knowing that I soon had to go back to school again. The classroom environment was like walking through a psychological minefield in the sense that one could never know when this sick person would have an outburst. It was surreal. The municipality allowed the teacher to continue "teaching" and potentially ruin more children's lives despite recurring warnings. This would of course not have happened if the signals were taken seriously. But we should be able to assume that a person with a title/role of a teacher must be doing the necessary things, right?

Needless to say, these years of psychological abuse in front of a class full of peers have had a huge impact on my life, and maybe will have for the rest of my life. It of course impacted how I view people in authority roles, especially if they don't consider it to be a role, but rather an entitlement to put people through psychological hell.

The only thing this teacher taught me during these years was that it was no use for me to even try, because I would never succeed with anything anyway.

The attitude and psychological scars developed as a result of my exposure of this person with the unfortunate assigned authority – more or less a brainwash that was allowed to go on for three years – propelled me down a path that no one should have to go; years of unnecessary suffering. It was when I had begun studying psychology in my early twenties that I understood that the self-image created during this years was not who I was, and the unsupportive mindset was not my own choosing, but rather a reaction to the abuse I had been subjected to. I managed to force myself through a number of limiting beliefs and receive a university diploma, and through it all I learned that I was not so worthless after all. Intellectually I knew that what I had installed in me was mere lies, but the feeling of the abuse lingers even to this day.

One might say that you have always a choice of how you react to something like this. Yes, that is right, if you are aware that it is a choice. However, many people are not, especially not children under prolonged indoctrination. Since there is a law that you have to go to school, I could not just extract myself from the situation – which I learned years later when studying cults and cult leaders is one of the six cornerstones of any successful brainwash operation; to control a person's time and physical environment. Children subjected to this type of madness think that they must be bad; otherwise a person of assigned authority would not act out in such a hysterical way. They don't consider that this might be a deeply disturbed person who acts out irrationally because of what goes on inside of them; they don't know what personality disorders are.

During the three years of abuse I had this abusive teacher in the majority of my courses, but this psychopath was not precisely going to let the rest of the lessons pass painlessly, and instead decided to convince other teachers to join the madness. I later saw this phenomena of teenage group thinking when I was working as a teacher's assistant in my late twenties. The teachers were sitting in the teacher's room and deciding which of the students to like and which to dislike, and then treated them accordingly. Sadly, too many of the teachers I have had in my life have been nothing other than teenagers in old bodies with an assigned authority, longing for students admiration and taking no personal responsibility whatsoever to ensure that all the students would actually acquire the results needed.

And so, at one lesson during this time of madness, my class had a substitute teacher. He was well-prepared and preprogrammed to think and do what the head teacher had decided for him to think and do, i.e. he was a puppet, and all of a sudden, out of the blue, I found myself flying through the air and into a wall. The other kids and I were, as usual, in shock. Did this just happen? Why did he do that? How is this possible?

This sanctimonious child abuser is now having a local horse show each year, and the local newspaper publishes a huge article about it every time. Most people probably don't have a clue about the true nature of this person. I would like to see this person try something like that on me today; I can assure you that it would have a rather different outcome.

It was layers upon layers of sanctimonious cowardice. To act out from an authority role against a child who is forced into the situation by law, and abused not just one time – which would have been bad enough – but over the course of three years. And to top it all off, they ganged up together to really try to ruin a child's life.

I would go as far as saying that sanctimonious authority figures are the root cause for many of the issues with exclusion, depression, learned helplessness, criminal attitudes, gangs and so forth in society. To be a criminal you first have to have the attitude or mindset of a criminal in place. People are not born with a predetermined mindset. The destructive mindset is more often than not developed as a reaction to abuse of some sort. These individuals feel cheated, violated and robbed of their dignity because of what they've been through, so they give up the idea of being a member of society; what is the point if you are arbitrarily singled out to be abused? It should be possible to put an end to societally-designated authority figures like the one I was exposed to, if society simply bothered to evaluate them. The more complex challenge is to reach informal groups, where a lot of minds are poisoned by using drama role play and storytelling, which is also drama in the form of a story. People have to know how this things works in order to be able to protect themselves and to be able to stop ongoing petty drama chain reactions that could lead just about anywhere – or at least stop their own part in it.

The personality type mentioned above, otherwise known as a "wolf in sheep's clothing" is a person that poses as a helper or leader (the position is the purpose or end goal of their leadership; to be considered a leader or authority figure), but wants nothing other than to see you fail or hurt, or to make certain you will never get the tools or perspectives or training you need to get where you want to go. This person will typically ask questions to find vulnerabilities – not in order to help, but to exploit. This type of person will deliberately hand you a puzzle with the key pieces taken away, so that they know you can never get what you need. This could be a business partner, a psychiatrist, a coach, a parent, a teacher or a "friend", it can be just about anyone and you cannot afford to let a title make you blind to this type of person's true intentions.

These people have issues, and they very often manage to make them someone else's problem. They feel that their formal or informal role is all they have, and that they would lose themselves if things would change. Who they are is coming from outside in, and not inside out. They are addicted to contrasts, manifested in the form of social dynamics, in order to know who they are in relation to others.

And since there are both good and bad people and everything in between in this world, if you cannot discern who is who in your life, then you will pay a price for that sooner or later.

Win-Win Or Nothing At All

So how do you get rid of this kind of person if you happened to have one or more of them in your life? People are many times able to play this game because they can sense that you are dependent in some way. So you need to get rid of those dependencies and realize that you have a free will. It would be unwise to use that free will to choose to surround yourself with people who do not want you to succeed, who will keep you down or make you feel bad in some way. So from now on I recommend that you use your free will, without any guilt (because there is nothing to feel guilty about in using your free will), and choose to only surround yourself with people who have your best interest at heart. If you have to, decide to be by yourself until you find people who fit your new standard of friendship. That is why it is vital to be independent; otherwise you would not have that choice. Independence is the way out of this prison. If you want a change, then you have to move on, and that is not possible if you are carrying around people whose intention is to drain you of everything you've got.

This will free up energy and possibility like never before, because now people that used to stop you no longer have the ability to stand in your way.

People who have been cut loose will sometimes try to talk behind your back and paint a picture of your relationship that seems flattering to them on your expense. However, people will soon realize that this person is just obsessed and bitter because you have decided to choose something else, something better, and he or she will look weak; which they truly are, since they are dependent on a role.

Since they have been addicted to you participating in a drama, they will have some resistance since the equilibrium has been disturbed. So they might continue talking behind your back for a while and dramatize with stories even when you are gone, but that is OK, it does not matter, because you are no longer unaware enough to blindly accept being included in other people's dramas. And sometimes the other person gets the message that it is time to change and actually does change their ways, because they realize that it's no longer an alternative to stay the same; then your decision was the best for all parties. Remember to forgive as you let them go. They don't know what they are doing, it's just their way of handling their fears; it is nothing personal, it is all about them. Playing the victim won't serve you; in fact, it will only guarantee more of the status quo. Just be happy that you know you made your life better and look forward to your much brighter future.

Hopefully this chapter was to some help to propel you on your way to getting unstuck from the level of drama once and for all.

Andreas Fredrik Djurberg is an entrepreneur, engineer and a certified coach. If you found this chapter interesting and would like to know more or perhaps publish a book with me, please send me an email on andreasdjurberg@hotmail.com

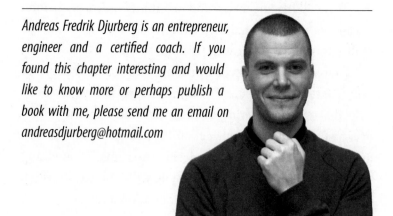

Be Your Authentic Self No Matter Where You Are

by Jessie Gao

The stream of life leads us to different places for the purpose of having new experiences. Sometimes we find it easier to adapt to the new environment, while other times we find it more challenging. How successfully we relocate ourselves depends to a great extend how we stay aligned with our own inner voice. Born in a small city in Inner Mongolia in northern China, I made my personal journey to the top university in Beijing, followed by an uplifting professional life in multi-national corporations before I moved to Sweden, where I today enjoy a new platform as an energy medicine practitioner and coach for personal growth.

Bold to dream

Born during the Cultural Revolution, I witnessed the

dramatic change in China after the death of Mao in late 1970s. My parents and teachers strongly encouraged me to pursue my own dreams, since they didn't get a chance to follow their own. I dreamed about studying at university in Beijing, I dreamed about seeing the world outside China with my own eyes. As the very first one in my whole clan with a higher education, I felt empowered to fly higher and further to broaden my perspectives.

Value of being authentic self

Few understood why I was bold enough to leave a top job in China to start a new life in a foreign country, where I had to learn the new language from scratch and reestablish myself in professional life. My inner voice has always been the most powerful source to listen to, when I felt right for me, so I knew I was making the choice I would not regret.

In the totally new environment I felt excited to explore opportunities with an open mind and open eyes. Knowing it was my childhood dream to live abroad; I focused on further study of new language and adapting myself into the new way of thinking and becoming economically independent. I travelled to other countries for short-time jobs, I learnt skiing and played golf and sailed with the money I earned, and I enjoyed the life style I had always dreamed of.

Competence brings added value

With fluent language skills in Mandarin Chinese, English and Swedish, I felt motivated within to present the cultural treasure of China to the people of the remote Scandinavia. Confidently I started teaching Qigong and Taichi, plus offering education programs to my curious students, who were eager to learn about Traditional Chinese Medicine and Quantum Self-Healing.

The more I teach others, the more I rediscover myself as a creative human being and the more I appreciate the diversity of world civilization. What an exciting time we are now living in! What a great added value we all experience when we are open to receive the wisdom and knowledge from other cultures!

Leadership from inside out

Many of my students and clients wonder how I can be so confident for being who I am and about what I do. I give them a very simple answer: I was brought up believing in self-reliance more than anything else. For me it's a natural manifestation of my inner strength to trust my own dreams and efforts and abilities to achieve my goals in life, without complaining about family background or social structures. Self-confidence and competence have formed a reliable self-made leadership for me, from the inside out. I always trust that things will work out fine for me. I make friends every-where I go and I keep learning no matter how others think about me, which makes me feel at home and secure as the leader of my own destiny.

Power of self-renewal

In ancient Chinese Taoism it's stated that the universe operates under the Law of Change and the Law of Balance. As part of the universe, our human lives also reflect these higher principles. When I shifted my professional life into energy medicine, I felt exhilarated to be able to do so! With hardly any fear of failure I focused on further study. In addition, I published my own books guiding others to embrace the power of self-renewal.

In my seminars, I share the exciting energy of inspiration with all I meet, and I smile within with great satisfaction.

Persistence of bigger dreams

In the ever-expanding universe we can never stand still. The motion of life calls on us to take a next step for further expansion of our consciousness. Old boxes of thinking and doing become out-of-date, and we must update ourselves with renewed perspectives and dreams. When our own dreams appear odd in the eyes of others, it's time to believe ourselves even more. Reaching any goal in life it demands persistence. Even in face of the toughest resistance wherever we are, we should always be able to move forward to where we really want to be.

Even though being in a 'comfort zone' makes us feel safe for short periods of time in life, our inner self is always seeking for new ways to further express itself. As creative human beings we just feel more dignified and more valuable to be able to stretch our thoughts and creativity - this is simply the way of life. If we really want to play safe, why do we bother to leave the womb of our mother in the first place?

Today, when I'm asked what the best feeling in life is, I always answer "Being your authentic self, no matter where you are."

Jessie Gao is a native Chinese with Bachelor of Science degree from Beijng University of Aeronautics & Astronautics, China. She is a well-travelled, multi-talented entrepreneur, currently working as a life coach and energy medicine practitioner, as well as a cross-culture consultant. Jessie has also written a number of books on personal growth, which are available at www.amazon. com. To get more updates about Jessie, please visit www.jessiegao.com.

Goals With Purpose!

by Luis Vicente Garcia

I am a firm believer in the Value and Purpose of GOALS, as they allow us to focus on what we really want to achieve. Over the years I have been able to talk, teach and write about goals and objectives, plans and strategies, and still I find there are a few issues that continue to be in the minds of people which, in many cases do not allow them – in my opinion – to truly understand what really works for them. And there are circumstances in which many people still find themselves not ready to act on or understand their goals; in many instances, they just simply give up.

I must admit that even though goals can be seen as a system or a process that we need to really grasp and understand, the real value to us is on identifying three main key factors that allow us to understand goals in their real meaning. We all know what a goal is that what we want to achieve, but very few people use goal setting and goal achieving in its true form. A more formal definition for goals is "an observable and measurable end result having one or more objectives to be achieved within a more or less fixed timeframe."

We might be experts in establishing S.M.A.R.T. Goals. We might even be experts in using other theories behind goals, which we now know are that goals need to be positive, need to be in present tense and also in first person. Yes, it is very important that we use all of these qualities; that they are in place for goals to work and be active.

And there are other two key factors that, for many people, are important to go from goal setting to goal achieving. One of the best definitions I have seen for goal setting involves a very important word for me: motivation! Goal Setting is a process that involves the development of an action plan designed to 'motivate' and guide a person or group toward a goal. On the other side, Goal Achieving is something a little more advanced; something that needs commitment. It is important to see that in order to achieve any goal we need to take the ACTION; both in order to achieve goals, and also to see them become a reality. Plans with no action are no plans at all, and goals will not be achieved.

Goal achieving is actually a step-by-step process that you - as the individual or as the company - need to be implementing on a constant basis. In a sense, every day we need to be doing something that takes us closer to our goals. Doing this, and making goal achieving a long term process and ideal, allows us to dream even higher and reach even bigger goals. As Zig Ziglar said years ago:

"What you get by achieving your goals
is not as important as what
you become by achieving your goals."

So goal achieving can be <u>transformational</u>. And here is where I would like to introduce the third element, besides setting and achieving, which is Goal Attracting. As we are reading so many wonderful chapters on the subject of the Law of Attraction, we must then realize that a goal is also something we need to attract towards ourselves to make it a reality. It is in the real sense of the theory behind goals: that in order to achieve a goal you need to see it, learn it, know it and, most importantly, work towards it.

Visualization is key to goal setting and achieving; and seeing your goal as being real is even more important. Now, when you start attracting every goal you are set up and ready to achieve, it will allow you to focus on what you really want to obtain and where you would like to be. One of the main reasons people are successful is because they are constantly setting goals; now imagine what you can do if once you set your goals you start attracting these goals to yourself and your life.

There are many areas in which you need to set goals both personal and professional; including your finances, relationships, emotions and your physical wellbeing. You also need to set goals in areas relating to your mindset health (I would recommend learning about mindfulness) as well as in every single aspect of your spirituality. This is why we see that those people who have peace of mind are the ones who have not only set goals in every one of these areas, but who also work very intelligently on developing a process for achieving them.

Over the years I have learned from my experiences, as well as from the failures and obstacles I have encountered through my journey; we all do. And by now you know that we can also learn by observing others and understanding what has happened to them as well. The value of the experiences we have accumulated is as powerful as we allow it to be. It is in our minds to be determined, to persevere, and to succeed. How we interpret our experiences and put them to work towards our benefit will determine how we act, how we behave and how we see our future.

This is then where we must tie goal attracting with our life's purpose. Even though, for me, PURPOSE is a more significant concept, we must understand that our goals must have purpose in order for them to be meaningful for our lives. In the end, it will allow us to touch other people's lives in ways we cannot even imagine. For me, there are two key ingredients in order to understand the purpose of our goals:

1. The first is PERSONAL MOTIVATION. Are you constantly motivated? Are you always looking for new ways to inspire yourself and others? What new improvements and ideas and dreams keep you awake at night? Which of those dreams and ideas have such a strong motivation for you personally that you are certain you will achieve any goal that falls into that category?

2. The second is POSITIVE ATTITUDE. Yes, it might sound strange that I first write about goals and motivation, and now about attitude. The issue here is that

the three of them are completely tied to your life's Purpose. So ask yourself the following questions: are you an optimist? Are you positive most of the time, regardless of the circumstances? Do you want to, and are you willing to, change?

Goal setting and goal achieving are processes that not only allow us to start dreaming and visualizing our dreams and ideas, and understanding the ones we will like to attract and achieve, but they also tell us how to start thinking, how to move forward and how identify all we need to do in order to reach our goals. Yes, we will have roadblocks, mind blocks and many other challenges along the way. Our real job is to get through them and come out stronger in every occasion.

Understanding how goals are tied to our life's purpose is of outmost importance. My GOAL PURPOSE is something even bigger – something that I understood once I started learning about my life purpose – and it is still in an evolving phase. Your purpose could be to change the world, to have a happy life, to teach others, or to change someone's life. And there might not be a main reason you would like to accomplish something, at least on the surface. But yes, there is a reason for you to accomplish all the ideas that exist in your very own purpose. There is a strong desire for you to do something in the right direction, and you'll realize it when you commit yourself to reaching that new level of your existence.

The main reason we set goals is because we are willing to make the sacrifices that are required to become better versions of ourselves. We want something better, something bigger or different. We want to be in peace with our self and with the world. Not an easy task, of course, but in the process of understanding how to be that better version of ourselves we encounter our purpose in our life. We learn from our experiences and we become that initial better version; as we encounter the many more experiences that allow us to grow, to have different perspectives, to put the important aspects of our lives in the right place at the right time, we move forward towards that better version of ourselves.

And as we embark in the process of goal setting, attracting and achieving, we then learn to find the purpose in our life, to reach that pinnacle and milestone that we want our lives to be. And then it is only a new beginning, a new starting place in a constant evolution to be someone better inside a continuum. This is how we grow; by empowering our very own purpose. As I recently said in a conference, "we personally select these new milestones, work to achieve them by attracting them to us and becoming that person who – after working on our goals – find the purpose and the meaning of our lives." It is what we really want our lives to be and to happen; this is how by attracting our goals we become purposely successful.

I have used goals in my life, adjusted them by changing my actions in some instances, and for so many years have taught and mentor people on how to see what goals can do for them. We know they are very powerful to our minds, to what we need and want to decide; to what we would like to do and achieve. And more importantly, by creating, defining and attracting a goal with purpose we are taken to that place where we really would like to be.

So as we embark in this journey of defining and implementing our goals, do not stop at the level that most people are on their goals process, which is setting and achieving. As in order to achieve you must dream, and in order to dream you must visualize. For that to work, you seriously need to be attracting that which you very strongly – in your heart and mind – want to become. By reaching this new milestone, you find your very own purpose in life.

This is why my invitation to you is to attract every single goal that will guide you in the right direction of your life's very own purpose. And by doing it, you will be always there, working on Goals that have a meaningful Purpose!

Luis Vicente Garcia is a motivational speaker, a Business trainer and performance coach, and a Best-selling author. He works with business owners and managers focusing on goals, leadership, entrepreneurship and teamwork. A radio host and a Global Entrepreneurship Ambassador, Luis Vicente inspires people to have a strong personal motivation with a positive attitude. He lives with his family in Caracas, Venezuela. You can visit www.luisvicentegarcia.com and @lvgarciag

Is Prosperity Just Wealth?

by Fleur Gessner

To me, prosperity was always something I was chasing. Meaning, others had it, I did not.

My view of what really constituted prosperity was very limited. At a young age, growing up in a beautiful neighborhood of Hamburg, Germany, a feeling of "not-good-enough" started to creep into my experience. I started school in the 80's and the focus on status symbols, fancy clothes, the right brands was tremendous. I quickly noticed that my friends had nicer things than I did. They lived in big beautiful houses, while we lived in an apartment. I started getting jobs as soon as I could to be able to buy the jeans or the sweater that was currently "in," but the feeling of "not good enough" just would not dissipate.

I was convinced that if I would just work harder and get a better job, I would be able get rid of that feeling. I moved from babysitting to tutoring and from tutoring to being a receptionist at a beauty salon. This drive took me all the way to business school. I did not go to university because I had passion for the topic, I went because I saw it as a way to get a better job and more money.

More Money Doesn't Mean More Joy

Soon after leaving university I was earning more money than my father ever had. And then, surprise! I found myself detesting my job. No matter much I enjoyed looking at my paycheck, a thrill that very quickly wore off, I could not get used to the demands of my job - of working long hours on meaningless spreadsheets, telling people what they should do, holding meetings that didn't interest me, and implementing processes I didn't believe in. I decided that there was only one solution...I needed a new job, preferably far away. I needed a job in the land of opportunity, the USA.

A Change of Scenery Wasn't the Solution

Working for an international company, it only took me a few months to find a job with the company's office in Sacramento. The thrill of the change and the high from disorientation lasted for a couple of months, until I couldn't avoid the truth that I did not enjoy this job any more than I had the previous one.

When I stumbled upon the movie "What the Bleep Do We Know!!" it felt like a door was opened to a whole other world. A world of truth and freedom that I had not felt before. This led me to "The Secret" and Joe Vitale and the Law of Attraction.

I felt empowered, I felt strong from my knowledge.

I thought that just knowing would make everything different, better. Knowing would change my life.

Knowledge Alone Is Not the Key

I quit my job and moved to the East Coast with my boyfriend, and we started our own business. We joined a franchise that promised work from home and a way to benefit from my business knowledge. However, just knowing the Law of Attraction did not help overcome the pit in my stomach when I went out to network. It did not magically bring clients to me, as I was struggling to explain my company's offering, and it did not fix my relationship problems as both my boyfriend and I became more and more depressed.

A New Low

I emerged two years later, back in Sacramento, broke, no business, unemployed, with $30k in credit card debt and nothing to show for it. My boyfriend and I were able to sell the franchise, but it did not even make a dent in the credit card debt that we had accumulated over the time that we had tried to get the business running.

I was living in my boyfriend's mother's house. No money. No job. No income. There were weeks where I had no idea how I was going to make the minimum payment on my credit cards.

I had reached bottom.

Eventually, I was offered a job at the same company that I had left, for less salary than I made when I had quit. I was hired as a temporary employee only. Gratitude mixed with embarrassment.

The pride I had to swallow was bigger at times than my will to get out of this situation, and there were days when the depression seemed to swallow me whole.

I Love You. I Am Sorry. Please Forgive Me. Thank You. – Ho'oponopono to The Rescue

I don't know how I got through those days. It was a haze where I tried to remove myself as much as possible from feeling the pain. I would sit in his mom's office and watch movies on my laptop, drink wine – anything to not hear my thoughts. In the mornings I would get up while my boyfriend was still asleep, as our relationship had become more and more strained and both of us struggling to deal with feelings of failure, anger, and fear.

The 60-minute drive to work, however, was my sanctuary. My time for myself. I started to listen to any and all self-help audio books the library had to offer. And this is how I found Ho'oponopono, the little prayer to God, the Universe, and yourself: "I love you, I'm sorry, please forgive me, thank you". Again and again, I would say it in my head until the persistent knot in my stomach would dissolve and in that moment I felt light and at peace.

Raising Consciousness

Perhaps we should be willing to trust one of the smartest men the world has ever seen, Albert Einstein, who said "no problem can be solved from the same level of consciousness that created it."

This implies that just working harder, thinking harder, and using your will power will not get you the results you dream of.

You need to work on raising your level of consciousness. This is where the work needs to be done; today and tomorrow and every day.

It also implies that you cannot trust your thoughts. Your thoughts will most likely still be stuck at the same level of consciousness of the problem. Why? Because that is how our clever minds work; they tend to focus on the problem, examining it from all angles, re-phrasing it, and re-naming it – but they make sure we remain laser-focused on the problem.

To raise the level of consciousness we can only pray, forgive, silence the mind, find relief, and find peace.

In my situation, there seemed nothing for me to do but to stay put for the time being. Be present, show up at work, and listen. In order to be able to do that, I had to get my own drama and my story that played in an endless loop out of my head. I thought my life was over. I had no idea how I would ever pay back the credit card debt. I was ashamed about living in my boyfriend's mother's house. In a relationship that was a farce, with each of us stuck in our own depression.

But I came back to "I love you, I am sorry, please forgive me, and thank you." Saying these words over and over in my head would reliably give me a momentary peace of mind. Something would shift in the pit of my stomach and I felt muscles relax that I did not know had clenched. The relief in those few seconds or minutes was reward enough for me to continue.

However, inevitably my negative thoughts and fears would come back to me, or something at happened during the day that would snap me back to where I was before.

Staying in the State

I knew I had to find a way to remain in that state longer than for a few minutes, and I needed to find a way to come back to it during the day, even with all the distractions at work. Every comment at work seemed to be a reminder of how low I had sunk.

I started to use other techniques in addition to Ho'oponopono to stay in that peaceful state a bit longer and a bit more often. The gap between where I was and where I wanted to be was so great that I felt I needed more help and constant reminders; I needed to re-program my mind.

During my commute I listened to audio books by Dr. Wayne Dyer, Dr. David R. Hawkins, John Assaraf, Asara Lovejoy, Byron Katie, and of course, Joe Vitale.

I would do a 10 or 15-minute guided meditation in the parking lot before I went into work. I would go back to my car at lunch break to do the same or a different one. I would take a five- minute break and sit in a stall in the ladies' room to say a silent prayer.

And after a couple of months I started getting more responsibility at work, I noticed that my voice was being heard, that I was able to provide good ideas and to make a positive contribution to the project. And miraculously, I was even able to enjoy my work! I had not expected that; I had only wanted to survive!

I believe that practicing the methods, prayers, and mediations so often each day allowed me to be able to be present, to be able to listen, to be able to act and speak out of peace.

And soon I found myself moving into my own apartment and ending a relationship that had become unhealthy for me. I am most amazed at how easy it was suddenly to make that change, but I am convinced it only became easy because I had programmed myself to moving my consciousness up slowly, but steadily.

More miracles started to happen, as within a year of starting this practice I was able to pay off my debt and get hired as a full-time employee, and then promoted again less than six months after that. And even more importantly, I finally began to realize not only in my mind, but also in my gut, that prosperity is so much more than just money. It is a feeling of plenty and possibility, of well-being and joy, it is a state of consciousness, it is a feeling that is within reach for you today!

What You Can Do to Achieve Your Own Prosperity

If you feel that you are in a dark place where prosperity and happiness seem out of reach, I encourage you to start small. At first, the Ho'oponopono prayer was all I was able to do, but it was a start onto a path. A path that led me to a major shift in outlook or consciousness as you may want to call it. And I fully believe that shift in me made all the positive changes possible.

Here are some ideas for you to try:

1. Start small. A short meditation, prayer, or gratitude list is a great way to start feeling better about yourself and help shift your mind into a place where miracles can become possible.

2. Take action. If you are too scared or depressed to hope or to make big changes, start with small activity rather than outcome goals. For example, make

the goal to sit quietly for 15 minutes in the morning or to listen to a guided meditation before bed. Remember that just "knowing" the Law of Attraction is not enough; you have to "do" it.

3. Embrace short breaks. Once you feel a shift, but it does not seem to last long enough for you to gain positive momentum, start taking short breaks during the day. Even a five-minute break to focus on your breathing will help to stay in that positive frame of mind.

No matter where your starting point is, you can always improve your level of consciousness. The rewards will be miraculous. Believe in yourself as all of us in this book already believe in you!

Fleur Gessner, MBA is a business manager at Siemens, a multinational company with an emphasis on green technologies. She is also a repeat business owner with a passion for personal growth and personal finance. Fleur is a German expat with a home base in Northern California.

Connect with Fleur at www.fleurgessner. com and discover more about reconciling your ambitions and dreams with the ability to enjoy the moment. She's passionate about personal growth and how to create a unique system of changing your beliefs and thought patterns and how to make work fun!

Money and Beliefs: Why Do You Settle for Less?

by Gail Golec

The path to abundance is an emotional journey. You must get beyond your limiting beliefs in order to manifest the money you desire into your life.

I work with people day in and day out, whether it be while consulting with business owners or in my coaching and even with family and friends; the focus on lack of money is prominent in their lives. People are living in fear as opposed to faith. They wonder where their next dime is going to come from. Should they make this investment or not? Will there be enough?

For those that are focused on being in a state of fear as opposed to faith, it is inventible that their self-fulfilling prophecy arrives.

There are also many who are satisfied with just getting by. Why is it that "getting by" is acceptable to you? Have you ever thought about that?

In reality, if you believe that you will have enough money to get by, you will. Think about it. You do. Somehow, some way you get by. It could be that you are walking down the street and you find the $40 you need just lying on the street. You could have a stranger out of nowhere follow his or her intuition and hand you the money. You can close that deal that you have been working on for months. Somehow money manifests into your life so you can just get by.

Why not dream big? You can you know.

Why is it that Donald Trump, Henry Ford and even Walt Disney can come back from bankruptcy and become millionaires again? Their mindset has always been one of abundance. They were also big dreamers. There was never a thought of "Now that I am bankrupt, I will never be able to achieve wealth again."

Do you believe that the love of money is the root of all evil? Do you believe that people with money are arrogant and you do not want to be classified in that way? Do you believe there are rewards in the afterlife for living an impoverished life now? What are your beliefs? What were you taught?

These teachings of our fathers, mothers, teachers, pastors and our life experiences overall have affected our subconscious mind. Our subconscious mind is truly the ruler of our actions on a moment by moment basis.

Driving is a great example of this. Most every time I get into the car and leave for an appointment, I take a right out of the driveway. However, on occasion, although I consciously knew I had to make a left to get to my appointment for the day, my subconscious overrules and a right turn I make. Therefore, I now have to turn around. Why? Because making a right has become second nature. It's a habit that has infiltrated my subconscious mind. I didn't make a conscious effort to make the decision to turn left and I turned right.

What your subconscious thinks about money makes a difference as to how much money you will receive. Why do we limit ourselves to just getting by when there is an abundance of money available to us all?

How do we get beyond this limited thinking? How do you attract money into your life?

It starts with awareness. You must be aware of what you are wanting. You must have a deliberate intention to bring into your life that which you seek.

How much money do you want to make this year or this month even? You need to be specific and write it down. Now, do you believe that you can achieve this? Really, seriously, do you believe it? You must believe it in order to achieve it. If you write down that you want to earn one million dollars this year and that does not feel comfortable to you, then don't write it down. Write down what you believe you can achieve and put yourself in the emotional state of actually receiving that money. If you are struggling with having a positive emotional feeling to having money in your life that is one of the main reasons you do not.

I also encourage you to DREAM BIG! There really are no limits to what you can receive or achieve if you believe it can happen.

Now, there is that conscious awareness that I was speaking about too. You must retrain your brain to want to bring in an abundance of money if you want to receive it.

A few suggestions I have are:

Memorize a mantra. Replace the mantra that is currently

in your subconscious mind. For example, "Money comes to me in increasing quantities through multiple sources on a continuous basis." Say it every day. Write it down and take ownership of the feelings that it brings you when you believe it to be true. Instead of counting sheep when you can't sleep at night, repeat this mantra. You have to feel comfortable with money coming into your life in order to receive it.

Become an excellent giver. There are many spiritual teachings that share the blessings of tithing your income to others. *The Law of Giving and Receiving* is always in effect. You sharing what you have with others will afford you the opportunity to share more. When you give you shall receive back in kind and in some cases in multitude. Does it have to be money that you give? No. It does not. You may give a compliment, a prayer of blessing, donations of food, water, supplies, and clothing. Whatever it is; expect that you will always receive back what you have given. The important practice is in the giving.

For example, have you ever gone through your closet and picked out shoes and clothing and donated them? Inevitably, your closet becomes filled again with more shoes and clothes.

Become an excellent receiver. When you do receive money, be grateful. Have an attitude of gratitude. Even if you find a penny on the ground, pick it up and say thank you. Being in a state of gratitude will allow more money to flow into your life. You can also practice becoming an excellent receiver through little things like receiving a compliment without giving a compliment back. It's not as easy as it sounds. When someone tells you they like the shirt you are wearing say "Thank you." There is a natural response to want to say you like something of theirs too. Practice receiving without feeling the need to make it even. It's ok to receive gifts with gratitude.

Do not focus on the lack of money. When your bills arrive, be sure to not focus on the lack of money you have. The more you focus on the lack of money, the more lack of money you will receive. What you focus on expands. This is how *The Law of Attraction* works. Start focusing on what you want. Take time to <u>write down</u> exactly what you owe each month plus more that you realistically *believe* you are able to obtain. It's ok to dream big. Know that number and focus on obtaining that dollar amount. Make it a game, knowing with eagerness and excitement that you will indeed receive that money. Look for ways to receive money outside of the box and take action when your intuition is leading you that way. Understand if you are getting promptings to receive money in an illegal or immoral way, you are not receiving that message from your true self, which only speaks to you with the intention of love. With this energetically vibrational shift and clearly defining your intentions, you will find that money you were not expecting will appear in your experience. Bargains will reveal themselves, so dollars will go further than you expected. All kinds of financial things will occur, and when they do, be consciously aware that these things are happening in response to your newly focused intentions, belief and expectation to receiving what you desire as opposed to the feeling of lack and fear.

Money is an object that is abundantly available. The more money you have, the more you are able to bless others. The truth is that you can never be poor enough so that everyone or even one other person becomes abundantly wealthy. There is abundance available for all that choose to seek it, believe it and take action to receive it.

There is also a sense of freedom that comes with having money and **we all want freedom**. Don't let the ways of your childhood determine your future. Take control of your thoughts, beliefs and actions and be ready to receive abundance. Expect abundance. Feel abundance as if you already received it and let money readily and abundantly flow into your life.

Gail Golec is a down-to-earth and compassionate speaker, author and spiritual teacher of personal transformation and reinvention. Inspired by some of the greatest spiritual teachings, she enlightens, empowers and energizes others to take action with deliberate intention to receive their "inspired desires" as it relates to their health, wealth, relationships and life purpose. Gail is an accomplished entrepreneur and a lifelong devotee of personal growth and development. Gail is also a Certified Angel Therapy Practitioner® and Certified Angel Card Reader.® To contact Gail Golec for life transformational coaching, Angel Therapy or motivational speaking engagements please visit her website at http://GailGolec.com

Your Time to Shine

by Carolina Gonzalez

We are all born with true purpose. Life calls us to remember and connect to our authentic self. I was born in El Salvador in 1977. I was born right in the middle of the civil war. As a child that is all I knew. I learned very early in that life is in fact precious. Our family was blessed with the opportunity to migrate to Australia and seek refuge. A new start in a new country. A wonderful country that welcomed us and has been home for the last 30 years.

As you're undoubtedly aware, life is full of surprises. My life now is very much a contrast from my very humble beginnings. Yet, it has been important for me to honor my past and keep in mind that all events happened for me not to me. Early on I fell in love with life. I was as also able to recognize what was truly important to me and what abundance meant to me.

Courage – leading with heart – has been a constant in my every day life. As I child, there were so many obstacles and challenges, starting from learning how to speak a new language, adapting to a new environment, and dealing with loss as I left all that I knew behind. With a courageous heart full of hope, I felt called to make it a mission to choose a field of work that would create positive change. A profession where I could make a difference and truly connect with amazing humans like you in an authentic way.

At high school I was fortunate to discover Chinese Medicine, its philosophy about prevention of disease as well as its fundamental belief that every thing in this world co-exists in constant contrast. An expansive world where the field of possibility is endless. It also taught me that where we focus our attention is where energy flows.

I love to see human beings shining and realizing their deepest wishes. Let me ask you – How are you? Are you ready to create a life you love? Do you remind yourself often that you are truly an amazing human? Are you willing to allow yourself to create a life you love? What would your life look like if you allowed yourself to shine?

Would you like to feel vital and connected both inside and out? Each person has their own definition of what it means to shine – to feel purposeful, to lead with heart – to be and feel passionate about life. Most of us don't easily find this path. The lucky ones stumble upon it or are guided (or inspired) by others to their best life. Just like a professional athlete, everyone can benefit from working with a self-development professional.

To shine and to feel your light radiating from within, there are paths to take and plans to make. I meet with clients every day, and work with them to create a well-being plan that supports them to shine. While each plan is unique to the individual, they all have some common threads.

Your Well-Being Plan Begins with Balance and Structure.

You already know that life is neither all play nor all work. The magic unfolds when you take full responsibility for all aspects of your life.

Life is only ever lived one breath at a time. With courage and enthusiasm, we are invited to connect with our authentic self. To really connect with what makes our heart sing. What we value most. We live in an expansive world. A world full of choice. Our life is so precious that we are called to choose what we are wanting to experience.

I have been a consultant in the healing arts now for 17 years, and I have facilitated many sanctuary retreats. In this time, I have been blessed to witness the power of intention, and the power of clarity. In a world where there are endless possibilities, a clear mind is invited to ask as well as be willing to receive.

At the beginning, taking responsibility for all aspects of life can seem daunting. It may be scary. It can be compared to a person learning to drive a car. It takes persistence, focus, commitment, willingness, commitment and courage. Soon enough, the learning driver starts to drive with ease, singing to a favorite tune and almost driving in automatic.

Initially, authenticity – speaking one's truth – can also be a state of being that needs to be remembered. We are all born with intuition, with a guidance system that connects us to what resonates as true for every single one of us. There is so much noise in the world at times. This authenticity can not be gained by anything external. It's an internal experience. It just is. Some call this the higher self; the wisdom within. The spirit that connects you the universe.

Once you are at peace with the magnificence in you, abundance becomes a vibration. It becomes your automatic set point, just like a radio that can transmit different stations. You now have access to the abundance station. In this station there are good vibes; they have positive talk back. There are many questions about what makes you light up.

It's not all struggles or all bliss. There's a balance to be found. Here is how:

Abundance requires attention, as this is what keeps it flowing. Remember your values daily. Nurture your inner world, your mind and your soul. Connect to your authentic self and lead with your heart.

Daily Practice Can Bring You To The Wonderful Space Of Manifesting.

On rising, breathe. Pause. Allow yourself some time to be still. If you have a meditation practice, then this is a great time to connect with the magnificence that you are. If you are a visual person, then give yourself 5 minutes to visualize what life would look like if everything was in flow, harmony, and abundance. Wake up, get up and nourish your body with nutritious live food.

Strengthen The Light Within Every Cell In Your Body.

Good health is fundamental for prosperity. You cannot shine if the cells in your body are struggling. Health doesn't have to be complicated. I invite you to look at five key areas of your own health.

Movement. You know you need to move your body and

exercise. Find movement that brings you joy. You only need to find 30 minutes a day to walk, do yoga, dance, hike in nature or work with a trainer.

Hydration. Water is essential for every cell to thrive, and for it to experience itself as plump and abundant. Hence, filtered water is also part taking care of the body. For every 30 kilograms of body weight, you should drink 1 liter of water every day. Sipping room temperature water is best.

Breathe. Meditating is essential, as it is the breath that connects our lungs to the universe. Breathe, one breath at a time – breathe in all that will expand your experience and gently let go of what your body no longer needs. Letting go is an art. It's only when we let go physically, emotionally and spiritually, that we allow space for what we really want to manifest in this one precious life.

Nutrition. Feeding the body what it needs is essential. Every cell requires vitamins and minerals for energy. I have found in all my years of private practice that most people need to supplement with minerals, as these are almost non-existent in our food supply. I love sea vegetation for mineral intake. I have a few favorites, including seaweeds and phytoplankton. Again, eating sea vegetation allows every single cell in the body to experience a plethora of nutrition. By doing so you're creating an environment of abundance.

Glutathione. This is the master-mother-queen-king of all antioxidants. It's endogenous, which means that we are birthed with a certain amount of glutathione genes. These are responsible for going around the body and cleansing the body, giving energy to every cell as well as preventing inflammation and disease. Through the understanding of my DNA, I know that I am one of the very lucky humans who were born with this pathway 100% developed.

However, once, I turned 20, this glutathione I was birthed with started to decline by 10 percent per decade. I therefore supplement with an amazing Glutathione Accelerator. Having my reserves of glutathione abundance in my cells means that every cell can work at its optimum. I have read thousands of DNA reports and most of my clients were born with this cell compromised, and have experienced illness and disease due to this lack of glutathione. This has manifested conditions from cancers to low immunity to infertility.

When possible, choose to only eat alive, organic, and local foods. Follow the best diet your DNA requires. Commit to giving all 50 trillion cells in your body what they require to function at their optimum. From my studies in Physiogenomics, I know that every gene responds to the environment in which it exists in. Therefore, you want to create a harmonious, abundant environment for every cell.

Get Clear

Mindfulness and being present allows you to see and feel what's important for you. You are able to stay in the moment, while also staying true to who you are, what you need, and what you want for your life. Meditation is the most straightforward practice for staying mindful. I have been blessed to have and continue to work with amazing teachers. My favorite meditation from all time is the "I am" meditation. Dr. Wayne Dwyer taught me this meditation at a gathering in Melbourne in the late 1990's. It's simple, yet profound. Life is full and wonderful—practicing self love and nurturing oneself is essential.

Spend time clarifying your thoughts, emotions, and values. Know what is most important to you. For me, I am clear that the values that I hold closest to my heart are health, family and achievement. A simple practice to consider is one that I use every day. On waking, I practice breathing and meditation. I want to feel with every cell of my body the very gift of being alive. I do this for 20 minutes. I then play a movie of gratitude, for my health, my family, my business, and the universe I live in.

Your journey will be different, but getting to the answers and creating your prosperous life begins with the same well-being plan and path to shine. Abundance is a way of living. It's seeing the gold in everyday life. It's about being able to connect with what is important. Creating a visual, a plan for what you would like to experience in the next 5, 10, 15, 20+ years. Living a life where you are feeling complete, and are working towards our dreams with enthusiasm and gratitude.

Next Steps

It's not always easy to find your abundance path on your own. I am always open for guidance, and you may be too. Books, retreats, and mentors can all help you not only get started, but also stay on your genuine path. Visit www. thenatureofbalance.com.au to learn more about Sanctuary; guided retreats that help you reconnect with your true potential. It is time to once more be passionate about life; to open yourself up to true happiness in your career, family and personal wellbeing. The retreat introduces you to tools you can use on a daily basis to keep you in your abundance.

Carolina Gonzalez is an inspiring force in the field of holistic health. Carolina is a Doctor of Traditional Chinese Medicine and a physiogenomic consultant. She's a passionate ambassador for holistic health and its ability to empower people to live life to the fullest. Carolina is a member of the Australian Acupuncture & Chinese Medicine Association and the Chinese Medicine Board of Australia. She is also a regular keynote speaker on lifestyle, balance and holistic health. Visit **www.thenatureofbalance.com.au** to learn more about enriching your lifestyle and improving your wellbeing.

Change Your Mind About Money & Transform Your Wealth!

by Elizabeth Mary Hancock

It seems like yesterday when I had an honest discussion with my husband on my earning capability. I'd tried to make two businesses work, and they were both going in the right direction – but VERY slowly. One was my passion; I was an EFT Practitioner and got such a kick out of helping people overcome their fears, phobias, limiting beliefs, past traumas and so much more. The other business was with a well-known UK network marketing company whose business model I really valued, but my heart just wasn't in it.

We talked about our goals for the year and I felt under pressure to justify my business and the reasons why it wasn't making much money, and why I still needed a generous amount of cash each month from my husband. We agreed that unless I was going to flog myself like I used to in my pre-children corporate HR & training job, we just had to accept and get used to the fact my job was only ever going to generate pocket money. But I knew my guilt around no longer contributing to the family income would stay with me, along with my feelings of "I must be capable of earning more money than this." I had a deeper calling that I just couldn't ignore!

Just one month later, after listening to a webinar about growing your business online, I found myself signing up for a free coaching call. A lovely lady asked me questions about my current life and work, how I'd like life to be, my fears and reasons for not progressing with my business because of my two very young children (and my fears and limiting beliefs around how hard I'd have to work to make it worthwhile), the impact that would have on my family and the fears around rejection, failure, and success too.

Would it be sustainable to keep working so hard, to keep earning the money, and would people still like me if I was making more money, or would they see me as obsessed with my business and my earnings? Was it ethically the right thing to do? My husband wanted to give up his well-paid job in the city in the next year to concentrate full time on his App business, which terrified me, but was also giving me a little nudge to step up and make more of my business.

I'd been so inspired by listening to Joe and other people, but I was still being held back from making that change to really go out there and share my gifts with the world (and make more money at the same time). Something had to change; I just couldn't ignore my calling anymore, even though the fear that was holding me back was big and real. Jeanmarie from Heart Core Business made such a strong case to me I thought, "Well if you are going to make me half as good as you, I'm in!" I had signed up with my first Coach!

I then had a crisis of confidence. "Who do you think you are?" was the voice I kept hearing inside my head. "You can't do this, who's going to listen to you?" I tried to back out, but I'd signed a contract and they rightly held me to it because I needed to be brave and believe in myself. I had to move forwards with my dream and answer my deeper calling, and I couldn't do it alone.

Because I was nervous about saying I was a "Coach" on a potentially global basis – I'd coached in a corporate environment, but didn't have any formal qualifications apart from my EFT Practitioner Exam and on-going assessment, I looked around at what could fill this gap. I had always admired the wonderful Tapping Queen, Coach and New York Times Best Seller Margaret Lynch, so I signed up to work with her too! Margaret took me through the processes herself and then trained me to do them on others – we had LOTS of practice and the results were unbelievable! The work goes deep and we uncover the programming we have grown up with around money, the beliefs like "you have to work really, really hard to earn money," "only the lucky ones have money," and even, "money isn't safe."

We re-set the way we think about money, which allows us to relax and create the space to think big and be creative, so that business idea you've always had, that desire to speak on a stage, that want for a pay rise or promotion, can become a reality and not just a pipe dream.

We go through many different processes, leaving no stone unturned. One of the most powerful is the session on Financial Trauma. Mine was an abusive relationship that ended with him keeping the money I'd spent on things for his house with the inheritance from my Nanna. I'd been contributing to the mortgage and paying his debts, but had nothing when I left. But it was so much bigger than just finances. It led me to have to move back home with my parents, which was REALLY hard, and for a while wasn't even an option because we'd had a falling out while I was in this toxic relationship. I felt so let down by the lack of love and support I had around me that I'd go on huge spending sprees to try to cheer myself up, racking up a large amount of credit card debt.

I was also pressing the self-destruct button in many other areas of my life, making other lifestyle choices I wasn't proud of with drugs, alcohol, the men and friends in my life, all to try to fill this massive void I felt over rejection, failure and emptiness. I was clinically depressed, was on anti-depressants (which at the time probably saved my life) and it took almost a decade for me to sort myself out, but even though I'd had counseling I still wasn't truly happy. I always felt I wasn't really in control; like I had to put on an act and as though I was always walking a tightrope that I could fall off of at any time. My mind and body never got to switch off because I was always on hyper-alert, trying to keep myself from falling in to the abyss below.

I know now, through doing these processes, that I have finally been released from the trauma of the whole situation and so much more. I now feel no bitterness over what happened or to anyone involved. I have accepted that my ex-boyfriend, my parents and others involved in my life at that time had their own stuff going on and were doing what they did or were stuck in their lives, for their own reasons – not mine. Through doing this work, I have completely forgiven my parents and my ex-boyfriend. I hope he has found peace in his own life and is now happy. I am even grateful towards him for the transformation that has happened as a result, and for being part of what was needed in my own life to now be able to help and heal others.

I really feel like I have cleaned out the disease of regret, hurt and betrayal within me and not just put a bandage over the top of it. I am now living my dream; a successful, growing business that is fulfilling on so many levels, a happy Husband who has been able to quit the corporate slog and follow his own dream, happy children and a happy home, but most importantly peace, calm and complete contentment in my heart and in my head.

If you change the way your body or nervous system reacts when you think about doing "scary" or "big" things, like earning more money, or starting a new business or project, then you will feel so much more comfortable and at ease, so that your true talents can shine through and not be hidden under nerves, stress and old traumas. If you can turn the volume of those doubting voices in your head down, or even off, then you won't be held back like you have been. We work together to open up the energy so that you can be relaxed around money, no more arguments, no more stress and no more scarcity or lack. I can't magically make you rich but what I can do is give you the skills and mindset to open up that inspiration, that passion, purpose, energy and creativity to generate a bigger income or grow your business or company, and I can promise you it works EVERY time!

Even with the best marketing in the world, I believe that you can't be truly successful until you get your mindset 100% in the game. Some people are strong enough and game enough to try the "feel the fear and do it anyway" approach. Of these, some will break through, others will fail, no matter how hard they try they will always remain loyal to the vows they made as a child to re-live their families' paradigm around money and struggle. Some will go against it and appear to be successful, but then sabotage it, or it may be a constant struggle, or they may even destroy themselves trying.

By working through my own issues and learning how to use the techniques with others, I am now able to share the gift that I was given to guide, support, coach and mentor my clients through their own problems and on to a better path. This better path is one that leads them on the journey they were always meant to be on, that leads them to their deeper calling and to the realization that the hardship we experience can often end up being the catalyst and gift that we need to make a difference in our own lives and those of others. I have clients who have never had anyone believe in their dream, but now are lit up and striding towards it. I know I am now doing what I was always meant to do, but I also appreciate that I had to make my own way to where I am now, and that it wasn't meant to be easy. Otherwise, what use would I be to my clients?

I help my clients to break through their barriers, their past programming and limiting beliefs to be successful in business and in life, by combining the deep inner work and mindset coaching – which makes the marketing strategies appropriate for a business SO much easier and doable. My clients are set free to think big and shine, and for this to lead to a life that is truly abundant and prosperous in all aspects!

A few short years ago, I NEVER would have thought that I would be collaborating with Joe Vitale, THE Joe Vitale, on a book! But I had a dream, and because I worked so hard on my belief system, that dream has now become a reality. So I ask you this: Do you want to carry on dreaming or do you want to start taking action so YOU can live your passion and share your gifts with the world?

Elizabeth Mary Hancock guides entrepreneurs and small business owners on a path to freedom, and helps them to think big and create their dream business! She makes the process fun and pain-free by blasting through their limitations and beliefs, and then coaches them through the cycle of success and beyond. She found her passion for helping others conquer their money fears and ace their business after doing the same herself, after many years of playing small and being fearful of shining.

Liz is the producer and host of the international online summit "Think Big and Shine" (thinkbigandshine. com), is an AAMET Level 2 EFT Practitioner, an accredited Tapping in to Wealth Coach, and a Chartered Member of the CIPD. You can talk to Liz directly by booking a complimentary discovery session at www.elizabethmaryhancock.com.

Prosperity Factor

by Marcella Vonn Harting, PHD

I believe there is an Entrepreneur in all of us, and it is our birthright to be abundantly prosperous. We all have a Prosperity Factor Gene, which can be activated through our own journey into self-development.

Growing up with a mother who was a waitress and a stepfather who worked at a gas station, I experienced the modeling of a working mindset; that you must work hard to get ahead, and you must work hard to hang on to what you get or someone will take it from you. Society also taught me that school would get me ahead in life, and that getting a higher education would give me a place in society and a good life!

At the age of 18, I discovered, through a course called EST, that I was the product of all my beliefs. This put me on a path of my own self-development; searching my inner world for my beliefs, values, ethics, thoughts-limiting and self-limiting, rules-conscious and unconscious, and if all of these were serving my highest good.

I studied a course called Conscious Language from

Robert Tennyson Stevens, where I experienced how my words created my reality. Changing one word in my daily vocabulary changed my life within 30 days. I realized that at every moment of my life I had the opportunity to choose to choose, instead of coming from reactions triggered by emotional experiences from my past. I could reset my mindset, which was formed by others of significance and experiences in my past, to an awareness of support for Grace & Ease, and Success.

Another great mentor in my life was Tony Robbins, who taught me through his seminars that success leaves clues. I started to look around at results, outcomes and success that I was searching for, and what others were doing to get the same results, outcomes and successes. On this journey into my own self-development, I discovered the 80/20 principle, which for me looked like 80% self-development and 20% basic skills. Many great books, teachers, mentors, coaches and courses supported me on this journey.

My journey of self-development was satisfying and productive, and taking me to little successes every day. Then an event happened that would change my life forever on this journey. Married and looking at starting a family, I gave birth to my daughter, with many complications at her birth; she survived having swallowed meconium inside me. Suctioning her little lungs for over 6 hours, I was finally able to hold her. Her health was fragile, and at 7 months of age she died in my husband's arms as we were rushed to the hospital. They resuscitated her back to life twice, with many complications that would play out into her future and mine. I was told that having suffered much oxygen deprivation to her brain she would need to be institutionalized. As I was given this diagnosis, my inner core screamed "NO!" I smiled and knew intuitively that if she received the proper nutrients and love she would Thrive. This put me on my journey where my Prosperity Factor Gene got activated. I was searching for education and knowledge, foods and nutrition, supplements, techniques, resources that I could implement into our lives to create a better life for my daughter.

I studied nutrition and Chinese Medicine and just about anything else that I thought could help my daughter. Through this search I was introduced to essential oils and aromatherapy 25 years ago. Having many tools and techniques in my personal tool box, and no one magic bullet, I used everything; all of what I was learning. My daughter did get better and graduated from college with a degree in visual communications. Married now, and a mother herself, she empowers me daily to share my journey. You see, when I was introduced to essential oils and aromatherapy 25 years ago, virtually no one knew what it was and what it could do. My journey into prosperity came from sharing my experiences with these little plant liquids, otherwise known as essential oils. I found myself being asked what I did for my daughter and I started to share the products and techniques that have become such a part of our lives.

Today I stand on the shoulders of great people in my life. I have the largest organization in a relationship-building business, or what you may call MLM or network marketing. This is where Joe Vitale's books and work have made such an incredible impact on my life. And I am honored to be writing a book with him. You see, on my journey I found that my successes actually came from basic skills, people skills and self-development. I found that the basic skills and rapport-building skills could be taught easily. The self-development skills were more difficult because of our limiting beliefs and saboteurs. I discovered that great success came from not re-creating the wheel. In other words, all we need to do is implement the teachings of great mentors who have shared their gifts with us. Joe's work with the Law of Attraction, The Secret, conscious awareness, self-talk, intentions, expecting miracles, how to be grateful and living in the present, the Hawaiian system for wealth, health and peace-Zero Limits, the Attractor Factor, and sharing Neville's work are the tools I have been sharing in my journey of self-development. Another great advantage from this is that my resources are not about me, but about getting great information, systems and techniques into many hands – which in my business is duplicable and very successful! I learned early in my career that there are two ways to gather wisdom. One way is to learn from your own life and the second way is to study the lives of others. If you choose to be successful, study success. If you wish to be happy, study happiness. And if you choose to manifest money, study the acquisition of wealth.

Success is a process; it is both material and spiritual, practical and mystical. It is both a journey and a destination for me, a collection of personal values clearly defined and ultimately achieved. It is creating a lifestyle of balance and, most importantly, having someone to love and love you; enjoying friendships, acquaintances for the betterment of both. A good life comes from a lifestyle that is fully developed, regardless of the size of your bank account; a lifestyle that provides you with a constant sense of joy in living; a lifestyle that fuels your desire to become a person of deep value and achievement. Activating your Prosperity Factor Gene enables you to live this lifestyle and share it with many.

In closing; I would like to share with you, my "why." I believe there is a better way of doing just about everything. I am always looking to improve both personally and professionally, for myself and my organization. I am going to share myself with you through my experiences and stories, to help us relate on all levels. I will put myself in your place; to build rapport and open the door to all possibilities.

I will partner with you to reach your dreams and outcomes. I will study, seek, and share anything I can to advance your life, from books, to systems, to strategies, and any resources available. At the end of the day, it's all about success with humor, fun, and movement, we can win together.

If this feels right, resonates with you and looks like something you can be part of, let's create a better life for you and those around you. Results matter. Together we can make a difference…

Marcella Vonn Harting, PhD is an internationally recognized author, speaker, facilitator and entrepreneur. Involved with Network Multi-Level Marketing since the 1980's, Marcella Vonn has built two highly successful businesses with more than 1,000,000 representatives worldwide. In her Leadership Play Shops she demonstrates how creating a residual abundant income centered in health and wealth can empower balance and purpose in one's life.

Marcella Vonn has lectured throughout the United States, Canada, Europe, Australia, Japan, Singapore, and Malaysia. She combines nutrition, conscious communications, face and body language into her dynamic presentations to assist people in creating the life of their heart's desires and dreams.

With certifications in Nutrition, Iridology, Reiki, International Aromatherapy through PIA, Master Practitioner of Neuro-Linguistic Programming, Master Practitioner of Hypnotherapy, PhD in Psychoneurology & Integrated Health, Anthony Robbins Digital Delivery Event Leader and as a Personal Trainer, Marcella Vonn is an inspirational mentor and coach in manifesting and teaching how to achieve one's divine purpose with grace and ease and fun.

Marcella Vonn has co-authored several books, including "Yes, No, Maybe" Chronobiotic Nutrition *with G.I. Atom Bergstrom, and the book* Guerrilla Multilevel Marketing *with Jay Conrad Levinson and James Dillehay, and she has been featured on CNN. She has also authored* The Harting Training System Book *and* Aromatic Essential Cards.

Marcella Vonn is an inspirational mentor in manifesting and teaching how to achieve one's divine purpose with grace and ease and fun.

Marcella Vonn Harting has achieved the rank of Royal Crown Diamond in Young Living Essential Oils. This is a monumental achievement – a Royal Crown Diamond rank is the highest level that a distributor can succeed to in Young Living's compensation plan. This makes her the top leader & top distributor of Young Living Essential Oils.

Married since 1980 and the mother of two children, she resides in Paradise Valley, Arizona.

Visit www.marcellavonnharting.com

Gifting to…and Honoring Death

by Pani Horgan

This chapter illustrates two different approaches to dying and death – one is cultural, and has been practiced since Ancient times, and the other, Access Transformation Energy, uses contemporary tools. Remarkably, these two different methods share the same message.

I am the fortunate and grateful recipient of both of these points of view.

I grew up in a culture that viewed dying and death as a natural concept. The subject was freely discussed by everyone – both young and old. The dying was visited by young and old, even babes in arms and funerals were attended by everyone – once again, young and old, as well as babies. Life was, and still is recognised as a season that preceded the next life.

Just as the forest accepts the passing away of the life that it houses, so too, do the Maori. There is sadness, of course. There is also a knowing that relinquishing all ties to the deceased, and setting them free, allows those left behind to be free to move on more easily, with acceptance and without guilt to celebrate life. Closure can come more easily when you acknowledge that you may be carrying other people's grief. Let it go.

Access, founded by Gary Douglas, is an energy transformation program that links seasoned wisdom, ancient knowledge and channelled energies with highly contemporary motivational tools. Its purpose is to set you free by giving you access to your truest, highest self.

Death is shown as a human point of view. The sum total of life here on planet earth seems to be that we are here to die. It does sound a little crazy, doesn't it? And the only way we know it's real, is if we have the intensity, like the heaviness of grief that everyone else seems to have.

If we are not behaving like everyone else, then we feel something is wrong with us. In our society, grief is something to bear, a burden to carry and some people live their whole lives doing just this. My goodness, does that feel light. No way. What if we are like sponges, absorbing everything around us? Once we become aware of this we can use Access or EFT to clear grief, pain and many other emotions and blockages.

Is it possible that death is transitional? That the body is simply a tool? When death comes this tool or, physical being is left behind, but the being within that body lives on. It has energy. Everything is energy. We are energy. We often hear people say of some-one, he is my uncle or she is my aunt resurrected. Realizing this, for what reason then would you not celebrate the letting go of that being with ease and love?

When someone is dying, he or she has a choice – to be healed or to be allowed to die. What we tend to do is take over. If the person is choosing to die, do we have the right to take control and behave as if we are God? What would it take to ask the person, "What would you like? Truth! If they choose to die, then make sure you spend more time with them. During these times, massage them ever so gently. This helps them stay connected with their body and you with them. Touching is one of the greatest gifts you can give, especially to the dying.

The Maori of New Zealand have observed and celebrated death since time began for them.

Three days are set aside when a loved one dies.

1. The first day deals with the shock. The extended family, friends and community offer their help with money, food and company.

2. The next day comes the acceptance of death. Visitors come from far and wide and are warmly welcomed, for they bring life to the place of mourning. Grief is shared, stories told, punctuated with singing, laughter, prayers.

    It is here that Maori oratory is at its best. Maori sayings abound where reference is made to nature and its forces at work. Some examples –"The Totara tree from the great forest of Tane has fallen." Or, this tribute and condolences from V Jacobs to Mr Rabin's wife and state of Israel. "Arise from your rest and take your place among the stars." Finally, homage to Papatuanuku, Mother Earth.

    Indeed the ancestry and those who have travelled the same road are invited to return and accompany this being to another dimension.

3. The third day is when the burial takes place. It is at this point that all ties are relinquished. There is much wailing and weeping. The ability to do this openly and without judgement is, for many, the most freeing part of the process.

Celebrations then begin.

To the Maori, it is this chain of events that cushions the blow of death that in our reality inevitably comes to all.

The energetic connection after death is also a choice. To the Maori, conversing with the dead is as natural as speaking to your next door neighbour.

Do the forests mourn the felling of its members? They may. They also allow. They are willing to receive everything. They surrender. They gift. What would it take to be willing to honor and receive death without judgement? We celebrate birth. What if death is merely a transformation – a new life? One is the other side of the coin. It is the same place from which beauty exists.

From Raz comes this, "Honoring Death gives awareness to the being and improves the possibility of knowing in each life time. That, is the gift we give to the spirit when we honor death."

Haere, Haere, Haere.
Farewell, Farewell, Farewell.

Going from life to death, from death to life.

EFT/TAPPING, founded by Gary Craig, USA, is a specialised form of acupressure, used by many doctors and healing professionals worldwide. It is very simple, effective, easy to learn, can be applied anytime, anywhere and often yields remarkable and long lasting results. No drugs or needles are used. Instead, simple tapping with the fingertips is used to input kinetic energy on to specific meridians on the body while you think about your specific problem – whether it is a traumatic event, an addiction, pain, – acknowledge it and voice positive affirmations.

With practice and persistence, you can overcome and heal yourself of many old fears and past beliefs that have kept you stuck.

EFT has been proven to lessen the intensity of the emotional attachment to the loss of someone dear.

Tapping on each aspect such as feelings of sadness, guilt, anger, resentment, losing interest in socialising or eating properly, can lead to becoming more focused and acceptance of the loss.

The technique leads you to forgiving yourself, the deceased, giving yourself permission to grieve, to your own feelings, whenever you want to, appreciate the process you are going through AND deeply and profoundly accept yourself.

Prayer and gratitude go hand in hand with this technique.

EFT offers tools for "Stress Free Living," and an awareness enabling us to appreciate ourselves and the abundant world in which we live.

Gifting to the spirit and honouring death would seem to complete the natural process of LIFE.

Arohanui (Love),

Pani Horgan.

Pani grew up in TeKao, a small Maori farming community approximately 30 kms from the most northern tip of New Zealand where the Tasman Sea meets the Pacific Ocean. Her tribe is called Te Aupouri and can claim its genealogy as direct descendants of the Mamari and Kurahaupo, two of the canoes that landed in New Zealand during the Great Migration of 1320. She has extensive experience in education and natural therapies and a love for sharing these therapies with people from all walks of life. Her skills and knowledge include Remedial and Therapeutic Massage, Access Transformation Energy, EFT/ Tapping and Meditation. Visit Pani at www.energytherapysolutions.com and learn more about how to take the next steps with your own personal and spiritual development.

4 Step Simplified Formula to Prosperity, WISH I had Known these Secrets Earlier

by Jayant Hudar

Prosperity is an amazing word that means money, wealth, abundance and being fortunate. For me it also means peace of mind, contentment and happiness. It means a sense of fulfillment in every sphere of life. However, prosperity never comes by merely wishing for or longing for it, and you can't even inherit it; you have to create it yourself. You have to create it inside yourself. It's a State of Mind. The word "prosperity" has a nice ring to it, which spreads gold in the air. It smells of happiness and has a spiritual taste.

> *Prosperity* is a way of living and thinking
> and not just money or Things.
> *Poverty* is a way of living and thinking,
> and ***not just lack of things***.
>
> — Eric Butterworth

"Prosperity" is the **root cause** of happiness and bliss, and you should do everything possible in your life to achieve it.

My Formula for Prosperity

Prosperous Life = Doing Well Financially + Experiencing Sound Health + Great Family, Friends & Relations + Spiritual Life, Full of Gratitude.

Anything missing from this equation represents something less than prosperity.

How do I get there? How do I become prosperous?

All this requires good focused effort and planning, Working on "**Project Prosperity**" itself is a joyous Journey.

Predictable Revenue Flow, Multiple Sources of Income

Money and wealth are obviously big parts of being prosperous. A consistent flow of money coming to you, every day of the year, is the first step towards a prosperous life. You are really well off when the inflow of money is "Recurring Passive Income". When this happens, your thoughts are not dominated by everyday problems of food, shelter and clothing. When your basic needs are already taken care of, you'll have something extra to share with people. This sharing and giving is the state when the real prosperity factor comes into picture.

You have to decide in very certain terms how much money and wealth you need to be financially secure. Calculate your monthly expenses, and then carefully plan to create that much revenue in a recurring and passive way. Create multiple streams of income; don't depend on a single revenue source like a job. Try to create an online income as a part-time additional source. Only then can you think of working on other aspects of your life.

There are so-called "rich" people (at least in money terms) who lack the prosperity factor. They don't enjoy life, and they can't share happiness. They are spiritually poor. We want to stay away from such people and such thinking. Instead, start thinking how you can make a difference in people's lives. For then the world will start changing for you for the better.

Wealth, like happiness, is never achieved when pursued directly; it comes as a by-product of providing useful service to others. You first have to decide to be prosperous.

Design your Life. Create a MAP of a dream Life and work towards it.

Do you know any lazy people who are prosperous? I don't. However, prosperous people may appear as if they are lazing around and enjoying life. That's because prosperous people don't have to experience "daily financial uncertainties" anymore. They know where they are now and the future they are working towards. They have a deep sense of peace and are relaxed because they know they are headed in the right direction.

To achieve anything meaningful requires setting goals and working towards them. Success is not an accident; you need to plan for it. Once the goals of your life–in terms of specific financial goals, health goals, family and relationship goals, spiritual goals–are decided, then focused effort and action is required to achieve them. Set goals to be prosperous.

Write down all things you would like to experience in life, places you would like to visit and see, things you would like to do and achieve.

Your ability to set goals and make specific plans for their achievement is the master skill for success. And this journey of achieving success, wealth and prosperity can be made joyous. How?

Learn the LAW of Cause and Effect

Everything happens for a reason. For every effect there is a specific cause. We live in a world governed by laws of the universe, not by chance. Every action has a reaction or an outcome. Whatever a person will sow, so shall they reap.

Knowing this law of cause and effect makes it easier to achieve anything and everything in life. Even to get the Law of Attraction to work for you, where all you want in life gets attracted to you like a magnet, you have to BE the person. Become more valuable as a person; be a person of charisma and charm. Once you have your Goals defined, you need to conduct a self-check and see what abilities and skill sets you need to learn. The more you invest in yourself, the more valuable you will become.

Sow the Seeds of Prosperity. The more seeds; the greater the probability of being prosperous.

Prosperity Seeds = Valuable Skills

Have you sown any new valuable skill seeds this year in yourself?

Learning New skills makes you more valuable and also makes your life Interesting

The "WORDS" you use can change your Life. Speaking skills are of utmost importance to succeed in life, including both verbal and non-verbal communication. Words have the power to move people, change people, and even to hurt or harm. Most important is that Words can make you rich.

Just speaking well is not enough. Learn the hypnotic words, learn NLP (Neuro-Linguistic Programming), and learn the art of copywriting. These skills are much more valuable than you may think; they transform lives.

Develop a winning edge in everything you do. Develop a mind-set of excellence, because every small improvement in your own personal abilities, knowledge and skills can lead to a major increase in your income, achievements and success in life. Your life can only become better when you do something every day to improve your skill areas. The sense of prosperity starts coming to you every moment you apply your newfound knowledge. Your imagination expands and creativity flows, new ideas come to you. And just a single idea can change your life.

How do you acquire new skills "Fast"?

Books are the Best source of Knowledge

Leaders are good readers, and reading self-improvement

books is the best shortcut to acquiring multiple lifetimes' worth of knowledge in a short time. You can take your books with you to bed and read before you fall asleep.

However, don't just read them as stories. Study the books and take notes and apply their lessons in everyday life. Your thoughts are the most valuable commodity; take great care to screen what thoughts go inside your mind. Avoid negative self-talk. Think about prosperity and how you can achieve it.

Lifelong learning is an absolute essential for leading a full life, resulting in personal growth on all levels - spiritual, emotional and mental.

As you develop into a new and improved you, you will attract fortune and likely, friends in higher circles. People are naturally attracted to the new positive and worthy you.

With such a vibrant you, a sense of control over life will come to you. You will experience a kind of happiness that no one can take away from you. The sense of freedom and prosperity will automatically come.

With these higher energy skills and competencies, you will grow as a person. Your body has limits to its growth, but your mind can continue growing year after year, provided it is fed and exercised with good thoughts and good books.

Appreciate your new skills and your achievements as they fill your heart with happiness and gratitude. It will give you peace and take you towards prosperity in the shortest possible time.

Give 100% to life and everything you do. Go the extra mile in everything. Focus on your goals. Your heart is your compass, Money is the energy, and as Brian Tracy says,

"Energy flows where the attention goes." Enjoy the journey to prosperity.

Health, Family and Relations are the Key factors of Prosperity

You can have all the money and wealth in your lifebut if you lack sound health, or you don't have family with whom you can share your happiness, then prosperity will be incomplete and superficial.

Know that in a human life, there are 4 things that energize you – Food, Sleep, Air and Thoughts. Thoughts control your emotions. As good news can lift your energy, bad news can hurt you emotionally and reduce your energy instantly. So guard what you eat, drink and Think. Be selective about the things you allow to enter your head.

You have to take care of your Health, eat food that feeds your body and energizes your Spirit. Study how "food effects your being", and how your body can last as long as possible. Exercise is equally important for health. There are special exercise techniques that connect your Spirit and Body and can help you to achieve your Material dreams in a very short time. Learn about them, through genuine Gurus. Find a Guru who will help you.

You have to work on your family and relations too, put in efforts in terms of time and love. Because it's the LOVE frequency or the Vibration you emit from your being which actually attracts all the things you desire in your life. The more you are in that zone, the easier it is to achieve your desires.

The Final step to real Prosperity

I feel that Prosperity also gives you the freedom to be generous and compassionate. When you are earning money and wealth, you should also be sharing it. Give away at least 10% of your income. "Giving away" is one of the Secrets of "getting more." Give away and you will actually feel yourself grow. Don't stop there. Give your knowledge, and share your experience. Make a Difference in other people's lives.

Important Note : When you give away money, give with a "**sense of gratitude**".

I agree with what Joe Vitale says "Give money to wherever you receive spiritual nourishment and you'll activate the money-attracting law."

Live Your everyday life with lots of GRATITUDE, and prosperity beyond your imagination will remain with you throughout your life.

Good Luck on your journey to Prosperity!

Jayant Hudar is a Founder and CEO of School of Business Wisdom. He is a Business Growth Consultant, Celebrity coach and an International Seminar Speaker. Visit www.schoolofbusinesswisdom.com to get free books and reading lists on NLP, Copywriting, Prosperity and Business Growth. You can reach Jayant on info@jayanthudar.com or call +91-9321812220

The Soul of Language

by Masahiro Iimura "Axel"

In Japan there is a belief that there is power in the words that you use and the names you choose. It's called "Kotodama," which loosely translates to "the Soul of Language." It's the idea that sounds can affect objects, and that language rituals can have a lasting impact on your life; your body, mind, and soul. The Soul of Language basically says that *what you say will be realized.* This belief aligns perfectly with the Law of Attraction, which says "what you focus your attention on, you receive."

Your language is more important than what you think.

Early on my dream and my life's work were focusing on becoming a teacher. I knew deep down that teaching was my purpose. I became a lecturer on preschool education. It was also my belief that I deserved to be rich. I wasn't rich at the time – far from it. I was poor, and yet the path to prosperity happened as naturally as my path to becoming a teacher. I believe that my language and the words I choose to say, think, and read supported me to succeed and achieve.

Focus on Gratitude

The words you use are more powerful than your thoughts. What you say is small in comparison to all of the thoughts you have each day. If these thoughts are positive, and the language you use supports you, then you'll realize your dreams.

Gratitude is one of the simplest ways to shift your thoughts from negative to positive; to shift your language. If you focus on something it will expand; this is the advice that Joe Vitale gives and I believe it is true. Every day, I focus on gratitude. I have created a ritual of praying and saying what I'm grateful for. It's difficult to be negative when you focus on all of the good and positive things in your life.

Practice Positivity

It can be difficult to stay positive. There's so much negativity all around us. I don't watch television or read the newspaper because of the negative information. Instead, I read books and watch self-development videos. I surround myself by positive and supportive information and people. Practice is the only way to shift your thoughts and your language.

Let Go of Fear

I no longer teach school children, I'm now fortunate to work for a friend and mentor, and I teach conversational English. Most Japanese can speak English, but they have a fear of making mistakes. This fear holds them back. It stops them from reaching their full potential. It makes the process of speaking to someone a negative process.

But no one cares about mistakes! It's more important to communicate with passion and intention. Whether you're communicating to someone else, to yourself, or to the Universe, let go of a fear of making mistakes or saying or thinking the wrong thing. Speak with passion and intention.

Find Your Dream

It's not uncommon for people to not know what their dreams are. If you don't know, then how do you go after it? How do you choose language and thoughts that support your success? You cannot. First, you must become clear on your dream. Go back to your youth. What did you love to do? What were your hobbies or interests? Your childhood often holds the key to your biggest dreams. If that doesn't work, close your eyes and imagine that you can be anything that you want to be. Now open your eyes and write it down. What is your dream?

Find Your Teacher

Most people have an ideal person or someone that they want to be like. Find this person and approach them. Follow them and their teaching completely. Keep in mind that this person must align with your dream and support your positive language. If they are famous and unreachable, which can happen with mentors, then read everything that you can about them. Read their books, watch their interviews and learn how they achieved their goals. They have habits and lessons that you can apply to your life. Personally, I have many teachers. Joe Vitale is the one of my mentors. I have read the books he has written and watched his videos. Joe has had a big effect on me and my life.

Take Great Care of Yourself

Your health has a direct impact on your mindset. If you feel tired, sluggish, or sick then your mindset will align with that physical state. On the other hand, if you eat nutritious foods, get good sleep and exercise every day, your mindset will align with that positive energy. And exercise can and should be something fun. I do something different every day; whatever I'm inspired to do. I might do bodyweight exercises like pull-ups, or I might choose to run or swim. Find an activity that makes you smile.

Speak Up and Talk Positively About Your Goals

Finally, I challenge you to positively share your dreams and goals with others. This gets the goals out of your head, where they can be forgotten. Now you're more accountable for your goals, and you may even find people who are willing and excited to help you. That's the Law of Attraction and the Soul of Language at work for you.

Take One Positive Step Today and Keep Going

There's power in the words that you choose and the wonderful thing about words is that you can change them right now, this very moment. Start shifting your thoughts and your language. Identify one small phrase or habit that can support you to achieve your goals. If you don't know your goals, then figuring that out is your first step. With each positive step you take, the momentum will increase. Your goals will become your reality sooner than you can imagine. Don't give up. Your new reality starts today.

Masahiro Iimura is the Marketing Director and Copywriter of Direct Publishing, Inc., which provides clients with access to personal development programs relating primarily to English conversational methods and goal achievement. He also provides clients with access to Psycho Cybernetics, 7habits, and the personal development programs by Lee Milteer.

His "Daily Inspiration," "Next leader," and "EQ English" magazines are enjoyed by over 150,000 subscribers. He was born in Kyoto Japan in 1978.

Destiny By YOU

by Akiko Ishikawa-Tyler

"You have BRAINS in your HEAD and FEET in your SHOES. You can steer YOURSELF in any DIRECTION you CHOOSE!"

– Dr. Seuss

Ladies and Gentlemen, welcome to your world of CHOICE. Let your journey begin!

Calling
Hope
Open-Minded
Imagine
Courage
Elevate

Calling

"Choose a job you love, and you will never have to work a day in your life."

– Confucius

Do you love what you do? When my 10 year-old heard me reading the Confucius quote above out loud, she in return gave me her favorite quote, "Love the life you live and live the life you love." My lovely eight year-old boy is ever in his imaginary dreamland and is a powerhouse of my joy and passion along with his sister. Yes, being the mother to my children is my calling although they may not agree. It is the most challenging and rewarding occupation that is 100% voluntary. In addition, I have three ongoing careers which I feel passionate about at this point of my life.

How do you find your calling? First and foremost, identify what you're good at and absolutely love doing to the point that you breathe, eat and sleep it. Second, ask others – who are close to you, who know you well and whom you trust for their honest perspective –what you bring to the table. You may be surprised to find out about what they say, and discover a new you. Third, build on it! Acknowledging areas for improvement is important for growth and that can be worked on.

"The biggest mistake people make in life is not trying to make a living at doing what they most enjoy."

– Malcolm Forbes

Hope

"Everyone has goals, aspirations… and everyone has been at a
point in their life where nobody believed in them."

– Eminem

Yes, we all talk about hope. What exactly is it? Hope is what drives us forward daily. It is that intangible, deeply imbedded positive in us or that we have created that's closely tied with goals, visions, and dreams. Malcolm Forbes states, "When things are bad, we take comfort in the thought that they could always get worse. And when they are, we find hope in the thought that things are so bad they have to get better."

I've experienced numerous times when some laughed at me, while others called me crazy, for what I have been pursuing. I'm knocked down for pursuing what I believe in because it's not aligned with theirs own ideas. But whose pursuit is it? They're not walking my path. I'm walking my path.

With hope, having belief in yourself is necessary. No matter how challenging your life gets, and no matter what others say to you about your endeavors, keep your sights focused and hold on tight to your hopes! Continue minding your own business. Take a look inside you and discover the abundant beauty existing and to be created in your life.

Open-Minded

"The mind is like a parachute. It works best when it is open."

– Dalai Lama

You have our own belief system. You have heard that the mind is a very powerful thing. It is what leads to what we do. Have you wondered why arguments occur? It is the extended version of being unable to understand our differences, and each person pushes his/her own belief. Is there a possibility that you may have been, in the past or may be in the future, in the other person's shoes? It's vital to reflect upon ourselves before pushing our own ideas forward.

The next step is to simply listen to what others are saying. You can agree or disagree, and it's perfectly fine. You recognize that there are ideas, thoughts and perspective other than yours. This will open up so many more possibilities and so much more potential in your life – not to mention perhaps fewer arguments and being able to build more understanding toward others.

Imagine

> *"You miss 100% of the shots you never take."*
>
> *– Michael Jordan*

Enter to win! What happens when you enter a contest? You'll have a chance and an opportunity to win. You know what happens when you don't enter. Nothing. When you choose to "enter" and take an active role in taking charge of your life, can you imagine yourself living your life to the fullest encountering abundant opportunities?

Need to polish up your creativity and imagination? You can do this by watching movies, reading books, going online to listen into success stories of those you wish to follow, changing your routine by engaging in out-of-the-norm matters. There are so many options. My favorite is to share some time with children. Many of them are the pros in freely expressing themselves and can be good role models in this area for us.

"You have many years ahead of you to create the dreams that we can't event imagine dreaming.

– Steven Spielberg

Courage

"All our DREAMS can come true if we have the courage to pursue them."

– Walter E. Disney

That's easy to say, but many people have actually done so. I have and am now reaching for other dreams in different areas. How about you? If you have, congratulations! If you haven't, do you really want to? As we all are aware, many things in 2016 are just a click away. Have you wondered where the icon that reads "to purchase your dream, 'Click Here!?'" So, really, what's holding us back from pursuing our dreams?

Such factors may be a support system in general, family, health, finance, etc… but as you write down these reasons, you may notice that there's a common ground, FEAR! Remove the FEAR and you'll feel so much lighter and notice that options to solutions of such factors open up.

I've failed countless times and returned stronger each time. What I can offer, by making the best of the opportunities I've given, and as a result of my risk taking, is much greater and more worthwhile. Some people say, "I have nothings to lose, so I'll try it." Believe me; I DO have a lot to lose and I think you do as well.

When the fear monsters kick in, remember, Marilyn Monroe's *"Fear is stupid. So are regrets."* and Babe Ruth's *"Never let the fear of striking you out keep you from playing the game."* Those of you who've experienced achieving your dreams, you know that *"Victory is sweetest when you've known defeat."- Malcolm Forbes*

Elevate

You are here on this globe for a reason. Define that reason today or work towards it now and take it to the sky! Moving forward is your choice, right? You've heard that attitude is directly related to the altitude we want to take. Yes, you decide. Along with attitude, what do we need? ACTION, ACTION, ACTION! First be a dreamer, and elevate yourself to be the DREAM ACHIEVER.

Do you sometimes experience that you're doing everything you possibly can, but there are times when taking action doesn't come so easily? What are your remedies and solutions?

Dr. Vitale advises that "...the more you can feel good, the more you will attract the things that help you feel good and that will keep bringing you up higher and higher."

What do I do when I feel "stuck?" Stopping (almost) everything and simply enjoying time with my children is ultimately when I not only feel good, but my absolute best. This seems to go over very well with them, as they're seemingly limitless in their ability to call out "Mommy" "Mommy" "Mommy" "Mom" "Mother" "Hello" "Are you listening?" "Can we go to a store?" "I spilled water." "Can you take me to the bathroom?" "Where is my backpack?" "She's (sister) being mean to me!" "He's (brother) being annoying!"

Whew.... and yes, this is my calling, my choice. What's yours?

Akiko Ishikawa-Tyler has been an international educator for 12 years, enjoying serving international students coming to the U.S. – giving back what she received when she was an international student 20 years ago. While engaging in full-time work and being an active mother of two young children, she discovered an additional passion of sharing with and helping others through a global organization called Kyani, as an Independent Distributor. She believes in creating time for what matters. Explore the possibility of your and your loved ones' beautiful and abundant present and future with Kyani. Visit akikoishikawatyler.kyani.net.

In Awe of Myself

by Maria Elena Iturralde

Faith is the "Eternal Elixir" which gives life, power, and action to the impulse of thought!

~ Napoleon Hill

To understand one's worth, and see the true miracle that we have been created to be, is the most wonderful gift we could give ourselves. For you see, loving yourself will swing open the doors of amazement in all areas of your life! You will start to feel good and have a different essence about yourself. You will exude confidence and will not need anybody to validate who you should be, because you already know who you really are or want to be! Unfortunately, many people feel guilty at the mere thought of loving themselves because they feel that it's selfish or egotistical. Nothing could be further from the truth.

Loving yourself means that you accept who and what you are, good and bad. Loving yourself permits you to grow where you stand right now! Falling in love with yourself is the most fulfilling feeling ever! Best of all, when you admire and celebrate yourself you send out positive energy which will result in attracting to you what you really want and need. It's better than winning the lottery, because money can't buy such inner peace.

I invite you to take a journey through my life, I want to show you that it doesn't matter what happened in the past or what is happening now; that you can live the life you want when you discover what a powerful individual God created you to be. I have decided to be very candid with details of my life in the hope that it will inspire and help others.

Growing up I was physically and verbally abused by my father who punched, kicked and whipped me with wet electric extension cords for simply looking at him in what he thought was the wrong way. I also had to see my mother – who was the positive force in our home – also suffer at the hands of my father. I witnessed him rape and beat her on an almost daily basis. As you can imagine, my home felt more like a torture chamber than a home a lot of the time. There were some good moments, but mostly negative ones.

In 1990 my father did the unthinkable and murdered my mother by stabbing her in the heart multiple times and robbing her children of the most wonderful and loving mother any child could ever ask for. My mother was only 34. I was left to care for my siblings at the age of 19 years old. I had four siblings who were 1, 3, 13, and 17 years old.

I was married at the time of my mother's death, and for two years we made the best of it. My husband was in the military and we were transferred to Yuma AZ. Once there, the burden of having to raise so many children including one of our own became too much for my young husband to bear and left our home. I was understanding of his decision. However, what happened next I did not expect. I did not expect him to leave me with no support of any kind; he left me in a town where I did not know one person, I had no job, no transportation and there were no modes of public transportation in that town in 1992. I had to walk in 120 degree heat to try and find employment. I recall that in walking around looking for work, the floor was so hot that my cheaply made plastic shoes were literally melting!

I was 22 years old. I lost a lot of weight that year, I went down to 96 pounds because I only ate if the kids left food on their plates and most nights I would only get a couple of canned green beans. So I know what it feels like to be really hungry! Must be the reason I love to eat till my belly is super full now! Even though I had endured so much at such a young age, unbeknown to me, I was practicing the Law of Attraction by default. I never asked "why me?" I simply stated, "God if you thought I was strong enough to put this before me, you have also put in me the courage and the stuff I need to see me through it." And I always said thank you! But when I said those words I really meant them; I said them with a heartfelt faith! Divine energy has always been with me and in me. I just didn't know the power behind it then.

That same year, a week before my little sister's prom, she became stricken with some sort of infection that doctors could not identify or understand the cause of. Three days after finding the infection, she was paralyzed. There has always been divine guidance in my life; I've always felt it just did not know how to explain it. And it was evident that divine source was providing for me when my sister was in the hospital.

Elizabeth was finally able to leave the hospital after about two or three months. My sister got depressed her first days and weeks at home which is to be expected given the circumstances. But I would not let her give up on herself. One day she was in her bed and she had a muscle spasm in her big toe. But I made such a big deal about that spasm that you would have thought she jumped out of bed running! I said to my sister, did you see that? You moved your toe! You see I told you, you can walk! I took her walker out and said come on lets go walk, she was so excited! For the first time I saw hope in her eyes! I helped her out of bed and onto her wheelchair; I wheeled her outside and set up the walker. I stood her up so that she could hold on to her walker and I began to move her legs for her and told her look you see, you are walking! You're walking!

I moved back to San Diego in 2004 after my son was born, and life was really good until 2007, when I started to suffer from debilitating panic attacks, they were so bad that walking to the mailbox was a horrible task. I remember telling God that I wanted to be happy and filled with joy again because after times of homelessness and failed relationships I was for the first time in my life feeling something that I had never felt before – "hate."

I started going to therapy. The therapist said it was normal but I refused to accept that because I had never experienced that feeling, no matter what had happened to me in the past, I always kept the faith that things would work out for me. Now I understand that life will try to send help gently, first the signs are subtle and I remember seeing the signs but I would not listen and what I found out the hard way was that the universe will make you listen one way or another, for me it was through panic attacks that imprisoned my mind body and spirit! That is the only way I finally paid attention.

For many years I thought I loved myself, yet I always felt a void. Even though I took the time to exercise and make myself as pretty as can be. One day as I sat in my room reflecting upon my life I realized that I didn't really love myself to the point that I thought. The day when I made that realization I was at the worst point in my life! I became what I criticized others for doing; I became a "victim" of my circumstances! I had been through so much in my life that life simply just caught up with me. Well at least that is what my therapist said. And for a while I accepted that, but I still couldn't shake off the feeling that it went much deeper than that.

In 2007, God put in front of me a little book entitled "The Secret." It changed my life! I was pumped! And realized that I had to a certain extent been unconsciously using the law of attraction all my life! That's how I was able to remain happy and calm during what should have been horrible times in my life. I remembered that it was not what happened to me that affected my life, but instead it was my reaction to what happened that had changed.

I started to say to myself, "you are stronger than you think, look at what you have gone through, yet you are here!

You are a courageous soul who can do anything she puts her mind to do. The trials have turned you into a warrior. This new warrior is full of immeasurable value!"

I wanted to know more about the Law of Infinite Abundance. How could I take it to the next level in my own life? I was infused with desire and faith to go after my dreams. I kept seeking and desiring knowledge.

I found that my curiosity had grown to more of an obsession, intrigued by what I was learning. I felt feelings I had never experienced before! And to my surprise, good things just started happening! I started to feel a peace that surpassed my own human understanding. One of the keys for my own growth was to be able to forgive the people who for whatever reason felt the need to do what they did. I forgave everyone in my life, oh, but most importantly, I forgave myself! I gave myself permission to finally say it was ok that I made mistakes, it was ok that I may have had bad judgment in picking a mate or whatever else I "think" I did wrong, so what! Forgiving myself was the most liberating feeling ever!

In my expedition of self-development I found my purpose in life! It felt amazing to have this realization. And at that moment I didn't know how I would do it, but I just knew I would and my feelings let me know I was on the right path! I finally understood what taking inspired action meant!

In March of 2015 I was looking for a graduate program to become a behavioral analyst inspired by my son's autism. At first it was difficult to find a program that did not require you to already have a teaching degree in special education.

But I put my desire out into the Universe and shortly after I came across a program that not only did not require the prior teaching experience, but it followed the curriculum to allow me to sit for board certification as a behavioral analyst. I was super-excited, but then I saw the admission requirements, and I did not meet the GPA standard. I said "ok, this is what I really want and I don't know how it will happen, but it will," and so I submitted my admissions package. The wait was brutal, but I eventually received an acceptance letter from Arizona State University! I was in! I was elated! I am currently working on my Master's in Education to become a behavioral analyst. Ideas just keep coming to me and I can't wait to see how they unfold. I am in a state of indescribable feelings! It is true that when you go after your heart's desire, you really do not have to worry about how it will happen, because the right people and opportunities are simply put in front of you! As I write these words, I find myself getting filled with so much joy at the thought of you finding inspiration and discovering your heart's desire in reading the pages of this book. You have everything you need to make it happen! God would not have put the desire in you if he didn't also equip you with everything to make it a reality! But you have to be the one to take action!

Maria Elena Iturralde is CEO of Iturralde Consulting, Subsidiary of Iturralde Immigration Consulting, LLC

Iturralde Consulting offers consumer financing for personal development products, services and other financial needs and services. She is a trained mediator, LOA practitioner, author, public speaker, advocate, and a trained immigration consultant. She is currently working on her Masters of Education in Applied Behavior Analysis

Maria Elena is passionate about helping others. Her mission is to empower and mentor people to recognize they are God's highest form of creation, and guide them through the steps of harnessing the Law of Attraction to attain their heart's desires.

For more information visit www.iturraldeconsulting.com.

Best No-Bake Success Recipe

by Kate Janik

Dear Reader,

This is a true story that I wish to share with you. I strongly feel that my message can be helpful to you and will give you hope and positive feelings towards your life and the people that surround you. I was once where you are now, and I know for a fact that life can turn 180 degrees in no time, bringing happiness and success, exactly the way it happened to me. Here is my simple recipe for your happy life:

I am a Slovak, living in Greece for over 15 years now. When I was 22, I finished my MA in English language, literature and culture. I was on the top of the world: young, healthy, good looking, sexy and clever. I had it all. All but love.

Studying literature proved over and over again that the biggest struggle throughout the history of humanity was always to find love, or freedom, or both. All classical literature describes those two feelings as crucial to happiness. So

I decided to re-evaluate the relationship that I was in at that time. The guy was great: really nice, good looking, polite, clever, gentle, respectful, intelligent and funny. He had it all, right? So where was the problem? We were together for three and a half years, but somewhere on the way I lost my love for him. I could not explain it, it just happened. Upon finishing our university degrees and I decided that the future of our must be decided once and for all. We would go on holiday, to spend some time together somewhere in a strange environment. For me this was the only way to see if I had feelings for him or not. And so we booked holidays to a Greek island of Corfu.

Once in Corfu, on this beautiful green island, I realized that not only were there no feelings for him left inside of me, I realized that the person is actually the complete opposite of someone I could share my life with. I ended the relationship almost immediately. I remember I was sitting on the beach on this magical island, looking at the dark starry night and saying: "Please God, you gave me everything I could wish for, please also bless me with love - that is all I care about now".

And the God or Universe, or the Law of Attraction (all of them means the same energy and power to me) heard my wish. The very next day a man came into my life and it was love at the first sight. I remember looking at the sky every night and thinking: "Really, that fast, huh?"

We have been together for over 15 years, married for 9 of them. We have two wonderful children and one crazy dog. We work together, we eat together, we sleep together, we dream together. And we never felt tired of each other's company after so many years of being 24/7 together. Imagine...

When I decided to stay in Greece, my parents went ballistic. My father cut me off financially, thinking that this is the only way to bring me back home. My parents had plans for my life, and in their eyes I threw all that away for LOVE, because I believe you can study or earn money at any point in your life, but love does not come as easily as career or money. I believe that when you finally feel the real love, you must put everything else aside because love is the highest feeling; it is the ultimate happiness we, as humans, can experience.

Today, I know that there is no difference if you desire true love or a car. The Universe has abundance of everything and does not care what you desire. The only truth that remains is that love is really the ultimate feeling, and if you can apply it to all of your desires and requests, you can speed up the process of acquiring your desires and objects of desire.

Now back to my story. Together with my husband we created four successful businesses, and today we are financially independent. We work when we want, how long we want, and we travel and enjoy precious moments as family – also whenever we want. I have plenty of help with the household, I do not clean or cook. I have a super nanny that helps to raise our children the way we believe is fit. My life seems like a dream on all levels.

So what am I doing right?

In my understanding, the success was determined the moment I decided to partner up with person I truly fell in love with. This person had a constructive impact on my personality, together we were strong team that created perfect conditions for success on business level, and happiness on the personal level.

Moreover, on daily basis I strictly follow these rules (the "ingredients" of my recipe for success):

- don't forget to be grateful for what I have (gratefulness)

- don't forget to express my love and gratitude to everyone around me (positive communication)

- always be true to myself and follow my inner feelings, and immediately act upon them (following of intuition)

- never allow negative thoughts to thrive in my mind (negative thoughts control)

- visualize and feel my goals and desires with all my senses (visualizing and feeling)

And the Universe is bringing me back more each day. That is it!!! The secret recipe to success revealed. It is that simple.

The main thing is to realize what each goal you set really means to you and why you need it (or desire it). What feelings (or outcomes) do you expect to experience once your goal is achieved? You see, it is all about FEELINGS, not things. When we wish to buy a great car, we do not imagine the actual object (the car itself). What we imagine are feelings we'll experience once we own that car.

We try to bring to life all feelings that our five senses will provide us with when driving that car; the sound of the

engine, the feel of the leather, the smell of the new car, the
thrill of its speed, the beauty of its design that makes the
other people turn their heads and smile – all feelings are
important. The more details you imagine and feel, the more
real the whole experience will become, until you will be sure
that you already own that car. We do not care for the object
of desire. A car is a car – simply a means of transportation.

And as mentioned before, love is the highest and strongest of all feelings. It is the most powerful experience that
can help you attract everything you desire.

How do we make ourselves to love objects?

Normally, we do not connect love with simple objects,
such as a computer. In our minds, love is connected with
higher concepts such as helping others, doing something for
the planet, etc. The trick is to apply love to smaller things
and objects as well. Simply re-program your sub-consciousness to accept love for objects and things. It is necessary that
you will stop feeling guilty for desiring material things. This
is very important technique, and once you will master it,
you will reap the fruits of your desire really fast.

How can you re-program your sub consciousness?

Firstly, accept that the Universe does not have any moral
code. It does not care if you love your car more than your
wife. Other common, but untrue, affirmations include:
Study hard and achieve good school grades! Find a good
paid job! Do not disappoint your bosses! Do not provoke!
Life is hard! You must earn your respect! You must get married and have children!

Your parents, grandparents, and teachers probably all
made sure that they showed you the old good and safe way

how to accomplish what they considered "a successful life." And a child, although a very strong being at first, becomes fragile at some point and will give in to the adults' pressure, and sooner or later will follow the proposed path.

To me it is a crime to suppress children's fantasy. Being a mother I always support all dreams my children have. When my son tells me that he wishes to be an astronaut I always back him up 100%. I tell him, **you can be anything you want**. I wish that I had been brought up that way.

The damage was done to most of us in early childhood. This means that it is deeply rooted into our sub-consciousness. The only way to fix this is to realize that the damage was done in a first place, accept it, define it, and then start over by creating a new set of assumptions and affirmations for your brain:

Life is to be enjoyed! Love exists and everyone has a counterpart in this world! You deserve time and money! You can have good health! There is no such a thing as bad genes! You can be beautiful, slim, sexy and attractive forever! You can love money and luxury goods, and there's nothing wrong with it! You can be happy and enjoy every moment of your life! You can divorce and start over at any age! You can be free! You can believe in whatever you choose to believe! There is no right or wrong! There is only what you feel is best for you!

You can be anything and anybody, all you need to do is to believe in it and persuade your inner (sub-conscious) mind that you are worth it. You deserve it and there is nothing wrong with your desires. From that point on, it is only a matter of time when you will transform yourself into that desired being, surrounded by all those cool gadgets and things, feeling happy, healthy, strong, admired, respected and loved at all times.

So go on and start now destroying the bad old affirmations and replace them by those great affirmations that will allow you to dictate the universe the list of YOUR desires and dreams. Then religiously use my daily ingredients and cook yourself a SUCCESSFUL LIFE A LA YOU that you 100% deserve and will surely enjoy!

Dr. Kate Janik (www.katejanik.com) is a successful entrepreneur located in Corfu Island, Greece. She manages and co-owns many companies, including: Next Holidays, a leading travel and tourism agency (www.corfunext.com); holiday design studios (www.ionianeye.com); an innovative excursion portal www.corfutrips.com; and luxury spa villa (www.ionianpearl.com). Kate is also very well known for being a leading professional wedding consultant and planner at www.weddingscorfu.com.

Kate studied in various universities some to mention are Cambridge and Harvard and owns a MA in English language and literature, a PhD. in translatology and intercultural studies, and has published numerous scientific articles in literary and translation studies. She is currently working on her new book explaining Greece's economic crisis, to be released in summer 2016.

You Were Born to Be Healthy

by Doctor Jof

As a qualified M.D. and Family Doctor, Board Certified in Anti-Aging as well as Acupuncture, I have been practicing Medicine for more than 20 years and I travel a lot. When people hear what I do and they learn how old I am, they always say "Give me the secrets. What do I need to do to be healthy, to lose weight and look younger?" This chapter is an attempt to capture that fifteen-minute conversation that I would have with that person beside me on the plane.

Here are a few nuggets to share:

Nugget #1 You are already healthy. You are healthy by design, genetically. Cells are designed to heal themselves and if they are not healthy, the first question to ask is "What do my cells need to function? What do I need to do to help them be healthy again?" This is powerful knowledge, because no action or habits change without you changing your thinking. Knowing that you are designed, genetically, to be healthy is a radically important element of manifesting or attracting the prosperous health that already belongs to you.

Having been trained in traditional conventional medicine, over a number of years I realized that I am not helping people get better or healthy only by prescribing medications. Not that I am against prescribing medications, but the answer to the question: "What do my cells need?" is usually not Prozac or some other medication. Drugs can treat or mask symptoms, and I am not against making my patients feel better to buy time to fix the problem, as long as we know we are doing just that.

The other answer that we often hear to that question is some kind of crazy and intense exercise program, or eating less fat and changing your diet dramatically. With both of those suggestions, I disagree. You have to work with the body physiologically to figure out where you, your body and your cells are at mentally, physically, physiologically –and go from there. This is called Individual Metabolism or Functional Medicine, and this is the future of medicine. It is what health and healing should be. I will also make a somewhat bold statement, not so much my own words, but in the context of answering that question, exercise, cardio or doing more cardio is almost the worst thing you can do. CARDIO IS DEAD. No one should be doing cardio anymore.

If you think of your poor struggling cells, does it make any sense to be beating or poisoning weak cells either with drugs, poor diet or with rigorous exercise? If you have poorer cells that are unhappy and struggling to function, then trying to beat them into health does not sound like a logical solution to me. When your house plants are suffering, what do you do? You water them, you nourish them, you give them light, fertilize and supplement. That is common sense. Shouldn't that be the way we treat our growing organic body cells? Your body is about 75% water. Hydrate those cells with water, nourish those cells, and treat them with love, respect, and kindness.

Nugget #2: Most diseases are now 90% environmental. You are genetically designed to be healthy and even if you have genes that suggest you may get breast cancer or celiac disease, that outcome (or whether those genes will be expressed) depends 90% on your environment, what you do, what you eat, what you drink, how you sleep, how you rest and how you exercise. To a lesser degree, where you live and what you do with the toxins you are exposed to also matters.

There is now evidence to suggest that breast cancer is 90% environmental. Another example of this is that 98% of people who have celiac disease have a particular gene, but only 2% of people who have that celiac gene actually get celiac disease. This means that roughly 98% is environmental. Just because you have a bad gene, you cannot blame mom, dad or your grandparents for your outcome; you have control. As I said, the good news, if you do things right 80% of the time then you will avoid switching on those triggers. I hope this liberates you to attract a prosperous life. You are not captive of your genes; you control your environment, your health and happiness.

Nugget #3: Your cells have not been designed to deal with sugar, or what I like to call white poison. Only eat sugar by accident. Read the labels; everything is full of sugar. By

the way, cancer cells primarily feed on sugar. If you have to
use or cook with sugar, then use sugar in the raw or organic
unbleached (not whitened) sugar. Avoid artificial sweeteners
at all cost. A good alternative is natural Stevia, but be careful
of chlorinated products that are commercially available. If I
avoid all the sugar (and alcohol as well, because alcohol has
sugar) then I lose, on average, one to two pounds per week.
I do sometime gain those pounds over the winter or over the
holidays, so this is one of the main ways to cut down and
make myself and my cells happy again. Sugar is also more
addictive than cocaine, so this makes for a difficult habit
to break, but it's relatively easily achieved with baby steps.
Sugar is very inflammatory. Any inflamed problem in the
body will be made worse by sugar, especially arthritis, myal-
gia and headaches. I also ask my patients, "Do you think it
is a good idea glycolizing bad cholesterol, brain cells, kidney
cells, eye cells or nerve cells?" This doesn't sound like a good
plan to me. Consuming sugar also usually can significantly
reduce your white blood cell activity, which is directly linked
to your ability to fight against infection or problems in your
environment. Stop thinking sweet.

Nugget #4: In the unforced rhythms of controlling
your environment with common sense, the most logical
next nugget to think about is, "How do I interact with my
environment and which barriers do I need to keep in place?"
This is like a country guarding its borders. It is really very
simple. Your body basically has four barriers that you need
to keep healthy; three directly with environmental and one
a little more indirectly. They are the skin, stomach/intes-
tines, airway and blood-brain barrier. Anything that pene-

trates through the other three, could potentially penetrate the blood-brain barrier, which gets to your central control system in the brain.

I will suggest a short recipe for basic barrier health. To illustrate the point, if someone has IBS, eczema and asthma, do think that they may be having a barrier problem? If you skin is eczematous, what do your lungs look like, what does your stomach barrier look like. Oh my goodness, if you have inflammatory triggers that cross the blood-brain barrier, could you be anxious? Could you be depressed? Could you have mental fog? Could you have poor memory? Hmmmm, that is a novel idea. Is there a connection between the stomach, immune system, inflammation and brain health? It is not rocket science.

Here is the basic barrier for stomach health recipe:

- Take a probiotic with about 10 billion colonies, including Saccharomyces boulardii. Take this one to three times per week, perhaps on Monday, Wednesday and Friday. Follow this recipe for the next three to six months;

- L-glutamine, 1000mg, twice daily for three to six months.

- Digestive Enzyme blend with every big meal of the day, this acts like a natural anti-inflammatory. Zinc 25mg, daily for one month.

- Vitamin D, 5,000 IU daily for three months.

- Olive leaf extract 500mg, twice daily for two weeks only.

Please be sure that you are not allergic to these items. You may want to contact your Health Care Provider or

Certified Naturopath. This plan is for people older than 12 years and weighing at least 120 pounds.

Couple this with proper hydration, good sleep, proper or organic diet and you are stacking the odds to attracting health and prosperity.

Nugget #5: How to exercise to build muscles and metabolism without adding rigorous routine or cardio to your program every day. This may make you look funky, funny or goofy, but you can do what I call "mini-squats" everyday without it taking any time out of your normal routine. What is a mini-squat? A mini-squat is literally just what I would say "cracking your knees" from a 180 degree normal standing locked position, to about a 160 degree angle at the knee. You literally just drop your torso four to five inches by bending your knees. If you do this every time you brush your teeth, or in the shower or when you use the bathroom, a minimum three to six times per day, doing ten mini-squats at a time, and you could be doing 30 to 60 mini-squats per day. This stimulates the biggest muscle group in your body, controls your metabolism, and strengthens your knees, back and posture. You didn't have go to the gym and it did not cost a cent. There was no need to change into gym clothes and no sweating. Just normal stimulation of growth hormone, testosterone, new blood supply, muscle growth and metabolism. Simple and easy.

Consider an energy rebalancing device or electromagnetic field protection device. I do a little Meridian Acupuncture Imaging, as well as Biofeedback. Sometime a computer can give you a score for your health. When people wear a Q-Ray or Q-link device, I have found that these scores can improve between 2.5 and 5%, about 90% of the time. This is one way to avoid negative environmental impacts and stack the odds one step closer to attracting and enjoying a prosperous healthy life.

A few final thoughts: To change your results, you need to change the way you think. "I am healthy, how do I stay that way?" "How do I improve or secure what I do?" "Am I looking for a quick fix, masking symptoms, or am I supporting function, physiology, psychology and mental health. Do I love to do or eat things that love me back?" If you can see a mental picture of yourself as a tree with roots, trunk, branches, leaves and fruit and you see a bad fruit on that tree, ask the question; "What is the root cause and how do I fix it?"

Want to find an American Anti-Aging Medicine Certified Physician in your area? Do you want to invest in better choices for your genetics and body type? (In other words, learn what foods are better for you to eat without changing volume, quantity, and counting calories.) Want to loose weight, feel better, have more energy? Restore your memory, have better sex and live more prosperous? Join me on your journey to a prosperous life, on my website: www.doctorjof.com

---

About Doctor Jof:

Born in 1971 and raised in South Africa, he qualified as a medical doctor in 1996 at the University of Pretoria. After 9 years in public and private practice in rural Limpopo province, he felt called to Canada. Knowing that he has a world vision, this was seen as a next step towards that goal. He left his friends and family to pursue this dream. He arrived in Saskatchewan, Canada, and has been living there since May 2005. He has 3 beautiful daughters.

Dr. Jof has a keen interest in preventative and Natural health. He firmly believes furthering the health industry and not the disease industry. What needs to be done to cure you, not just manage your symptoms? The world of conventional Medicine and natural health collided, and this website is a product thereof.

As a Functional medical doctor, Dr. Jof started looking into Simple Physiology for answers to disease, the origins, the cures and prevention thereof. Join us for the discoveries already made and still to be made, during this journey.

During his in time in Canada he has re-qualified as an MD, and is registered with the College of Physicians and Surgeons. He is registered with the Canadian Medical Council, the Canadian College of Family Physicians.

He obtained his Acupuncture Designation in Canada in 2008, through the Acupuncture Foundation of Canada Institute.

He obtained his Advanced Fellowship in Anti-Aging and Regenerative Medicine through the American Academy of Anti-Aging and is Board Certified in Florida, USA. Visit www.doctorjof.com to connect with Dr Jof and to learn more about how functional medicine can change your life.

Prosperity and the Body, Mind & Spirit Connection

by Sandra Kimler

We all have dreams, and most of us love to dream of prosperity in our lives. We visualize ourselves living in that house, driving in that car, married to that person, earning a lot of money and going on holidays, but what are we actually doing for it? I do not mean working yourself to the bone. No, I mean are you actually "being" a person of prosperity? Do you wake up with a song in your heart and a dance in your step?

I hear people say: Once I am wealthy, then I'll be happy. I say to them: Be happy and then you are wealthy. Oftentimes it is hard for people to feel happy because they feel so burdened down with life. And even though they might have the best intentions of being happy, they just don't feel like it. As a Nutritionist for almost thirty years, I have studied and put to the test the correlation between the food that we eat and the mood that we are in after eating certain foods.

Did you know that there are foods that help us become happier?

Every food comes with a story and every food has a vibration. When we eat healthy foods like fruit, vegetables, green smoothies, sprouts, salads, nuts and seeds our body gets all the nutrition it needs and feels satisfied. The brain releases serotonin, and in return we feel happy and good about ourselves. Serotonin is a happy mood chemical. Eighty percent of serotonin exists in the gut and is governed by our state of hunger. Junk foods have no nutrition, therefore we not only feel unsatisfied physically, we also do not feel mentally good about ourselves. An unhappy mind keeps the stomach too acidic, causing ulcers, bloating, reflux and physical weakness. When we are happy and relaxed, we digest better.

You must heal the whole person from top to bottom, inside and out, including your environment, how and where you live, work, love, diet, exercise and the level of connection with yourself and your higher self or spirit.

We've known for the longest time that the Body, Mind and Spirit are connected.

Our body follows our mind, which means that when we are emotional or sad, we tend to grab the comfort foods like sugary cakes, chocolate and ice-cream. When we are uptight or stressed, we crave salty and fatty foods. Unfortunately, all these foods create brain-fog and are low in vibration. The foods we eat have the power to make us sick or they have the power to heal us. The obvious foods that harm us are junk food and fast foods, which are really not foods at all. The obvious foods that are kind to us are organic fruit and vegetables, superfoods like berries, kale, rainbow salads, avocado and drinking lots of room temperature, non-carbonated, water.

Which foods do you think our higher selves want us to have?

Our higher selves want us to be the happiest and best we can be. So when we look at the foods we eat, we find out that there are indeed foods that are kind to us and foods that harm us. Junk food is very addictive, and addiction is a separation from our higher selves. The more we eat the wrong foods, the more we are separated from all that is good. When we eat foods that are high in vibration, then the connection to spirit becomes stronger and the flow becomes easier. We get messages all the time from our higher self, but if we feel tired, depressed and feel sorry for ourselves, then we'll miss these messages.

You can make the change today! There is no pill you can take for this, but there are foods that can change your life forever. When toxins have been removed from our head-area, we lose our brain-fog and our mind becomes strong again. The channel between our third eye (6th chakra) and our higher self becomes strong and clear. Increasingly we feel grateful for what we have and give thanks to our higher self. This is when the magic happens.

First, we need to accept that we want to prosper and therefore we need to live as a person of prosperity. That means we must accept that we are going to change our lives as we know them today. A person who is prosperous eats healthier foods. Would a wealthy person eat McDonald's, cheap junk or take away foods?

Therefore, work on yourself, get rid of old thinking habits and old habitual lifestyles, say yes to new ways of living, and get out of old patterns. Our path has been universally laid out for us already, so don't worry about that. All you need to do is raise your vibration in order to walk this path. Work on yourself, work on your personality. Raise your personal vibration!

It's ok to give up alcohol, coffee, junk food, sugar, fat, smoking, dairy, gossiping and keeping up with the Joneses. Find new groups to exercise with, learn new 'live food' recipes, eat organic, become a volunteer somewhere, forgive, go hiking, be with yourself, grow some vegetables, meditate, do yoga or tai chi and stay fiercely curious about what is out there. It's a vicious circle. This way of life will become your normal 'new' way of life which increases your vibration at that time, which in turn gets rid of karmic residue, opening you up to more life lessons of a higher vibration.

Fresh organic fruit and vegetables have a higher vibration, a higher frequency. These are 'alive' foods. How can you feel alive when you eat 'dead' foods? Lots of fruit and vegetables will eliminate toxins out of our bodies, but more importantly they are eliminating toxins from our brain.

Also, eat lots of live sprouts, activated almonds, berries, kale and green juices. Stay away from dairy. Dairy produces mucus and phlegm in our bodies. This mucus is the cause of many allergies, asthma, osteoporosis, brain fog and ear aches. When we stop having dairy and instead eat high frequency foods, then our bodies will cleanse themselves, become more youthful, our muscles become firmer; we lose weight and guess what?

We become happier! When we are happy the thoughts we think are different to those when we are depressed. My observation is that depression is nothing more than being unhappy about an outcome that ended up differently to what we thought it would be. When we are happier we have a different energy, which people notice. Different doors will open for you, different opportunities will become available to you.

Often we learn or return to meditation, we enjoy our own company and start to visualize our lives in a more prosperous way. We need to work on our own personalities, we need to improve ourselves all the time and eating high vibrational foods is a key element here.

In order to change our behavior, we need to let go of our old story.

Our old story gave us the attention we needed as it fed our emotional needs. So how do we start? It starts with a decision. This is the hardest thing because a true decision comes with commitment. If a person goes back to an old behavior then it wasn't a decision to begin with.

I call it 'replacement therapy.' Stop drinking all sodas, supermarket fruit juices, alcohol and animal milks. They cause brain fog, as does sugar. They interfere with clarity. They are also addictive. Drinking plain water is brilliant. Replace all snacks between meals with fruit or carrots. When you go out, grab a piece of fruit such as a banana, some grapes, a mandarin or an apple. Eat as much organic and raw food as possible. Have brown rice instead of white rice and use the absorption method to cook it. Don't have pasta. Pasta is dried up glue and should be considered a junk food, as should all breads and pastries. Use black-bean spaghetti, lentils and beans instead.

Your body will thrive on organic and raw foods because these foods were designed for your body and everything else is a burden. Animal food products like meat, chicken, fish, eggs and dairy do not contain any fiber. Generally, we do not eat enough fiber, but on a plant-based diet there are plenty of foods containing fiber, such as fruit, vegetables, beans, nuts and seeds.

God helps those who help themselves. Through strengthening our spirit, mind and body connection, we can achieve many wonderful things, including being prosperous, and with that comes a whole new life through eating healthier, thinking kind and positive thoughts, meditating, becoming aware of life's messages and not becoming a victim to our story. We can all flourish and thrive through eating healthier, and in this state of wellness and prosperity our spirit, mind and body connection will be strengthened. Our lust for life will shine through our eyes and be evident in our actions as we achieve many wonderful new things with the body, mind and spirit connection.

Sandra Kimler is an International Speaker and Author on the subject of nutrition. Sandra was born in The Netherlands in 1964. She immigrated to Australia with her family in 1978. Sandra received qualifications in nutrition and iridology studying the teachings of Dr. Bernard Jensen. Sandra is a passionate animal-rights activist, a devoted mother of three wonderful children and lives in Byron Bay, Australia.

Sandra is the author of "So, Why Become Vegan?," "Tap into Transformation - The Spirit, Mind & Body Connection," "Saladmaster," and two lovely children's books, "ABC for the Gentle Soul," and "Jack's Trip to India."

For more information on Sandra and her books, please visit her website at www.sandrakimler.com or contact her by email at sandrakimler@gmail.com.

The Number One Prosperity Factor –
The Power of Self-Healing
9 Steps Into the Wealth of Health

by Alexandra Kleeberg

Just imagine:

Wouldn't it be exhilarating if you could heal yourself from any sickness? Would it not change your life into one with fascinating freedom, desirable dignity and fortunate flow if you would be equipped with the power of self-healing? Would it not be a holy and healing bliss, which gives you trust to float and fly prosperously in what we call "real life?" Would it not be beneficial to all of us and our togetherness if we all lived with knowledge at a great height and the energizing might of self-healing?

Prosperity comes from the Latin word *"prosperus,"* which means exhilarating, beneficial, desirable, blessed, and fortunate. Prosperous might be an economic term, but etymologically it stands for a life in abundance and bliss. Abundance and bliss are also pillars of health and healing, as well as feeling whole. Feeling prosperous is predominantly an inner attitude rather than a large bank balance.

You cannot buy health, you do not earn health, but you can learn health.

My medical doctor colleague Michael Schlaadt puts it that way:

"Health is the normal state of our wonderful body. Our body is the most brilliant self-organized being, which has ever existed on Earth. Programs that have been perfected and stood the test of time for millions of years control all important metabolic processes in the background, without us to take care about it. Genetically, we are almost identical. Therefore, the control depends on the influence of our living conditions. This gives us the possibility of active self-influence via targeted imaginations."

Most of the behaviors that damage us are learned in a collective spirit of the times, which demanded and demands adaption, functioning, perfection and reason. Often healing is a way out of this so-called normality into the individuality of an emotional, empathetic, enthusiastic, creative and vivid being.

Would you like to understand your body and to heal it? Would you like to bring joy into every cell, inner peace into the magnificent network of your brain, and deep love into your heart? Would you like to blow up your inner walls and to experience yourself in your very own existence: pure, free, creative energy?

Then open your heart and start!

Nine Steps into the Power of Self-Healing

I have divided the process of self-healing into nine easy to follow steps.

You can take a page out of Heidi's[1] story. With these nine steps, she has healed a life-threatening disease, as well as a traumatic family history, all on her own.

1. You are awareness: get conscious of any sort of pain or discomfort

Write down all situations in which you feel fear, pain or any kind of discomfort. Should they last longer than half an hour, then they are likely learned and unnecessary. Discover all of their underlying dogmas like a detective.

Heidi was not expected to live much longer. A crime has happened in her body. As a detective, she daily investigated all her wounds. Every day she scanned her body for tensions, pains, wounds. She learned to understand their language. She recognized how wounds develop into diseases. She wrote down her observations.

2. You are release: let go of self-destructive dogmas

Realize the unconscious patterns of all the painful situations you experienced. For example: I am not lovable, I always have to be good, I have to function, I have to be perfect etc. Write down the thoughts that have led to feeling sick. Read them aloud. Then burn them with fire, drown

---

1 Heidi's name and history are changed

them in the water, send them on the wind or bury them into the earth – again and again and again...

Detective Heidi found the offender: 'You are worth noting. You were not planned. You do not have any rights. You are damned in misfortune...' Always and always she dismissed fear, anger, shame, pain, sorrow and many more powerful emotions. Then she burned all self-damaging dogmas in an imaginative way. She forgave her torturers.

3. You are freedom: choose a new life

Use emotional relaxation to discover which patterns have led your former life, and how you have repeated them in an endless process of pain. Decide now to live a happy and fulfilled life, because today is in every way the most beautiful day.

Heidi assured herself every morning: I choose love. Today is a wonderful day. I choose joy. In every moment, I choose to see the good inside me and in others, and feel it too. I am prepared for new learning.

4. You are trance: dive into flow

Start to play, putter around and do handicrafts, to become engrossed in the nature or whatever turns you into trance and flow. Or shut your eyes and feel what is deep inside - dream, dream, dream.

Every day Heidi sat between two trees – one of the trees was her loving mother, the other one was her good father. She let the trees speak to her. She dreamed herself anew in the womb of the trees, the wind rocked her, the rain kissed her – she experienced deep security and fundamental trust. An angel and a lion guarded her and protected her new beginning.

5. You are vision: embody your goal

Write, paint, and imagine the vision of your health and of your luck: in an upright position, the crown sparkles on your head, the eyes exude pure love, the ears are pricked up, the lips are sensual, the spine swings, the wings of freedom flutter. All organs are working in perfect harmony in a body that swings in a wonderful way. Pure love streams out of every pore. It flows into your social environment and into your vision of a fulfilled, happy, healthy life.

It was Heidi's vision to write a book for children, to help them find their paradise inside, even if everything around them storms and raves. Heidi painted, did handicraft and wrote her vision with an enthusiastic attitude. With shining eyes, she told people about her goal.

6. You are creator: build a new mindset

Develop new dogmas, which create a pleasant resonance in your body: I am valuable, I am lovable, I can manage everything step by step. Write down these dogmas, paint them, dance them, sing them, live them – so that they manifest deeply inside you.

Heidi looked for sentences, which brought happiness into her body, so that it streamed with relish and pulsated warmly. She wrote in her diary: I am welcome, I am dearly loved, I love me.

7. You are exercise: practice, practice, practice

Practice your new attitude and the vision it presents passionately with every beat of your heart and with every breath. Manifest it wholeheartedly and in a creative way in your life, in your contacts, in your dreams and in particular in your every-day life.

Heidi copied the sentences, which had healing effects on her. She stuck them on her refrigerator, the washroom door, the wardrobe door – every time she passes one she read the sentences and jumped joyfully while doing it. With every standing up Heidi imagined that she opens for an inspiring day, with every sitting down she did this in silent patience and relievable, relieving forgiveness, with every step she confirmed her healthy, wealthy, fulfilled life.

8. You are growth: overcome all obstacles

Mistakes are our best friends; they help us to grow. Welcome every obstacle, so that you learn to jump. Consider them as mirror images of your old attitudes, which you can now overcome and dissolve. Jump: You are a victor, not a victim.

Heidi had developed a mantra for the hours of desperation and despondency: 'Every obstacle takes me quicker and nearer to my goal, to my health and to my luck.'

9. You are bliss: bless your life

Bless your conception, your birth, your steps in life, your wonderful body and all your cells; bless these nine steps on your way to luck. Bless whatever you like to bless.

Heidi blessed her ancestral line of painful readiness to make sacrifices until she could develop pictures of her grandparents and parents as bright living cordial people, she blessed herself in the womb, her childhood and her youth, her profession and her new calling. She blessed the earth, the stars, the vastness of the universe and everything beyond space and time. She blessed her healing path.

Today, after 4 years of healing, in which nearly all physical and psychological symptoms disappeared, Heidi is on
the way into a healthy, wise, vivid future. Together with the
many other participants of my groups, she goes into a new
life with dignity, freedom and her very own power.

Do you know that you can also reach the heart of wealth
with only one step? Are you ready for the big jump that radically takes you directly into a healthy, prosperous, fortunate
life? Are you prepared to take a run-up and to bridge the gap
that separates your current life from its fulfillment?

Open your heart and start:

Jump, leap, spring, vault – in the very midst of unconditional love. Stay there forever.

Please remember always:

You are love: float in love, radiate love, share love.

Just imagine:

Would it not be thrilling, if everybody learns how to
heal? Would it not be most democratic, if self-healing would
be taught in kindergartens, in schools, colleges and universities and in the retirement homes? My medical colleague.
Michael Schlaadt and I founded **Network Self-Healing**.
We collect healing stories around the globe – healing by
one's own power. Our vision is:

1. a free Internet portal with healing stories for all sort
    of sicknesses, so people can get inspired, motivated
    and competent in the power of self-healing,

2. teaching the wisdom of the body – our body: dura-
    ble, curable, miracle – and many, many exercises

to heal organs, body-systems and of course ways of thinking,

3. lectures in kindergartens, schools and retirement homes, so that people learn how to heal themselves, and

4. international scientific exchange on self-healing.

Watch us under https://www.youtube.com/watch?v=mqY1gf_WYiI

Join us.

Open your heart and start.

With all my love,

Alexandra

My work: As a licensed psychotherapist I teach self-healing imaginations to groups every day, I have written two books in German and forthcoming in English: **Healing Every Day** and **Nine Steps into the Wealth of Health**. I have published some CDs and DVDs and many little videos on my YouTube Channel. You can get my brief daily imagination **HeartLight** and much more for free under **www.imagienatium.com**.

My heart:

- *I am inspired by learning.*

- *I am enthusiastic about every kind of new wisdom I gain.*

- *I am very thankful about the creative field and support I am living in.*

- *I love to dream, to write and to float through times, myths and space.*

- *I love to dive deeply into the wisdom of time and emerge with a glimpse on the treasures of humanity and the universe.*

- *I love to connect with people, their experiences and their potential.*

- *I love to expand my consciousness, clear my heart, and sensitize my body*

- *I love to build new networks, to engage and most of all: to create.*

My vision: *Together with medical doctor Michael Schlaadt I founded Network Self-Healing: We collect healing stories around the globe and teach the wisdom of the magnificence of our body: just durable – curable –miracle. Find out more under **www.heal-your-self.org***

Photo by Dietrich Busacker

CREATIVITY – Pillars for Building Your Creative Palace

by Ken Lacy

s children, we create our own reality through imagination. In those moments, there is no guessing as to illusions or false fantasies. It is a reality that we experience in that given space at the time. As we navigate the growing years, that childlike imagination becomes diluted over time. Based on what we hear, what we read, and what we're told, the imagination is deemed untrue, based on restrictions created in our minds. What if we take that same creative energy that was used to establish those boundaries, and instead apply those efforts to validate our imaginations? Life evolves in a cyclic fashion, giving us the opportunity to learn, and then apply those lessons for another chance to pursue our ambitions. Children may be our greatest asset to learn from at times, when we realize that imagination fuels our potential for unlimited creativity.

There are three parts to the brain, and I'm not talking about the logical and emotional sides. I'm talking about part #1, which is "what we 'know.'" Part #2 is "what we don't 'know.'" And part #3 is "what we don't know that we don't 'know.'" The largest of these three is part #3; 'what we don't know that we don't 'know.' Albert Einstein supposedly used more of his brain capacity than anyone, at around 12%. It had been said for many years that on average, humans used 5-6% of their brain capacity. Now there are studies that claim we use less than 1%.

As we understand the two points above, childlike imagination and our brain capacity, take a look at technology. Technology is a continuous work in progress. It constantly gets better and better, with more advancement and constant improvements. The reality is that any and all enhancements within technology begin with a thought. There is no technology without a thought. So that childlike imagination launches the creativity within the freedom of one's mind to bring a new idea to fruition. The fact is; the same space that limits us between our ears is the same space that offers us free reign – no barriers and no boundaries to live life to the fullest.

I love analogies, so let's consider the process in which an architect prepares for constructing an establishment of some sort. When he/she goes to design a building at a particular site, they already have a vision for the result. They have a specific scene in mind, and he/she knows what that scene should entail. However, there is a design process to create that specific look with a distinct appeal. Notice the word 'create.' If one phase in the design process is missed, then the project becomes altered and produces a result that does not correspond with the intended design.

Now follow the analogy. When you wish to pursue your ambitions, the artistry of the mind creates an architectural design to formulate your vision. Just as there are special tools for architectural drawings, there are special tools that we are each equipped with to design our own destiny. These three tools are obvious with each of us having the ability to use them, but yet often times, we don't use them properly. These three tools are your *thoughts*, your *tongue*, and your *actions*. Just the same as when an architect designs his/her drawings, the key is how we use these tools to satisfy our dreams.

Now let's take this concept to a different level by digging deeper into understanding how this works and, more importantly, how to make it work. As we begin to "peel back the onion," we will transition to another parallel, but one that provides a clear cut snapshot in applying the process.

We will use the analogy of building a house as we navigate through the various tiers to fulfill those aspirations. Once this process becomes a daily routine, your ability to tap into the limitless field of creativity opens the real estate market of your dreams – to continually build new structures to expand your community of ambitions.

Excavation

In the building process, excavation is clearing the land to construct a home. As the ground is prepared, a platform must be established to level the ground and to ensure stability before any building can take place. When our creativity ignites, the excavation phase is where our thoughts begin to create an idea. Our thoughts create that space to birth an idea, and a vision begins to develop with substance created to formulate what that idea looks like. The excavation phase is critical before beginning the building process, and can be the difference in building your house on solid ground or something less durable that does not withstand time. So the creativity in our mind is laying the groundwork in order to build upon something that withstands any adversity. In other words, this is the conviction that if you can believe it, you can conceive it; the idea that you wouldn't have been given the ability to dream it if you didn't have the ability to achieve it. So now the ground is prepped for building, just as the mind is ready to exercise your creativity.

Pillars

Pillars provide the additional support for a home when there is no basement. They serve as fortification to enhance the foundation. Without the pillars, the foundation may not remain intact. The pillars to optimize creativity are your *thoughts*, your *tongue*, and your *actions*. Your thoughts hold the blueprints, the floor plans, and the materials to produce the reality of your vision. The thought is the reality that is already created, the idea that gives life to your vision. Your tongue navigates the process. It has been said that the tongue is like the rudder of a ship. The tongue serves as your compass to maintain proper bearing. We can think and we can talk all day long, but nothing happens until we take action. So your actions of course do the work, and move the process forward to bring reality to your creation.

Creativity is a positive energy, a positive force, and a process to move us forward. Therefore, when we create a new desire, create a new dream, create a new idea or concept, we MUST exercise our belief in that vision with total conviction. That means all five senses must be tuned in to the vision. In other words, you can 'SEE' it, you can 'FEEL' it, you can 'TASTE' it, you can 'SMELL' it, and you can 'HEAR' it. Granted, in some cases that might be easier with some senses than others, but when you're continually engaged with the creativity aspect, you WILL discover that you can exercise all five senses with any given scenario in some way or another.

Foundation

Once the pillars are in place to support a stable foundation for building your home, it is extremely important that the concrete is poured evenly. That means pouring consistently across the entire foundation with even density, level, and strength. That foundation must be set up properly, settled, and created to support the rest of the construction for the home, in order to last long term.

The foundation in your creativity to pursue your destiny is that same consistency, applied towards your _thoughts_, your _tongue_, and your _actions_. You cannot be thinking of the wonderful results from that creative idea in your mind, while at the same time speaking of all the reasons that it may not work. Just as when you may be seeing all the results as you exercise your thoughts, and even when you may be talking about all the great possibilities that could come from your creativity – if your actions show that you're preparing for failure, it simply isn't going to work. The alignment between the three is crucial. Your _thoughts_, your _tongue_, and your _actions_ must **ALL** be painting the same picture, sending the same message, singing the same song, and sharing the same results synonymously within the established vision.

Your thoughts, your tongue, and your actions must be in alignment. Notice it has to be all three, not one of the three, and not even two of the three. Once the mind (thoughts), the tongue, and the actions are in alignment to where that habitual congruence becomes a lifestyle, we can only succeed, we can only see our dreams come to fruition, and we can only reach our goals. At that point, it's just a matter of time. You simply must be willing to stay the course. Remember the foundation to aligning the three is consistency.

So now you may be wondering what determines the level of consistency. It simply comes down for forming a new habit, one that just becomes your DMO (Daily Mode of Operations). In other words, it's your newborn way of living. There are various theories on how long it takes to form a new habit. Some say 90 days, some say 30 days, and some say 21 days. You'll never go wrong when striving towards the longer term. However, most will never reach the 21 day mark. That isn't pessimism, just reality. So I would encourage anyone to strive towards the 21 day mark because as you strive forward past that mark, it really becomes moot, and at some point the number of days has no relevance because you'll already have a grasp on making this work for you.

The Walls

As the walls go up in your home, you start to establish

boundaries within a given space. You are beginning the construct within the blueprints that become the early stage of shaping your home. Within the walls of your creativity is where you begin to shape your destiny. In other words, you've established the pillars and the foundation, the consistency has begun, and you are now in the early stages of groundwork to form your vision. These walls establish boundaries, not to be confused with limitless creativity, and they exist for the purpose of securing your place in that space. But they should not cause you to let go of your creative vision. In other words, hold your ground in that space and with non-wavering focus.

Plumbing / Electrical Work

When construction reaches the point where it's time to begin the plumbing and electrical work, you know the home is taking shape. All the extras begin to differentiate your living space from any other. The framework is now in place, and these amenities add the luxury of running water and power that we've become accustomed to. The plumbing and electrical work are those daily practices to keep you on the path to your destiny and chasing your aspirations. Take the time to journal and meditate on the reality of your vision. Read books that lend the same positive energy as when you visualize the success story that you've created in your mind. Associate with those who share the drive to be creative, and those who recognize change as a process to move forward with your endeavors. Those practices keep the path clear in order to see the road ahead for pursuing your dream.

Roofing

The roofing process protects a house from inclement weather, and provides the ability to regulate the indoor environment with a controlled climate. When you've put in the sweat equity and stayed the course, your conviction becomes so strong that it cannot be penetrated. Applying the success tools to develop a daily habit creates an imaginary shield around the plan of your dream. That shield acts as your roof to protect the dream, keeps the opposition away, and although that shield is invisible, the drive to your destiny has made it invincible.

Landscape

A home can be built properly, it can be built strong, and it can be well designed with all the right rooms to accommodate a comfortable living space. However, the landscape is the finishing touch that creates that special look, an estate of beauty, a welcoming atmosphere, and even someone's paradise. Once you've created an action plan to build your dream and that plan has been executed to fulfill your vision, the landscape is where you build upon those accomplishments. It is all about continuous growth. Growth is not limited to age, income, titles, and/or material possessions. We should always be learning. When we're learning we're growing, when we're growing we're progressing, and when we're progressing we're moving forward.

What allows the above-constructed success house to become a community is our willingness to teach others the same. When we take our eyes off of ourselves and put them on others, it redirects our focus to contributing and seeking ways to add value through others. The greatest gift that we can give is that of ourselves. What we give we receive. So, in other words, when we bless others through our giving, we become blessed. When the key elements that we've described, our thoughts, our tongue, and our actions, are all in alignment and congruent with our vision, we create reality in our dreams, and we create belief for others.

Ken Lacy is a retired US Army veteran with 30 years combined experience of leadership & management, and has a diverse professional background. He has served as a Program Manager in defense contracting for the past 10+ years, managing contracts of various sizes, various types, and managing large staffs of contractors. Ken was also part of a leadership and training team within the direct marketing industry. His career ambition is to contribute in a way to move humanity forward, and to add value where others can identify their own internal gifts to make a difference within society. You can reach Ken via email, kenlacy@ aol.com, or on LinkedIn: https:// www.linkedin.com/in/ken-lacy-7048b915

The Prosper Factor

by Claire Langlois

S tanding behind the wired fence, I was feeling the pressure of the well-known sensation. The wait was getting long into the short season of summer in Quebec, Canada on this very warm day. I was starting to question the situation... till I heard the whistle blow.

I know; like I knew what I always have known. The freedom of being in that space of sensing the water all around me, submerged, no bottom to confront limitation, no empty space to touch my skin – it was soothing my heart. At the age of 5, I had revived my memories of feeling safely alive on earth. There was no other place I would like to be then, the basin of water called the swimming pool.

The strident sound was signalling to the boys to get out of the water and leave the perimeters of the pool area because for now, it was the girls' time, according to the free swim schedule. There were many little girls and boys in the 60's in our up and coming neighborhood. Being the fifth of five children born in a 5-year period, I was part of the baby-boom era. But surprisingly so, what I can recall clearly is being alone – from inside out – with my extreme sureness of being happy exploring the element named water.

Here I am like it was, now and forever, being in the flow of my life. With all the swimming I was doing in the summer and winter, I was progressing faster than expected. At the pace I was improving, I would soon finish all the courses, but would be too young to enter the Leaders and subsequently the Lifeguard program.

Eventually, with the mixed feelings of pride that comes with recognition, and of frustration of being held back, I was to repeat all the courses to complete the full program of the Red Cross. So by age 16, I was at the pool as an apprentice lifeguard. I knew from an earlier age the power of trusting the water to keep me afloat.

Our public swimming pool offered my siblings and me many opportunities to become very confident swimmers, and consequently comfortable practicing many water sports to say the least. What I got from being in this community setting marked one of the strongest memories of my child-hood. I was feeling good in the presence of the lifeguards; Roger and Liliane. They were so kind to me and saw my potential as a swimmer. One special day, which is dear to my heart, I gave them bottles of perfume that I careful choose to express my love for them. To love and be loved is the foundation of prosperity because it is the source of Joy.

Interestingly, the period of my life when I was living my dream job as a lifeguard. I felt miserable because I was not loving myself for who I was. At eighteen, feeling depressed at not having an ideal body shape, weight or boyfriend, my inner waters started to swirl big time, and I lost not only my happiness, but also my perception of my own self-worth.

I tried to escape Earth on an ordinary summer night. In my mind, I could not grasp the deep meaning of the essence of life. My lack of faith in life, and my lack of connection with significant others, got the best of me. My brother happened to come in our empty house, the light turned on in my heart to confess my action to him. A lifeguard himself, he was very effective at helping me to save myself from my limited perception of life.

What happened? The secure state of feeling safe in the water was up against the need for prosperity. Prosperity is derived from the basic need to change for the best, to become who we are, to transform in our full potential of being. I had to move out of the water, walk on the ground and find out what I was leaving behind – which I could not give a name to yet. It's all about going beyond your limits or success knowing it is a partial view of the whole scenery. We are naturally curious of who we have the potential to be.

Each one of our living moments is the fabric of our imagination; they unfold smoothly in front of us or spread out under our feet or on top of our head. Knowing it or not, we follow the pattern imprinted on the fabric created by our mental activities such as thinking, feelings sprouting to become concepts, principles, rules, and values that determine which hat and shoes you will wear tomorrow, as well as 10 or 30 years from now.

I fabricated strong beliefs, like billboards on the side of the highway, such as that I had to be anything besides chubby, round and heavy. What came up was exactly what I was rejecting, fearing, focusing on: I gained weight and I lost sight of the love of myself. Life projects what you create in your mind.

Love remains the bigger picture. The young man I was attracted to at the time said to me "you are loving, whether you are yourself or trying to be a flower of a different seed." This belief resonates with my heart soul, and I integrated this belief – which became: "if I am love whether I want it or not, I might as well enjoy loving myself like I am; quite fit like a fish!"

At that point I got back on track, and I went back to swimming. Do we need to follow a straight line that is a result of a rational calculation, or some pattern that the mind fabricates? Really and clearly, you need to do the next step, which is going through the smooth or troubled waters you're already in. Be lovingly true to yourself. Connect to yourself in any way but in a space of love; it is all good because that is where you are... but there is so much there to be.

Up and down, we go around and we move along on our journey. We prosper. What is true is you can make yourself happy now, by shining with contentment. Now is an infinite and eternal well of revelation. The fear of losing track with our development, our journey, prevents us from surrendering to the line (the flow of the stream) of our inner light (the captain of your ship) from inside out. Take action as the designer of your own life. The joy of the soothing presence of embracing all there is of me, on this blue planet, shows up time and time and again, including when I spend time learning, writing, swimming, designing, visioning, conversing, meditating and coaching as a certified Emotion Code and Body Code practitioner.

Claire Langlois is an interior designer who earned a Bachelor degree with a major in counselling from Université Laval, Québec,1994. Self-healing and self-care through knowing oneself and daily practice of awareness has been her way of living since her teens. She has practiced daily meditation for over 37 years. Being a mother to two young adults has made her who she is today. After receiving a certification in life coaching from Erickson International, she became a certified practitioner of The Emotion and the Bode Code and has been active since 2012. You can connect with Claire at www.clairemariedellalanglois.com

A Miracle A Day Keeps the Doctor Away

Viktor Lazarevic

Hello to you my new friend! Welcome to the world of wishes fulfilled, abundance and overall wellness! It is not coincidence that you are reading this. It means you are looking for the truth, for something greater in life!

My name is Viktor Lazarevic, I'm a doctor, and thanks to the Law of Attraction, I have discovered my true passion: being a life coach. My mission is to tell people around the globe about the Law of Attraction, to help them manifest real miracles, unlock the secret powers they already have, and help them live their lives in prosperity and abundance. I love to empower people, and more than anything else I love to see people taking their lives in their own hands, and creating the lives they deserve.

My story starts when I was very ill as a child, and almost died. I was 4 years old. The doctors didn't give me any chance of survival, and told my parents that I was living my last days. My parents went against traditional medical advice and took me away from the hospital, deciding that no doctor would decide whether their child would live or die. Empowered by an amazing, invisible force, my parents saved my life! My mother literary gave me her blood, for the second time! And I survived! After my illness, my parents had to teach me to walk and speak again. My parents knew I was a born winner. My mother knew this even when she chose my name – "Viktor" means winner.

The day of my survival will always be celebrated in my family, almost as a second birthday. Since then, every day is a continuous celebration of life for me. This experience taught me to be grateful for every breath I take, and to see the positive side in every situation.

Years later I became a doctor. Something within me was guiding me to save people. Later, while fighting with my own personal demons, I discovered that I needed a life coach to help me work through things that my scientific brain could not explain. I'm grateful every single second that I made that decision. Sure, there are ups and downs in life. And every storm is easier if there is a lighthouse to guide us. My lighthouse was my life coach. All of the sudden, I had this incredible drive and desire to become a lighthouse for my friends, for my community, and for the world.

So I did!

My life is changed thanks to Law of Attraction. How do I see life now?

Imagine for a moment a nice coffee shop with tables outside. The weather is perfect; you sit comfortably, relaxed.

The aroma of freshly made coffee is so inviting and tempting. You can hear all the pleasant sounds around you – birds, distant conversations, children playing on the street. All of that is making you even more relaxed, even more calm. You are looking at the nearby fountain, and you see drops of fresh water jumping towards the sun. There is a rainbow around every single drop, and around the entire fountain. That is life for me; that rainbow, fireworks of colors– red, yellow, green, blue, thousands of colors, I don't even know the names for all of them. All those colors and sounds and smells, feelings, emotions and experiences – I am completely amazed with life.

Yes, I am in love with life, deeply in love, with small butterflies in my stomach, like on a first date. Life is full of miracles, every single day. The first of those miracles is that life always finds the way. Think about a small seed that falls into a crack in asphalt. At first you see only a bump on the sidewalk, then a crack, and eventually a tree is reaching to the sky. There are no obstacles, no limits.

The secrets that I have discovered are priceless. All thanks to my desire to understand life, to live it fully and freely, and to help create abundant and fulfilled lives for the people around me. I have met amazing people, and forged memorable friendships. But, the most brilliant accomplishment was to gain the understanding of one of the most amazing forces there is: the Universe.

I am ready to share this with you. I am ready to be your guide. I am ready to show you what true love for yourself means.

And, I will introduce you to my exceptional friend, The

Universe, and teach you its principles; his unique mobile phone is always on vibrate – a very special vibration of LOVE and POSITIVITY. And guess what, he is expecting your call!

You and I, we are the same. I am a winner, and YOU ARE A WINNER TOO! I create miracles in my life every day – you will soon become aware that you have the power to create miracles too.

Remember, for you, there are no obstacles, no limits!

Love and be grateful, The Universe will respond every time.

Viktor Lazarevic was born in Serbia. He lives in Kuwait and is a practicing dermatologist, with a PhD in immunology. Viktor is a certified Life Coach, with the great experience in applying the Law of Attraction, manifestation, and creating miracles. He has learned and developed secret tools that can help with introspection, boosting creativity and motivation, empowering and personal growth. Positive self-talk is one of his favorite topics and is often found telling his friends, clients and patients, "A miracle a day, keeps the doctor away."

Remember that life is now, while you are reading, so decide to transform it. Decide and get in touch, let me transform you into powerful attracting magnet, so you can live in abundance and prosperity, like you deserve! You are not alone. Connect with Viktor on Facebook or at his blog: http://mind-building. weebly.com/

Level Up Your Life

by Ariel Lee

I was raped while I was sleeping when I was 14. I felt like dirt. Different from my friends and ashamed. At the time there was not a word for sexual violence. I didn't have anywhere or anyone I felt I could turn to. I cried a lot and I thought if I could just stop crying then no one would know about it and nothing would change. So I buried it and I forgot it.

It was kind of like having amnesia. I truly forgot about it, and later wondered whether the whole thing was just a dream. I was confused. After 11 years, when I got first help, I got counseling. The counselor made me to write about all the things I'd been through. Then I suddenly remembered that I cried a lot in middle school age, and I felt horrible. But still I don't remember that night fully, just couple of scenes in my mind.

I pretended to be okay and normal because I was too young and my friends were too young. I tried to study hard; it was the only way that I knew to be successful. But studying wasn't easy. Whenever I tried to study I found that I couldn't focus, but I didn't know why. I could not understand myself.

And when I said something about my anguish to my friends, they simply couldn't understand. They just said, "You're different." That was hurtful. So I could not express myself. I was afraid of what other people thought about me. From then on, I pretended to be okay and tried to be normal. I understand now that they were too young to understand me. And I was young to go through that.

It's difficult to set aside a violation and pretend it didn't happen. The more you ignore it, the more invasive it becomes.

It was painful.

It got worse when I went to college. I felt incredible shame and constant embarrassment. Still I didn't know why. I was afraid of what other people thought about me. I wanted to hide myself, even though I had no reason for my shame. I was depressed, but I pretended to be okay. I didn't want anyone knowing about me. It was like a shadow that followed me everywhere I went. When the shame was there, I couldn't think of anything else.

Guilt soon joined the shame. I had lost control of my thoughts and emotions. I was in despair, hopeless. I lost my faith in God. There was no hand to hold me. It was like I was in a deep dark well, alone with no light.

I thought about suicide. It was a war inside me. What if I killed myself? What if I didn't and things got better? What if I tried and failed? I'd have a scar on my wrist and it would be weird. I was afraid, but I also hated myself. The rage in my mind was getting stronger and out of control.

Suicidal thoughts continued to plague me and then, at the most hopeless time, just when I could give up, help came.

I reconnected to my God.

When I was in 3rd grade, I was also going through difficult times, so I went Europe a month with a friend during my summer vacation. In Europe there are many churches, and my friend and I visited many of them. In one of these churches, I found myself sitting in chair with my eyes closed. I found that it made me very comfortable. I think, in a way, I was kind of praying.

After I got back to school, I sat in on a human character and behavior seminar. It was held by a Christian group, but I didn't know that. I met someone in the seminar who helped me. I got counseling, and then I met God.

During my last year of college, I took another important trip. I arrived in the mountains in the late afternoon. It was the end of March; I had the deep dark forest and the lodge to myself. After I arrived I unpacked my bag and went for a walk, and later sat beside a stream, where the owner of the lodge found me. He expressed his relief and explained that he thought I was trying to kill myself. "I'm not dying," I said. I shared a meal with the owner and his wife. Afterward, I went to the lodge to sleep.

I was all alone in my small room. It was empty and there was one small light and a candle. I wrote in my diary there. I was quite afraid with the solitude, but also quite comfortable. It was like I was lying in the tomb. I felt like I was facing my own death.

I sensed a light around me, with a color between white and ivory. The light wasn't critical of my sins. I felt death accept me as who I am without judgment. The blame was gone. I felt the light embracing all my faults, all my sadness, all my pain, as it is. It comforted me.

At that moment, I clearly understood what is important in life and what is not.

Social position and material goods were not important. Living a worthy life was. I was a little bit afraid when I tried to sleep, but I felt warmth and comfort when I woke up in the morning. I felt I was not alone. It was like God was with me.

After that I went down the mountain, and went to some temples. I saw many people. And I thought if I hadn't reached the bottom of life and found complete despair, my approach to life would have been "I am more intelligent than you. I've read more books. I have a better job, and I'm better than you."

But having reached the bottom, my thoughts were, "I was worse then you, I was a worse person then you, I hurt many more people than you. It just became better. I have nothing better than you. You will get better also."

I felt my life level up. I began to focus on helping others and living a life that was purposeful. I shifted my idea about what "worth" meant. It's not about money; it's about offering value to others.

Pain is a Gift

Without the pain that I endured, I would not be where I am now. I am a wife, mother, and have had an accomplished career as a dentist. I'm now on the path to becoming an author, and I know what the future holds.

The pain was a gift. We can learn something from the

gift. It's a process of growth. It teaches you what's important, what you're worthy of, and what you're capable of achieving. When you feel pain or discomfort or unhappiness, don't avoid it. Don't run from it, bury it deep, or ignore it. Just accept pain as it is. Pain is not a bad thing. Do not judge it. Let the pain go through you. We can learn something from it. Pay attention to you. It's a sign.

Clue into those signs. Ask yourself the important questions. Why are you in pain? What is causing the unhappiness? Why are you uncomfortable? Look deep for the answers. The surface answers are rarely the correct ones. You can't just say, "I'm unhappy because my job is terrible." Look deeper. Level up. Allow the difficult times to elevate you.

The Law of Attraction and true prosperity can only happen when you allow it, and when you dare to look pain and discomfort in the eye and learn from it. Be grateful for the difficulty in your life. It's there for a reason and it's an opportunity to take your life to the next level.

My life is ongoing process to level up. I think I'm still going up right now.

We have to develop and grow ourselves until we die. That is our mission. We can have faith that after suffering there comes a gift, a better situation and something good. Suffering is a chance to change and grow ourselves. That is something I learned through my own experience.

Even through hard times, we have to protect ourselves. Love ourselves. We can't blame ourselves or hate ourselves.

Because it is ongoing process. Because it will be better and circumstances will change.

I like one phrase in Bible: 'But he knows the way that

I take, when he has tested me, I will come forth as gold.'
Job 23:10.

We can free ourselves to live the life we want. Life
beyond other people's expectations of us.

And I can be grateful for everything around me, because I
know I could have nothing. All the things around me are gifts.

---

*As a young Korean-born girl I had an innate desire to study and learn. I read
books from all genres and found literature to be an escape and adventure. I still
love to read. My youth was filled with Girl Scouts, art club, choir, English circle
and many other activities. I was repeatedly elected vice president or president
of my school classes. Though I was active, I was also introspective. I wrote in
my journal as a young girl and still continue that practice today.*

*I was raised by a mother who had great faith in God and she taught me to also
have great faith. I prayed diligently, even as a girl, and continue in my spiritual
practice today – which also includes breath work and meditation.*

*Currently, I enjoy music of all kinds and have developed
my mind in the sciences, as well as an artist, and
actor. I graduated from dental school and practiced
for ten years. I still love to read and study Personal
Development, and my current focus is wealth and how
to enrich my life and others.*

*I have spent a month touring Europe and love
to travel, which has brought my family to
the United States for my husband's career.
We have two beautiful children. We enjoy
concerts together.*

www.facebook.com/ariellee99

Prosperity and Love Mapping for Your Home "Creating Your Energy Atlas"

by Sybilla Lenz

Several years ago I was a struggling, unhappy, and broke single mother of three children. I was searching for hope and answers to make my life better or simply a life that I loved. I found those answers in an ancient practice used by kings and emperors. This practice is known today as Black Sect Tantric Buddhist Feng Shui (BTB). It is also known by the title Western Bagua and was introduced to the United States by Professor Lin Yun. I knew nothing about this practice nor did I really believe something like this could change my life to one that I would love.

The philosophy of Feng Shui is now proven to be a science based on quantum physics. If you really want to change your life then change your home or surroundings and I will explain how. I experienced a profound career shift, my wealth increased, and my soul mate entered my life, along with travel and plenty of mentor opportunities. I was so excited about all the changes in my life that I went on to study Classical (Flying Star) Feng Shui and would never think of not doing an annual update on my home or offices.

Unlike other forms of Feng Shui where a compass may be used to assess the environment, BTB does not use a compass for direction. Instead, BTB uses a Bagua or 9 square grid that depicts 9 life aspirations that a person is looking to enhance. I call this grid an "energy template." In his book *The Divine Matrix, Gregg Braden says "There is a place where all things begin, the place of pure energy that simply is."* When you establish a Bagua template on your home, or office, or property you are now the facilitator for harnessing and enhancing energy for your benefit and the benefit of others.

In the study of Feng Shui you will learn that the foundation of all the schools are the five elements, better known to some as the "Five Element Theory." This is the study of nature and the universe, from the foundation of the elements in the forms of Fire, Earth, Metal, Water, and Wood. Everything in our lives relates to these elements, from the organs in our bodies to the colors we look at daily.

Each element has a specific inherent trait that makes up the element, such as fire is depicted by the color red, by triangular or pointed shapes, and by some experts in Feng Shui as very fast highly charged energy. Earth is depicted by the color, yellow, or off-white, or brown and is symbolized by a square shape. Metal can be elements of silver or, gold, or round in shape and white in color. Water is blue or black in color and wavy in shape or simply the element itself in pure form like in a fountain. Wood is green in color and rectangular in shape and wood energy is considered to be healthy and abundant energy.

These elements are important to understand and get comfortable with as they have a nurturing cycle when implemented and a destructive cycle when not used harmoniously in the environment. Another dimension not mentioned here but when used with the elements can have a major impact on the body or environment is sound. When you combine sound with color or the physical elements you have an opportunity to create a prescription for peace, abundance, love, creativity, and joy. Unfortunately when there is an environment lacking uniformity or a harmonious use of color and sound it can aid in destructive or inharmonious thoughts and actions.

When I first encountered BTB Feng Shui and used the Energy Template on my home I was very confused. The template has what appears to be a directional chart with the North direction noted at the bottom of the chart or at the front door and then the East is noted to the direct middle left of the property with the Southeast quadrant to the back left of the property. South is directly in the rear middle and Southwest is in the right rear or furthest corner to the back right with West located in the middle right of the property and back to the North directly in the middle.

In the teachings of BTB Feng Shui there are many good

reasons for the layout of the Bagua but due to the limitation of space it is more important for you to understand how to use this "energy atlas" to enhance your life. Each directional location as described above also has a life aspiration associated with it. For example in the North, career is the desired aspiration. In the Northeast it is spirituality, East is family, Southeast is wealth, South is fame, Southwest is love, West is creativity and children, Northwest is mentors and travel, and Center is health.

Now let's discuss this 9 step formula for attaining a life you love by energizing or changing the Chi in the quadrants I mentioned above. When you apply the Energy Atlas to your home, apartment, office, or property you first overlay the map onto the space. You then start by looking at the North section of the map and see that this area is the Career aspect with water or the colors black and or blue representing water. You look for Wealth and find that section in the Southeast of your property on the map. What is there now? What colors are there? The element needed to be represented there is wood. You may want to add wood energy there in the forms of either color such as green, or plants like bamboo etc. You will continue this throughout the entire space.

When I first started using this form of Feng Shui I also had a huge love of music, and later discovered the powerful effects that sound also has on our bodies. Using color, sound, and powerful intentions will not only enhance your home or office environment but will also change your energy and life. Intention is also a powerful and necessary component of BTB Feng Shui. In the book by Wayne Dyer, *The Power of Intention, the author states "intention is a force that allows the act of creation to take place."* In each area of the bagua it is suggested, for the very best results, to use intention after you have created and changed the area with color, shapes, and sound.

Feng Shui has been a profound gift of knowledge enabling me to have a life that I love and to teach others so they can know that the beginning of change must start at home. Love your space and enliven your space and remember; If nothing changes, nothing changes.

Sybilla Lenz, is a certified Feng Shui consultant in both classical and BTB Feng Shui. She has over 15 years of experience in both practical applications and presentations to schools, hospitals, and businesses. She's the author of several books including: Living an Abundant Life, Designing Hospitals Of The Future, and Welcome Home. Sybilla attributes her own peace, harmony, and abundance along with amazing and positive changes for others to the science of Feng Shui. Visit www.positivelivingbydesign.com to download your own free "9 Step Formula To Increase Wealth And Love".

Forward in Faith

by Kim Ileen Mercanti (KIM)

"I am not afraid; I was born to do this"

Joan of Arc

Warrior, Military Leader

Dedicated to: Michael Arnold and Martin "Marty" Bodrog for their dedication and devotion to the United States of America, Department of Defense (former colleagues and victims of the September 16, 2013 Washington Navy Yard Shooting, Washington, DC)

Joan of Arc was a young lady when she embraced the power within her to fight as a fearless military leader. Her relentless faith and courage made her uniquely qualified to undertake her enemies and win. Like Joan of Arc, we are all uniquely qualified in our own individual ways. Each and every one of us posses knowledge, skills, talents and desires that can be brought into existence if we move forward in faith and believe in ourselves. I am living proof that a "Forward in Faith" mindset will move a person forward in any area of life. As for me, I chose it for my career after a major life-altering event.

Prior to experiencing a major life-altering event, I had it all…I owned a successful federal contracting business, was married to the father of my two children, had a beautiful home and multiple cars (including a Porsche Boxter – I loved that car!), made an incredible income, had an amazing spiritual life, owned commercial real estate, owned residential income property, as well as a large stock portfolio. From every perspective, I was living a dream life. Then, as you may have guessed… my world came crashing down.

It was late 2008, and I woke up one day to find myself broke, divorced, forced to move back into my parents' home, with no car, no money and no idea how I was going to make it through the day, never mind the next chapter of my life.

The hard reality was staring me in the face. The way I looked at it, I could sink or swim. I chose to swim with the sharks. As harsh as my life situation was, I put a smile on my face, brushed the dust off and moved "Forward in Faith," without looking back.

At this point in my life, I did the only thing I knew would help me get through this season of my life. I prayed. I was born and raised Catholic, with a strong faith base. The first day of my new reality, I prayed the rosary. Praying the rosary always brought me peace, and that is exactly what I needed on that awakened day.

The next thing I thought about was to come up with a plan. I have always lived my life to be simple, so my plan had to be simple. I had to take a leap of faith and just move forward. I decided to keep God first in my life, and not look back or think about the past. From that point forward, I began to appreciate life while reminding myself that I served God and not man. I will be the first to admit that this took constant focused thought on the present. Taking action by moving "Forward in Faith" changed my life in a radical way.

As I discussed previously, I decided to stay focused on the next version of myself, and that was to take my career to a higher level.

I had worked in the shipbuilding industry since the age of 14. My father is a retired Marine Engineer, graduate of Kings Point Academy in NY. As a matter of fact, my father even named all of his four children with names that are acronyms. My father is a character, and I had the honor and privilege of working for him for over 20 years. He taught me everything I know today about the United States Navy shipbuilding, which was more of an education than my BS degree in Business Management, MBA and Certificate in Financial Management from Harvard Business School of Executive Education.

Spending twenty years working for my father proved to be invaluable in terms of setting the foundation of my comeback. My father was very strict, and he was harsher on me than any of his employees. But he taught me solid work ethics, how to work efficiently and, most importantly, to provide strong customer support. During those twenty years, I spent five years studying and mastering finance; then another five years each in production, sales and business operations. I believed that the combination of my work experience and education would enable me to bring my career to the next level.

This was the point in my life when I decided that I wanted to start my life over and work in Washington, DC. I next took action in small steps to accomplish my goal. At the time, one of my business associates worked in Washington, DC, so I contacted this friend and told him I wanted to start my life over and move to DC. As I look back today, that small first step of making that phone call changed my life forever.

The second step was taking a temporary job as an administrative assistant, even using a friend's car as transportation until I was able to buy a used car. I gave this job my 110% and as I became efficient, I would continually as for additional work while keeping a cheerful disposition. I knew it would be a matter of time before a better position would present itself to me. Again, praying every day and moving "Forward in Faith."

Six months after taking my first step, I moved to Washington, DC to start my new job at a Fortune 500 Federal contracting company. It was a dream job doing the type of work I enjoyed best – U.S. Navy Shipbuilding. My prayers were finally answered. I was persistent on my part by praying the rosary every morning while keeping God first in my life.

In moving to Washington, DC, I only knew one person, but I wanted to make the most out of this experience. From that day, I made it my mission to meet as many people as possible, and to learn as much as I possibly could from everyone I worked with. I emerged myself into this position with the thought of moving up the corporate ladder as quickly as I could.

During my first month of working at this Fortune 500

company, the Vice President would have an interview with each new employee and an exit interview with employees leaving the company. At my interview, I was shown the division's organizational chart and was told that it was up to me to see myself anywhere on the organizational chart and that the company would support that choice and help me move up the corporate ladder. There it was right in front of me; and I chose to be a Deputy Program Manager. I worked diligently each and every day and learned my job to the maximum level of efficiency. I keep asking for more roles and responsibilities, and after nine months was promoted to Deputy Program Manager. I will be honest with you, during those months I was tried and tested through what I thought was almost my breaking point. I had fellow employees try to prevent me from getting a promotion, was told by management that I was not management material. Co-workers would sabotage my work then report me to senior management for making mistakes, but I prevailed. During these times of trials, I constantly reminded myself that I serve God and not man.

I ignored what I call "outside noise," and kept my focus on the organizational chart. I got myself through the first step; now for the next step. I began to focus my attention of the next level that I wanted to achieve, which was Task 1 Lead (Program Management) of a major shipbuilding program for the US Navy. That took a lot more focus and determination. Over the next five years I gave my life for this program. I worked long days learning this new program and providing a high level of customer support.

During this five year period, I was again tested and tried,

but to an even higher level than I had previously experienced. I was accused of being a poor manager; had people quit tasking with short times prior to delivery; people refusing to do taskings; handling high demand signal tasking of emergent nature on a regular basis; being accused of harassment; and again, held down from moving up the corporate ladder by the very man who told me I could move to any level on the organization chart that I could see myself.

One day, I seized a window of opportunity to speak my concern about moving up the corporate ladder with the past vice president that performed the exit interview. I was accompanying an employee that was leaving the company in an exit interview, as I was his manager at the time. After the interview was conducted, I requested five minutes of this vice president's time. I shut the door and asked why I not able to move up the corporate ladder to a senior management position. I told him that I was being held back and wanted to know what it would take to succeed within our organization. I was told that I had caught him off guard and he did not have an answer for me. I never received my answer, but shortly after that time, this man was no longer working at the company. In fact, after looking back, I realized that all the people within the organization that was holding me back were no longer working at the company. They either left on their own, or were terminated. The takeaway from this experience was to continue to be diligently focused on the end result in order to create it.

The next phase of my career moved much quicker now that I had conditioned my "Forward in Faith" mind set and continued to put God first in my life. In February 2013, I received an email inviting me to consider an opportunity to work at the Pentagon as an Action Officer on the Amphibious Class of new construction shipbuilding. I responded that I wanted to learn more about the position.

I had to read the statement of work, which intimated me, so I decided that I needed a few days to think about the position. Deep inside, self-doubt tried to creek into my mind, I did not even understand what having the responsibly meant, never mind how I would learn three shipbuilding programs as well as the missions carried out by our troops. Well, before I could give my answer, I received the job offer the next day, requiring a decision in less than 24 hours. I was flattered that I received a job that I did not apply for, so I decided that God got me this far, I would rely on him to carry me "Forward in Faith." After all, although this was not the job I was focusing on, it was a great opportunity, as I always wanted to work at the Pentagon.

The job at the Pentagon was by far the most challenging position that I had encountered in my career thus far, but I was determined to succeed and make a name for myself. The first seven days on the job were intense, in that it was sitting for eight hours each day with Marty Bodrog in doing a turnover of roles and responsibilities. Marty was extremely knowledgeable about this position, and on top of that he was compassionate about keeping the troops safe. I had big shoes to fill, but Marty provided me with the tools and means for success. Life was going well until September 16, 2013. There was a shooting at the Washington Navy Yard. I had received word that two of my colleagues were victims. On that devastating day, Michael Arnold and Marty Bodrog lost their lives.

My heart sunk that day, and I still remember that day like it was yesterday. It was surely a devastating day for many families, the US Government, the US Navy, The US Marines, The Chief of Naval Operations (OPNAV) and myself.

After this tragedy, it was a strong faith base and "Forward in Faith" mindset that brought me to focus on continuing the legacy that Marty started decades prior. This was a difficult time in my life as well as my career, but knowing how much these two men unselfishly served their country is what kept me going. There was important work to be accomplished, and I know that I had to contribute to keeping the programs on track.

It was a privilege and an honor to have known Mike and Marty, and to have had the opportunity to have worked closely with both gentlemen on successful shipbuilding programs was a blessing in my life. I will never forget them or the impact that they made on my own life. My heart goes out to their family and friends, as well as all the hearts that they have touched.

In going forward, I worked the next two months on the Pentagon until I received my next opportunity. I was offered the position of Task 1 Lead (Program Management) with the company I had previously worked for. This was the very job position on the organizational chart that I had wanted and had focused on for five years. I had finally accomplished by dream position.

I left the Pentagon and began working at the Washington Navy Yard, directly interfacing with the client. I again, gave it my all to be successful in this endeavor. I worked long hard hours in managing client expectations and striving to deliver high quality customer service. The team was over 100 people, all working at a high pace and with rapid turnarounds. I was in my element and thrived on working with a great team of experts and delivering quality products to our customer.

I always keep my eye on the organizational chart and am laser focused on meeting my next level of achievement. In looking back and considering the fact that it took seven years to accomplish my goals, but as I kept focused, the accomplishments came at a quicker rate. I count my blessings each and every day for being afforded the opportunities to make my desires into reality. I have always focused on the outcome, taking many leaps of faith and relying on my dearly beloved rosary to help me through each and every day. Focusing on the outcome makes it easy to achieve any goal. I am living proof that what you want to achieve is possible. Everything is possible when moving "Forward in Faith."

Authors Note: As I write this story today, I am being considered for another promotion within my organization. This position has yet to be defined, but as history repeats itself, this new position is the next one going up the corporate ladder. But the position is not actually on the organizational chart yet, as it is being created specifically for me.

Kim Ileen Mercanti was born and raised Catholic, and as an adult she rededicated her life to Jesus Christ. Being a strong believer in the Catholic faith, Kim has also borne and raised her two amazing children in the Catholic religion. In fact, of Kim's greatest accomplishments, raising her children will always remain on the top of her list: Andrew is an Aerospace Engineer and Amanda is a Certified Horticulturalist.

Having a strong faith base, Kim has lived her life based on serving God before serving man, and as a "Forward in Faith" believer, will continue to put God first and foremost in her life. In her professional life, Kim has spent her entire career in the Federal Contracting industry, supporting the United States Department of Defense, and currently works for CSC Government Solutions LLC, A CSRA Company. Her current position is that of Program Deputy Director. Kim has an open door policy and can be reached at kimercanti@ gmail.com

A Hymn for Freedom

by Federico Miraglia

We live at a turning point in the history of mankind, and an unprecedented crisis is rapidly coming down on our lives. However, the sky is darkest before dawn, and as one civilization sinks another one rises. Science can be a powerful tool to redirect us to the divine course, if used with the noble intent of pure, objective and injudicious knowledge. A new spiritual Science is emerging and opening the eyes of the ones who are ready to see, leading them to joy, love, awareness and freedom.

Science set me free because it made me believe. This is my story, and also the one of many other seekers of truth.

During my personal research into the non-officially-explored fields of Physics, I came to learn about the Ether. Throughout history, philosophers and scientists understood that we live in an ocean of unlimited potential. Every existing thing comes from this omnipresent fluid. The most relevant contributions to the subject were given by Nikola Tesla, who is nowadays remembered only for a few, less important discoveries. His groundbreaking studies regarding the Ether and its links to the physical forces of electromagnetism and gravity, received a complete damnatio memoriae. Infact, the astonishing scenario of providing the world with infinite, clean and free energy would have caused a drastic and unwanted subversion of the status quo.

In the last century, many other heretical scientists have proven the existence of this viscous and elastic substance, putting forth the basis for a theory of everything that could easily and elegantly reunite all the known forces of nature, without recurring to incorrect, perverse and mathematically inhuman speculations. Math is not a meaningless mental rumination, but a sacred discipline which reflects the order of the cosmos through numbers, shapes and proportions that recur in the most different contexts, revealing the divine Matrix behind our world. The circle, the spiral, the Pi and the golden section are all basic units of this universal fabric, beautifully described by Fractal Geometry. Hence, every physical phenomenon can be easily reinterpreted as an oscillatory perturbation of this texture, as a whirling motion of the Ether: the quantum-entangled field that permeates the entire Universe, the *Zero Limits* point that humanity has been looking for since the dawn of time.

Moreover, the final acceptance of the true structure of the cosmos will radically transform also our conception of Medicine. A century ago, even without including the Ether into their theory, the fathers of Quantum Mechanics peered behind the veil of Maya and found out that reality is an illusion shaped by a self-conscious observer. "There is no out there." The yogis that reached enlightenment described it as seeing and feeling nothing but themselves in every aspect of the creation. We are all one thing. Therefore, the investigation in the external world comes down to the study of Ourselves, wonderful Gods whose inner mechanisms are still shrouded in mystery.

The medical materialistic model of the human body has proven to be completely incorrect. New discoveries have shed light on the profound nature of humans, simply complex, emotionally intellectual quantum beings, able to draw their "bow of rainbows across the waters" with thoughts and feelings, waves of energy which propagate through the Ether: the divine medium that keeps us all united on a deeper, spaceless and timeless level. A new quantum informational approach to Medicine is reinterpreting our body as a marvelous, self-sufficient and self-healing transceiver, an ensemble of highly receptive cells governed by our conscience. The body is an extension of the mind. Our enemies are the false beliefs, not the genes, unfairly feared as jailers in the prison of disease. Instead, they are a tunable frequency, a ductile and malleable piece of information, a gift for you to express in the physical world any desire of your soul. You are above your genes: it's the field of your conscience that rules them.

Any vibration which you accept in your vortex has the power to heal you: a thought, a sound, a glance, a tear and, most of all, an emotion from the heart, the one who speaks the universal language of love, the ambassador of your spirit's wishes at the court of the quanta. An untiring valve for the pumping system of the lungs, a rhythmic beater surrounded by a magnetic field much stronger than the one emitted by the brain, an electrical cloud of intuitions, a mosaic of neurons whose inner microcosm is a masterpiece still mostly unknown. Electricity and magnetism are two faces of the same coin; each of these two forces cannot exist without the other, exactly as mind and soul, intellect and emotions, rationality and irrationality complete one another in a perfect and powerful harmony: when these couples get married, any possibility in the infinite Space of Variants can be manifested! If only we could hear the unceasing symphony of the electrochemical signals and biophotons which are constantly exchanged by our organs to keep us alive and connected to the field, regardless of our unwitting transgressions!

And yet we have inherited a vast knowledge about physical wellbeing from great masters such as Herbert Shelton and Arnold Ehret. We should all rediscover *The Secret*! The body is the temple of the spirit, and only purity and health will ensure an earthly experience full of pleasure and happiness. Everything starts from Food Education and, at the moment, life on this planet is a "tragedy of nutrition." Despite what we have been brainwashed into believing, we are a frugivorous and fruit-eating species and the internal Biology of our body demonstrates it conclusively. Besides, our hands have no claws and are shaped with the perfect morphology to cuddle our animal friends and reap the fruits generously offered by Mother Earth. Gaia is the garden to tender. The Prana, the sunlight and the air will one day be our primary source of nourishment and humans will experience a spontaneous reconnection to the Universe, becoming pens in the hand of the Great Writer. Only the return to this atavistic condition will revive a new Golden Age, where women will give birth without pain, men will work without effort and "the wolf shall dwell with the lamb." No more "fore-bemoaned moan."

The glorious past of our species will repeat itself. Gaia has endless stories to tell, and a forbidden Archeology is now starting to disclose them. History will be rewritten. The ancient mythologies, passed down to the present day, contain far more truths that we could ever imagine, and a growing number of independent explorers are unearthing impossible finds that challenge the orthodox dogmas from the ground up. Many cycles of extremely advanced civilizations have followed on this planet, but we are familiar only with the last one, characterized by war and destruction. A long time ago, peaceful beings lived in harmony, creatures so aware of the Etheric essence of the world that they could break the laws of physics to develop unimaginable technologies. Monumental structures scattered all over the world, mirrors of the sky on Earth, books of stone designed to reproduce the geometry of the Matrix, should be massive reminders of that!

What The Bleep Do We Know about who we are, if our origins have been concealed? We are not children of the random, and the probability that the irreducible complexity of our organism has evolved following a Darwinian process is a non-sense which exceeds the probabilistic threshold of impossibility. Besides, where is the cemetery of fossils that testifies the wrong tries of Nature to create environmentally-compatible living beings? The devaluation of ourselves to mere biological machines, without divine intelligence and accidentally originated by fortuitous genetic recombinations, is not supported by any scientific evidence, and has led to a society based on a rampant materialism. Shocking truths will unveil an unexpected past for our species, our planet and its mysterious moon, which, like an abandoned spaceship, preserves the remains of a lost time, while carried forward by the current of Ether. This luxuriant expanse of lands and waters, gently protected by an atmosphere and a magnetic field, is a perfect cradle of life and has always attracted much attention for its unique features! We have to return to the past to understand the present and choose our future. A genetically-enhanced, DNA-fully-activated and inspired offspring will soon initiate an incredibly prosperous phase for the history of Gaia, and it is up to us to start the change by completely revolutionizing our knowledge, lifestyle and beliefs. "Be the change that you wish to see in the world."

We are mirrors of the world, and by cleaning our interiority we purify the entire system. We are the Universe that becomes aware of itself. We are a hologram, an inscription of the Whole. God is a miraculous state of conscience, the moment when the struggle ends, the joy of being in the present instant, the extraordinary which becomes ordinary, the flow of the quantum flux, the still contemplation of the emptiness, the Peace of I and the abundance that Earth multiform and multidimensional community of lives is ready to reach. God is within you, peak of awareness in the pyramid of the natural reigns. From sleep to awakening, from knowledge to awareness, a quantum leap, through a leap of faith, that will elevate us to Satori and make all suffering disappear! There is always a way out. The therapies of Energy Psychology will free the meanders of our subconscious from the negative programs, the emotional blocks and the fears which prevent us from attracting all the wonders that resonate with the divine purpose of our highest self. Let's go back to seeing the world with the eyes of a child, without the filter of our past, let's go back to Zero and *Expect Miracles*!

The ripples of the Etheric sea are filled with compassion, the force that keeps the atoms together, the essence of the cosmic consciousness, which hears every imperceptible wail of frustration coming from any form of life. Would you believe that, in the depths of the Tibetan mountains, heremit monks, freed and fed by the blissful feeling of their heart, live in a constant meditative state to elevate the vibration of the world? Their vow is to keep praying until every single being on Earth is out of suffering. Even if you don't know it, the Universe is always at work for your own best, in this very moment! He just can't wait for you to make the most impossible wish so that he can take you, by hand, to its realization! Be grateful and ask for more. "If you express an intention, consider it the intention of God. How then could you doubt that it could be fulfilled?" In the world of quanta anything is possible for the one who truly believes, and remember that "if you have faith and do not doubt, not only can you do what was done to the fig tree, but also you can say to this mountain, 'Go, throw yourself into the sea' and it will be done." The truth is that you are free and loved, always.

We live in a world where nothing is what it seems,

and the truth is masked, manipulated, distorted, mocked or pushed away from us. Religion has imposed itself as an intermediary between us and God; sciences as intermediaries between us and our body, mind, world, past and even future! No more intermediaries. Cleave through the turbid swamp of obscurantism and take flight towards the evergreen oasis of verity within yourself. "Γνῶθι σεαυτόν." The truth lies in the simple and beautiful things that are right in front of us, therefore "the real voyage of discovery consists not in seeking new landscapes, but in having new eyes." We are here, part of this amazing Universe. Our mission is to become aware of what is already here, inside us, around us, in order to reach physical, mental and spiritual wellbeing. In my imagination, a new ego-less, corporation-free and innocent Science will rise, pursue pure knowledge and lead mankind to an Era in which the hidden truths will finally be revealed. That's when we will evolve from creatures to creators, from victims to victors. Imagine, In-Me-Mago-Agere: in me the wizard acts. We have been imprisoned in our own ignorance because a lack of knowledge is a lack of power. The truth will set us all free.

The definition of freedom is: "the power or right to act, speak, or think as one wants." I believe that we are like wild animals in captivity, so disoriented and far away from their natural habitat, to have completely lost the capacity to feel their true needs. The real freedom starts when we allow ourselves to follow the path of our heart and live in unison with the "freile" of our soul. Human race, get off your knees and break free from the chains of slavery! "You were born into bondage, born into a prison that you cannot smell or taste or touch." Your bars are not made of steel but false ideologies, which can be broken only by the revelations about the true meaning of life. The joyful chant of the uprising is getting louder and louder, the end of the collective hypnosis is near! "The lion sleeps no more."

Federico Emmanuel Miraglia is a Particle Physicist oriented towards the Science of the Spirit. His research involves the investigation of human subtle energies, plants vital force and consciousness-related physical phenomena.

Currently, he is studying to become a Quantum Doctor and an Alternative Medical Practitioner: Federico's work aims at developing a new Energetic and Holistic Medicine for the Third Millenium by reconnecting the principles of modern science with the ancient traditions of oriental spirituality.

In his free time he likes being in contact with Nature and taking care of his family, friends and animals.

Email: federicomiraglia90@gmail.com.

The Gifted Heart

by Trisha Niedermaier

I am deeply honored and I am so full of gratitude for this wonderful opportunity to write this chapter in "The Prosperity Factor" with Joe Vitale.

How did this happen? I may have to write an entire book about it. In the meantime, it may help you to understand that in October of 2014, I went to "You Were Born Rich" conference by Bob Proctor in Los Angeles, California. The best part of all was meeting Bob Proctor, Arash Vossoughi and Sandra Gallagher of the Proctor Gallagher Institute (PGI). This was one of the very best intuitive decisions I made. These people are the world's greatest leaders in growth and change for personal and professional development. Their love, energy, wisdom and passion reach people through the best sources possible – your heart, your mind and your spirit.

I mention this because I have learned so very much from them as my mentors, and I am deeply grateful and honored to know them. Thanks to PGI, I had the right paradigm when that chance came to become a co-author with Mr.

Vitale. I took immediate action, allowing my heart to guide me.

Now, whether I know you or don't know you, I sincerely want to "thank you" for each and every time that you touched the lives of so many people. Thank you for giving of your time and of yourself in order to make someone else's life that much better.

It is a gifted heart, your gifted heart, that in a single moment, with your pure and genuine care for people, you can change the course of time in a person's life – with warm thoughts, silent action and spoken words from your heart. "Thank you." You are an amazing human being and the heart value you generously share will hold true forever.

It is my hope that you are living your life from a mindset of abundance. I learned to do this. The time that I have spent with my faith, deeply immersed in my new abundance paradigm, is time wisely invested. This new paradigm in which I live my present life is a gift just to know, as well as a joy to share.

The paradigm holds the answers to showing you how to truly create the life you want. If you want to experience more abundance in your life there is a way to do it. Study abundance and study your paradigms until you are the expert of your own paradigms, and knowledgeable how to naturally and almost effortlessly manifest all that is meaningful to you to have in your life, for you and your family.

Love. This is the reason we all do what we do and go to the extent that we go. Love of all people. To promote human growth is a significant way to contribute to our evolution as human beings – keeping in mind that we are, in fact, first and foremost spiritual beings. We are fundamentally the same and the expansion of one is the expansion for all. The gifted heart is completely full of love, experiences the deepest love, feels the purest joy, the most profound gratitude, and everlasting abundance. Much of this is experienced simply by allowing.

You may set the ego aside to allow your heart to step up to the plate. Your heart and spirit work together like a team, and your heart is full of gifts for you to discover and enjoy through this growth process.

There was a time that I myself did not allow these gifts from the heart to touch my life. I did not know how. Logic and being analytical definitely works where applicable but I wouldn't be where I am today if I had not made the decision to follow the leads of my heart. When I came from that heart place, everything changed and continues to change.

Is there some area in your life that you want to improve to it's greatest potential? Are you interested in experiencing increase in your life? If so, then may you take comfort in knowing that you are just where you need to be to get started. With a calm and peaceful mind, look into your very own gifted heart where your natural talents reside. There you will begin to feel and to see the life-changing information that awaits you.

Accessing this information happens through the applied process of study. Study paradigms and figure it out and as you study, you will greatly expand your awareness and grow the greater faculties of your mind. It is the development and growth of these higher faculties that can and will change your very own paradigm to so much better.

For those of you who may not be familiar, and as Bob Proctor teaches, the higher faculties of the mind are: reason, memory, perception, will, intuition, and imagination. These faculties of your mind are real assets that you can continue to build upon all throughout your life.

In Napoleon Hill's book, "Think and Grow Rich," he said "An educated person is not necessarily one who has an abundance of specialized knowledge... Educated people have developed the faculties of their mind so that they may acquire anything they want, or its equivalent without violating the rights of others."

When you read for enrichment you grow the greatest part of you: "yourself." When you allow your mind and heart to grow, you allow abundance in, and allow the new paradigm to begin. This new paradigm of yours will be worth heaven and earth to you. If you are familiar with the very laws that govern this universe, then you are familiar with the infinite creative powers that you have and hold within your heart.

You are the owner of these gifts, so it is you who must decide to release them, allowing them to manifest in your life and then share them with the world. After all, you are in this world for a reason so allow yourself to act on the creative ability that you have. Live a life of prosperity through your gifted heart, opening those gifts that only you have, and put them to work in your life. The time to do so is now.

Embrace your life with love and compassion and embrace you mind with a new paradigm of thinking...get ready to welcome abundance and prosperity into your life!

Trisha Niedermaier is a Transformational Consultant with the Proctor Gallagher Institute. Trisha coaches the "Thinking Into Results" program, inspiring and motivating people to achieve their desired results in life, through a positive and effective coaching experience. Trisha is a partner of Bob Proctor, a leader in the field of personal and professional growth.

The Boy with the Rainbow Sack

by Ivan Nossa

Once upon a time, there was a little boy called Ivankor. He lived near Athens with his parents, who were farmers. He was an enthusiastic kid, always cheerful and in a good mood. He loved playing with his friends and, slightly less keenly, helping his father cultivate the land. One of the things he enjoyed the most was going along with his mother to the town market, twice a week, where they would sell the products from their farm. The city was colorful, full of life, sounds and scents, and these sensations made Ivankor giddy with pleasure. They would fill his heart with a great joy and he always waited impatiently for those days when he could accompany his mother to the market. At a small stall, in an alley just off the main market road, Ivankor and his mother carefully arranged the fruits of their family's work. The goods, the colors and the scents varied according to season. Ivankor was very careful in arranging the vegetables, cereals and spices on the stall.

The colors were always ordered and combined with chromatic skill. His mother was well aware of the talents of her young helper, and she was happy to let him handle what we would nowadays call "window-dressing". Although small, that stall always drew a great deal of attention. It was impossible to pass by and not take a look, or be captivated at first by the hues of the perfectly arranged colors and then by the enchanting and intense scents.

The mother counted and weighed the goods in a careful and humble manner, making sure that the figures would balance at the end of each day.

All this love they put into their work bore its fruits. Things went well. Every time, they would come home with their baskets nearly empty. The many customers, attracted by that magnificence, just kept on coming, and they would grow fond of that boy so full of love and enthusiasm for what he did.

Ivankor knew gratitude. His heart was filled with it. On every market day, he was the first to get up, check the goods and prepare the baskets. Once in town, he was so happy about everything he saw and the people he met that his pulse always raced. He was in love with that world and often he would stop and gape at everything he saw. All those people, always different, who often came from far away with beautiful dresses and exotic perfumes. And then those stalls laden with goods which had often travelled for so long and from places so far away that it was difficult to recognize them. But he smelled the scents and admired the colors. He enjoyed watching the peddlers, who, in loud voices, praised their merchandise. When he met peddlers of animals, he was so fascinated that he was unable to move on and his mother always had to pull him along. His favorites were those who sold talking birds with long green and blue plumage. He didn't know where they came from, but they were astonishing. He knew a peddler with a turban who played with them and Ivankor could swear he talked to them as well. They had become friends and every morning and evening he stopped by for a chat with those amazing birds. He was fond of one in particular, called Cocò, because it hummed a greeting as soon as it saw him. I almost forgot: there was also Abdul's stall. Well, I know that this name is not very original, but I couldn't think of a better one. It was his favorite. It sold Egyptian spices. There were many with hundreds of different colors quite unlike those at Ivankor's stall. He envied those spices a little. The shades of color were quite amazing. And the scents were so strong that they could be smelled throughout the entire city. Ivankor imagined that Egypt was a country full of sweet and powerful aromas. A country you could identify with your nose! Every morning, he would stop at Abdul's stall, make some suggestions on how to combine the various colors and then they would wish each other a good and successful day. Ivankor always thanked everybody, every person he encountered and every customer who passed by their stall. It didn't matter how much stuff they bought or even if they didn't buy anything at all and just stopped by to admire the goods. It was enough for him that he put such care in arranging them. And he always noticed the magical effect of that special word "thank you". He called it the magic word: the magic word of his feast days, those of the town and the market.

Then a downturn year came along. The crops were scarce and business for the town merchants was not so prosperous anymore. Even Ivankor's father's crops were well below expectations and, after subtracting the family's consumption, the goods for the market were less and less. The people at the market were less cheerful, they spent less money and negotiated everything. Regular clients were now stopping by barely once a fortnight. In the town's inns, there wasn't the usual animation anymore. Ivankor had not lost his good humor and, despite adversities, he continued to be thankful. He said "If not for this year, I'm thankful for what will surely come next year."

But his mother had lost that sweetness and serenity that she always had. The stall was half empty, the goods for the market were few. Ivankor, as only he knew how, had to prepare the stall with half of the goods there used to be and make it seem equally full and pleasant to look at. He always managed to do it one way or another, and it was a new challenge every time. But he was sad to see his mother sitting down, with no more smiles left. The market was so wonderful to him!

He thought and thought. He wanted to find a solution. Going to the market with a miserable half-full sack made the start of the day already seem gloomy. Somehow they had to fill that stall and he really wanted his mother to smile again. He stayed awake that night. He snuck out of bed and stared up at the stars until he came up with an idea. He gave his thanks, went silently to the granary and started to fiddle about.

The next day, they set off for market at the usual time.

His mother was busy preparing the same small sack with the goods to sell. At the time of departing, she saw Ivankor with another sack on his shoulders. A big and apparently full sack. "Ivankor, where did you get those goods? What's in that sack?"

"Don't worry, mother. They're goods for the market."

"We don't have anything else to sell. The pantry is empty. What are you bringing along?"

"Don't worry about it. They're wonders for our customers."

Giving a second look, she realized how beautiful that sack was. It had all the colors of the rainbow. In the sunlight, it reflected a maze of harmonious colors.

For the entire journey, his mother thought incessantly about the content of that big sack.

Once they arrived in town, people could not stop admiring Ivankor's sack, with all those colored reflections. They started to smile and greet him, and everybody complimented him for such an unusual and beautiful sack. People sort of woke up when he passed them by. A tiny bit of the numbness and sadness of the last period seemed to slip away, leaving behind greetings and smiles.

Once they got to their place at the market, they prepared their stall as usual with the few goods available, trying to stretch them out to make them seem more abundant.

Ivankor's sack remained on the ground, closed.

His mother continued to stare at it.

"What's in there? I want you to tell me right now!"

"Something to make customers come back to us and, maybe, who knows, even ensure a good harvest!"

"Tell me what's in there!"

"Alright, now I can show you."

Ivankor opened the sack and emptied it out on the stall, revealing just a little bit of wheat and a few tomatoes.

"My son, what are you doing? That sack is useless, what are we going to sell?"

"Try a little bit harder, mum, don't you see anything?"

"No, apart from those few seeds and 4 tomatoes..."

"Come on, focus, think about it!"

"I don't see anything, my son."

"Mum, do as I say. Close your eyes, take a deep breath and look again. Now trust me! This sack is full! Full of all the things we had and all the things we will have in the future. They are all coming together to form a rainbow. Even if it seems small it is a big sack if you want it. It's time to be thankful for the fruits of our land, for our customers and for our entire lives. We have been sad for too long."

Ivankor started to smile at the passers-by, at everybody, at old and new customers. He donated heartfelt thanks to each and every one. His mother decided to trust him and started to act like Ivankor. Slowly people started to come back to their stall, the vibe started to change and, regardless of how many goods they really had, people smiled. And thanked them!

His mother, closing her eyes once again, asked "Son, it works! But for what are we giving our thanks?"

"For the things that have been, for the things that are and for those that will be. For all the things that, if you take a careful look, are all around you at this very moment and make our life a miracle."

Ivan Nossa is from Italy and he is the bestselling co-author of The Midas Touch and The Prosperity Factor. After majoring in foreign languages he became a successful entrepreneur. His love for spirituality and self-development brought him to study Law of Attraction with Dr Joe Vitale. His passion for writing led him to became a journalist, lyricist, poet and author. His new book "Thank you (the power and magic of gratitude)" will be published in 2016. www.ivannossa.com

The story is an extract from his book "Thank You, the Power and Magic of Gratitude".

The G's To Prosperity

by Sandra Petgrave

A key component to living a prosperous life can be found in two words that begin with the letter "G": God - (Also referred to as The Divine, Infinite, Spirit, The Universe) and Gratitude – The secret door to prosperity.

God - The source of all wealth and prosperity.

God has given us dominion over everything on this Earth. This Infinite Power is ever present in us and it seeks to express itself fully through us. Through our talents and abilities the Universe can have a fuller, freer and more expansive expression of itself.

Some people have no clue of this power existing in them. I was one of those people. It took me years of dissatisfaction and discontentment with my life before I discovered this power. It would be accurate to say I had a serious problem with my identity. As a child I knew about God, but I didn't have the belief engrained in me that this divine power existed in me. Nor did I believe that I could achieve whatever I wanted and desired by tapping into this great power that is within me. So I lived a life that was less fulfilling and with what I call self-identity problem. I didn't fully understand who I was and what my purpose was.

As a child our parents give us a name which then becomes our identity. In some traditions great thought is placed on naming a new born baby. The circumstance surrounding the birth of that child or the anticipated future of that child is considered before a name is chosen. A friend once told me a story about how his great grandfather got his name. His great-grandfather was called Njokanma, which has its origin from the Igbo tribe in West Africa Nigeria, considered descendants of one of the lost tribes of Israel. The name Njokanma means "it's better to be bad to people than to be good." His great-grandfather was given this name because his great-great-grandfather was the king and he tried to be nice to his people by eliminating the compulsory payment of part of their proceeds to the king. He wanted people to willing give to his kingdom instead of being forced to do it. Think of it like paying taxes only if you want to. People stopped paying to the king and the grounds of the king were no longer being maintained as before.

On one stormy, rainy night the king's wife went into labor to deliver their first child, who turned out to be a son, the roof of the hut where the baby was being delivered was leaking due to lack of maintenance. The king became very hurt and disappointed in his people, thinking he was trying to be nice to his people, but they paid him back with evil. He called his son Njokanma and this son grew up to terrorize the whole village and lived up to the expectations of his name.

If we don't each discover our true identity, then we'll settle for mediocre lives and our destiny will be determined by the environment in which we grow up. This would confirm the erroneous saying that we are a product of our environment, rather than the ideology that we are a product of our mindset, which is greatly influenced by our environment.

You are not just your name; you are a spiritual being, living in a physical body, with the power within to achieve wealth and prosperity in every area of your life. If you are reading this, then you are responding to that longing feeling inside that knows that there is more to you. It is the Infinite part of you looking to guide you towards creating the wealth that you so desire. Knowing how to access this Infinite power is essential to creating wealth. Thomas Edison was a master at doing this – he learned that through his catnaps (similar to modern day meditation) he could access The Infinite, which he referred to as the land of the solution.

Gratitude – The secret door to prosperity.

Gratitude keeps you at a higher vibration, which allows you to attract more of the good things you want in life. I refer to gratitude as the Great Attitude that nurtures the connection between you and the source of all supply. Having a great attitude is being grateful for the gift of life, regardless of what the circumstance may be. It changes your focus from complaining about lack of what you don't have, to being grateful for what you already have.

For instance, I woke up early one morning to find my laptop had been moved from my home office to my kids playroom, I took it back to my office, opened it up to start working and to my surprise the screen was broken. My first inclination was to wake up my kids and start yelling to find out who had moved it and broken it. I immediate felt this feeling inside of me that said be grateful. Then I thought to myself *'what is there to be grateful for with a broken laptop, I have to spend more money replacing it.'* I quickly realized that I could be grateful that my kids are healthy and only a kid that is physically able to walk would go down to the basement where my office is and take the laptop upstairs. In times of difficulty, consider your problems as manure, when you add manure to a plant it stinks but it makes the plant grow. Every disappointment is a blessing in disguise; you may not see the physical blessing in a bad situation but choose to believe that it is a blessing in disguise, and as such be grateful.

To Sum It Up

There is enough wealth for everyone in this abundant Universe. The divine source of all wealth has given you the power to achieve everything good that you desire. Every answer that you seek is in your heart. Knowing who you are and taking possession of your own mind is the first step to changing your world. Finally, be grateful. Gratitude is the great attitude that invokes the vibration which attracts wealth and prosperity to you.

Sandra Petgrave is a speaker, Certified Life Optimization and Dream Builder Coach with a passion for helping people life an abundant life. She offers inspiring workshops and in-depth coaching programs to help clients achieve new heights of success, fulfillment, and spiritual aliveness. Visit www.SandraPetgrave. com to schedule a complementary strategy session.

My Journey to Success

by Chi Phan

I remember my childhood and my young adulthood as a time where I was quite lost and lonely. My family immigrated to Perth, Australia in 1978, shortly after the Vietnam War, and the transition to a totally different culture was particularly difficult for all of us. My mother started to learn English, but then gave up on it, and my father picked up just enough of the language for us to get by. So I grew up essentially in a household with parents that did not speak the local language.

My parents were quite forceful in instilling collectivist Vietnamese culture into my siblings and me. They had an authoritarian "tough love" parenting style that would leave scars on me for the rest of my childhood and into my adulthood. In order to survive the harshness of home life, I learnt to keep quiet and not ask for anything. We were particularly poor and I remember growing up without a lot in terms of material things.

I grew up in a large family with five siblings, and yet still felt isolated. At school I was painfully shy, found it difficult to make friends and was often a loner. Deep inside, I longed to be in a different world; a world where I was successful, popular and felt loved.

When I left school I studied primary school teaching, but found studying at times challenging, especially since I was so broke. I resorted to gambling to make some money and developed a gambling addiction. This gambling addiction, fuelled by my low self-esteem, would continue to haunt me for the next 14 years. I was so broke at times I did not have money to pay the rent or to buy food. I dropped out of studying to become a teacher (after having studied for two years), and drifted from job to job without much direction. I suffered from periods of depression, and at times had thoughts of suicide. I had no idea what I wanted to do with my life, and I continued this way until I turned thirty two, where a life-changing event would alter the course of my life.

I was persuaded by a colleague to attend a seminar with her. During this weekend-long seminar I experienced healing that I can not put into words. Amongst a new understanding of myself, I also experienced a major breakthrough where I was able to dissolve the deep resentment for my father I had been harboring up to that point. Shortly after this seminar weekend, I worked with my coach in intensive professional self-development, somewhat like counselling, where I continued to experience many more breakthroughs. It was in this period that my calling or purpose in life was revealed to me. I wanted to become a counselor so I could help people experience the same healing that I had gone through.

Shortly after this revelation, though, I began to doubt that I had the capacity to fulfill such a tall order. In my fear, I turned my back on my calling for the next eight years. During these eight years I continued to work in jobs that I was reasonably good at, and all the while I tried to block out my passion and purpose in life. At the end of this eight year period, however, I knew I could no longer continue to live an inauthentic life.

I mustered the courage to quit my job and to start studying again. I enrolled in a university degree in psychology and counselling, and began the next step in my journey. I found that things started to fall into place for me shortly after I started following my calling. I achieved a sense of peace knowing that I was on the right path, and I had a mission to fulfill. Three years later I finished my bachelor's degree with academic achievement, in the top 15% of students in my university.

Soon after graduating I set up my own business. I created a seminar where I now teach people how to achieve success in their lives by following their personal passions. I use the lessons I have learned in the course of my life to fast track people to their own success. The "Formula to Success" seminar is easy to understand and is taught in a step-by-step process. In addition, I also set up my own counselling practice, where I work side by side with other counsellors and healers. Counselling is particularly useful if an individual is experiencing challenges in their life and wish to work with a facilitator on a one on one level to overcome these issues. This then clears the path so they can now move on to achieve success.

Chi Phan, B.A. Psychology and Counselling.

Chi lives in Perth, Western Australia, and is the founder of "Chi Phan Seminars and Counselling Centre," where she works with other experts to achieve her vision of helping others achieve success by finding and following their purpose in life. She does this through her "Formula to Success" seminar, and through the process of counselling. She has a bachelors of arts in psychology and counselling, and she graduated in the top 15% of her class. Her extensive working and education background includes retail, reception, sales, coaching and teaching. You can reach Chi and her team at her business website – chiphanseminars.com.

SFQ – Your Path to Prosperity

by Elisabetta Reist

SFQ: What does this stand for? I am going to explain it to you right now.

S = Spring; F= Forest; Q= Qigong. The basis of this method is the Chinese discipline, which goes back thousands of years. It has helped millions of people achieve health, wealth, love, relationships, and peace of mind.

I am obviously speaking of Qi = energy; gong = work. And what does all this have to do with your prosperity?

SFQ stands for Spring Forest QiGong. The developer of this method is Master Chunyi Lin. When he was in the United States, he realized that this ancient Chinese method of QiGong was too complicated for the Western world, and he therefore created a simplified version of it. SFQ is based on movements, sound, mind, deep breathing, and meditation. You may also add visualizations, and the three fundamental values Master Chunyi Lin added to it: Love, Forgiveness and Kindness. Master Lin's vision is a world without pain and suffering. He was born a healer and he says that we were born healers too! We can heal our world, be it our personal world or the surrounding world. And if we, as a community of wealthy and healthy people, are a sufficient number on the planet, then we can contribute to its healing in a major way, thanks to our high level of energy and wealth.

It is a simple method to learn that gives us the tools to achieve better health. But it is not limited to one's body. In fact, working with the energy is working with the whole human being, not merely the body. The method starts with simple movements, mostly carried out with the hands. We move the energy in our body. Energy should flow smoothly in our meridians, which are the highways of the energy. But many times, the flow is not smooth because there are blockages, which can represent all sorts of things. They may be found in our body or in our mind, and more often in our subconscious mind, which is much stronger and influences the human being much more than the conscious part of the mind.

By moving the energy we are able to break up those blockages that hinder our spiritual growth or any positive aspect of our life. If we do these exercises regularly, the first thing that happens is an opening of our mind. Thoughts might change. We will look differently at our world or at ourselves. Why is that?

Blockages are opening up, or they may even be removed completely. Whenever a major blockage has left our system, we get more space for positive thoughts and values. And that's exactly what we want to happen. Our state of mind will no longer be ruled by anxiety, by worries, or by any other negativity. The more we slow down in doing our movements, the more we get into a meditative state of mind. Meditation brings us closer to the Divine, to the true Source of everything. As you know, everything is energy. Energy cannot be created, nor can it be destroyed, but energy can be transformed. The best way of transformation is that of meditation, of breaking down the barriers found in our conscious or subconscious mind.

Our subconscious mind is very powerful. It's said that it contains 90% of our energy. That's why it's so important to work with it and to cleanse it continuously. The subconscious mind is directly connected with the Divine, which is the infinite Source of everything.

While doing meditations, or the small and slow movements that become meditations, you will get a first glimpse of the Divine with its golden light, and you would like this state to continue all the time.

It's where no movements take place, or where you don't perceive any movements. Energy is always in motion but at the zero level it gets so fine that no motion is perceived. SFQ helps you to get into that state.

At a certain point, everything falls into place. You will get many manifestations of all kinds. If there are challenging manifestations, you now know they are road blocks that are there to help you grow in all senses. Just let go of everything that doesn't serve you. Often this is not easy to do, and you may initially resist changes. Letting go of things that don't serve us any longer is the best cure and way of cleansing. You will arrive at a point where cleansing and letting go is no longer a challenge, but pure pleasure. In fact, the more you let go of your old thoughts, of your old beliefs, and even of things, the better your life becomes. Being attached to old stuff gets in your way. Sometimes it's painful to let go of people, but sometimes it's very healthy. Letting go of people mostly involves forgiving. Work on it as long as you are not completely clear.

One very important thing is also gratitude. Be grateful for everything, whether it seems challenging or joyful to you. Gratitude is the word that opens gates, that lets good things flow into your life. Make a list of all the things you are grateful for. This list will never end.

We said that the method also uses sound. There are powerful sounds present in songs and in words.

The six-word chant helps you cleanse your energy. It also builds your consciousness that all human beings are here to live a good life, to enjoy abundance, perfect health and joy; in other words, whatever comes with heightened levels of energy. The six-word chant should (and will) penetrate your whole being. Sometimes you can hear it in your heart, which is truly awesome. There are other sounds used in meditations, and in the long run they will also become part of you. These higher energy levels will also help you see that the poverty in the world and all the suffering can be changed into a more human world, and that you can contribute in many ways to make the world a better place.

The more people become wealthy, thanks to spiritual practices, the easier it will be to erase or at least lower the incidence of poverty and violence where these still exist. It is the spirituality that makes prosperity a better value. Prosperity is not only being wealthy, having a lot of money and every-thing money can buy. Prosperity stands for a rich life in every respect, be it health, relationships, love and whatever positive values you can think of. SFQ will help you achieve this Prosperity.

Elisabetta Reist is a professional translator, and active in the field of Success, Personal Growth and Personal Achievement. She lives in the Southern part of Switzerland where she works with clients of all ages, to help them release anxiety and experience the peace and joy that comes from being freed from emotional traumas. She's the author of many books including:

- Anxiety, Goodbye!
- Kiss Anxiety Goodbye
- Overcome Anxiety, Embrace Joy
- Releasing Anxiety, Inviting Peace: Small Changes That Make a Difference

Elisabetta provides customized coaching to help clients release limiting beliefs and achieve their dreams. Thanks to her knowledge of various languages, she helps people in English, Italian, German and French. Her personal journey to peace led her to achieve certification as an instructor of EFT, Agegate Therapy and Spring Forest QiGong. She currently focuses work with SFQ. Elisabetta is a certified instructor for level 1 and 2 and a Masterhealer. Visit www.reistlingue. com and www.kissanxietygoodbye.com for more information.

How To Attract Prosperity Through Relationships and Building A Network!

by DJ Richoux

Too many people believe that the path to prosperity abundance, fulfillment and happiness is through hard work to gather and accumulate possessions.

When I was a teenager I dreamed about owning fast cars and racing around in them on weekends. I also dreamed about owning a summer cottage on a lake and travelling to exotic places. I was all about outdoor adventure and adrenaline rushes.

I always thought that James Bond had the perfect lifestyle. He got to drive fast cars, visit exotic places and have an adrenaline rush at least three times a day. You see, James Bond has access to fast cars, speedboats, yachts and the latest gadgets, which he never had to pay for. And of course he never worries about maintaining or fixing anything he damages or crashes like an Aston Martin DB7.

There is also an emotional and energy cost to owning things. Not only do you have to earn and save up the money to buy your dream possession you also have to protect and maintain it. What if someone steals it, scratches it and breaks it. One can worry, fret and be distracted by their possessions. In too many cases, the headaches begin once you finally get your prize when you have to maintain and fix your prized possession. Ask anyone that owns a sailboat, yacht or a collector's car.

When I was in my late twenties I came to the realization that what I really wanted was access to fast cars, sailboats and summer homes. I decided let someone else deal with all the maintenance and fixing, just like James Bond does.

When I graduated from university I could barely afford a Volkswagen, let alone a Porsche (my favorite car). So my first job out of University was working at a luxury car dealership that sold Porsches, Aston Martins and Jaguars. I got to live what I call the "James Bond Lifestyle" in a small way. I was able to drive not only one Porsche, I got to drive all kinds of Porsches and then I got to compare them to Aston Martins and Jaguars. For me having access to all these cars was better than owning one or two Porsches.

The thrill and excitement of driving fast and exotic cars diminishes over time. When you have driven a Porsche for the fifth or tenth time the thrill and excitement is generally not that the same as when you drove a Porsche for the very first time. In economics they call this the law of diminishing returns.

I have also been able to access sailboats, power boats and small yachts through the relationships and networks I have developed over time. The experience I was always looking for was being out on the water, enjoying the marine life and the beauty of the ocean. I didn't want to own a boat and deal with all the costs and headaches of repairing and maintaining a boat.

Around the time I was thirty I discovered that a lot of smart and successful people attract abundance and prosperity by building and developing relationships and networks that give them access to the abundance, wealth, experiences and connections they want.

That is when I came to the conclusion that I could attract prosperity through relationships and by building a network.

That is when I knew that the secret to getting what I want was through focusing on building relationships and developing networks.

By building relationships and networks you can apply leverage.

Leverage is one keys laws of prosperity. **You won't attract prosperity by trading time for money, and you can't do it all yourself.**

Attracting abundance and building wealth is about working smarter, rather than harder, by applying the following principles of leverage:

1. **Financial Leverage:** Other people's money and resources so that you are not limited by your own pocketbook.

2. **Time Leverage:** Other people's time so that you are not limited to 24 hours in a day.

3. **Systems and Technology Leverage:** Other people's systems and technology so that you can get more done with less effort.

4. **Communication Leverage:** Other people's books, magazines, newsletters, radio shows, and client lists/databases so that you can communicate to millions with no more effort than is required to communicate one-on-one.

5. **Network Leverage:** Other people's resources and connections so that you can expand beyond your own.

6. **Knowledge Leverage:** Other people's talents, expertise, and experience so that you can utilize greater knowledge than you will ever possess.

Leverage allows you to attract more prosperity than you could ever achieve alone by utilizing resources that extend beyond your own. It allows you to expand your abundance without being restricted by your personal limitations.

Leverage is the principle that separates those who have prosperity from those who don't. It's just that simple.

However if you want to have true prosperity and abundance you will give more value than you take.

When you give more value than you take you begin to measure success by how much you have given to the world. Adding value to the world by giving more than you receive makes everyone better off. That is how you build true prosperity and wealth. **You improve other's lives by improving your own.**

History is full of accounts of people who have built massive financial empires by taking advantage of others and exploiting the environment, however just taking can never lead to happiness or fulfillment. Exploitation may bring riches, but giving value brings happiness and fulfillment as well as riches – and that's true abundance and prosperity.

By giving more value than you receive, success becomes a measure of how much you have given. The wealthier you become the more you are giving to others. It is a rewarding and satisfying way to live.

"From what we get in life, we make a living.
From what we give, we make a life."

- Arthur Ashe

How do you give more value then you take? One place to start is by asking one question to your teachers, mentors and thought leaders... it's just 5 simple words, but it can and will transform your life and your business…. **HOW CAN I SUPPORT YOU?**

That's it.

But you have to truly "mean it". Your offer to help/support someone can't just be lip-service. It can't be fake. And it can't be self-serving. You don't ask how you can help/support someone – and then never reply to their email. This is the beginning of a *relationship*... and you have to give from the heart (and ask for nothing in return). Remember your goal is to deliver more value then you take.

The next time you meet someone at an event or you are trying to connect online with a person you'd like to do business with, stick to these five words, "How Can I Support You" – and you'll see how your life will change.

DJ Richoux is known as the "Profit Maximizer". Since 2001 he has been helping business owners maximize their profits in minimum time using simple and highly effective strategies. He has an unique ability of adding additional revenue streams to a business that most entrepreneurs don't realize exist. www.djrichoux.com

UpDogLife

by Robby Roy

A few years back, I found myself in a state of unhappiness. I wasn't really sure how I had gotten there. I had a great upbringing, loving parents and did well in school. I had a pretty good career in terms earning enough to live a comfortable and adventurous life. I had many friends. I had traveled the world a few times over. Yet I often felt empty inside. From an outsider's perspective my life seemed like a great one. But I didn't particularly feel that way. I kept asking myself what was missing. Like many people who have felt this way before, I tried to fill the void with external stimuli. I develop some bad habits. I partied way too much and took my liver for a ride along the way. I became stuck in this whirlwind of an illusion of self-pity and loneliness. I started blaming all of the circumstances in my life on past decisions that had led me this low point. I was so tired of feeling that way and replaying the same day over and over again like an old Bill Murray movie. How could I make this endless cycle stop? I had to do something else. I had to make a new choice. I had to do SOMETHING.

You know, a strange thing happens to us in moments of despair. We are put into a position of having to make one of two choices: give up altogether or change in the most meaningful way – the fight or flight biology response. It exists in pretty much every living organism on earth. Down to our cellular level, this holds true. So what did I do?

I made an intentional, absolute, non-negotiable decision that I was going to change my outlook, my habits and my life for good. No more feeling sorry for myself, no more making excuses and no more useless negative thinking.

I immediately started to put a plan in place to set myself up for success. I knew I would have to replace some negative habits with positive ones, so I quit drinking. Just like that. No more partying. Then, I made a second decision that would change my life forever. I decided I wanted to adopt a dog.

For the following few weeks I immersed myself in everything that had to do with dogs. Growing up with pets I understood the lifelong commitment it required to live with a dog. So I read articles, I read books, I watched countless hours of training and educational videos. I made absolutely sure that I was as ready as I could be for this adoption. This part became a healthy new habit for me. Instead of living in a Groundhog's Day of self-destruction, I was changing my paradigm one thought, one action, one habit, one day at a time. I was full of enthusiasm. I had a new purpose in life, something new to look forward to, something different and positive. I was ready to adopt.

I had searched a few rescue groups in the area and planned to go meet a few potential dogs. Then, the most amazing unexpected thing happened. I was so focused on bettering myself, on making this commitment to adopt a dog for life that I didn't even see it coming. Just like magic, my future wife appeared right before my eyes. Now, she may have a different romantic view of how we first met, but for me at the time, while I was happy to have this amazing girl pop up into my life, I was still focused on changing myself from the inside out without needing someone to fill that void for me. I knew that I had to continue on my path of developing new positive habits and committing myself to a lifetime with a dog.

I believe that having that kind attitude when I first started dating my wife was really beneficial for me. She quickly became interested in my self-improvement mission and she loved dogs. In fact, a few weeks after meeting, she's the one that found a dog for me. A big, bear-looking, scruffy Rottweiler mix named Wallace. He was found eating garbage at an old dump site. I called up the rescue group and adopted him. I knew he was the one the second I saw him.

The following weeks and months were all committed to attending to Wallace's every need. I established a daily routine for myself and Wallace. Every single day I got up early to walk him, then a training session, and walked him again at night. Every day! I remember one day it was -42C. I had to put special mittens on his paws so they wouldn't freeze. I was extremely committed to his well-being and his needs. These became my new habits.

I didn't realize it at the time, but I was creating a new life for myself through these habits. The more action steps

I took, in every area of my life, the more I was getting what I had envisioned. This is truly how the Law of Attraction works in my mind. You not only have to envision your ideal life, you need to take action every day. Develop new habits. Even if it's the smallest thing, it makes you move forward. It made me move forward in a way I could have never imagined. I met my wife unexpectedly through this process, without even trying to find her. I built a bond with a dog like no other before. I changed the way I thought and the way I acted. I grew into someone new and thrived.

That is really what the Prosperity Factor is to me. It is about developing positive habits of continual growth in every area of my life. And it all started with a single decisive intentional thought that I ACTED on to change my outlook, my habits and my life for good. And I did.

Robby is an entrepreneur, a coach, a trainer and world traveler. He is very passionate about living a life of freedom and health in mind, body and spirit. His love for personal development has inspired him to be of service to people who want more out of life but feel stuck.

Visit www.robbyroy.life. It is time to discover your inner power and create the life that you really want.

Persistence Is the Key to Success

by Kandasamy Thaninathan

"Wish You a Happy and Prosperous New Year". Year after year, when the New Year begins we wish others, and receive the same wishes from them. Every human being certainly does have the right to live in this world by leading a happy and prosperous life. But at the end of the day, only a few end up truly achieving successful lives. For many it is the same old story. Why?

I had a serene and joyful childhood. I never felt worry or sadness. I had no idea what those things even meant. When I was a teenager, my beloved mother passed away after a sudden illness. For the first time in my life I experienced sorrow and sadness. Ever since sadness glued itself to me, forming what seemed to be an unbreakable bond, I was never the same carefree person I once was. I started to watch sad movies and read sad stories. After a while, I started to enjoy sadness. It really is no wonder I started to silently attract negative energy into my life.

I have had to swim against the tide throughout most of my life. Things always go wrong at the right time for me, and I kept asking myself why? Why? I started to search for the answer. One day I discussed my problems with one of my relatives, Mr. Nadarajah. He is an old gentleman bursting with knowledge, and he has lots of spiritual and self-help books in his library. He gave me a book about Prosperity, and it was the first book I ever read on the subject. And now, many years later, the title of the first book I co-author has also turned out to be "Prosperity Factor." See how the law of attraction works?

The same old gentleman gives me books every time I meet him, and he encourages me to read. As a result, I started to realize there is another world out there; a new world where I have the power to change the direction of my life. I am always grateful to this great man, Mr. Nadarajah, for introducing me to personal development. He also gave me the hit movie "The Secret." In that movie, I connected with two teachers. One of them was Dr Joe Vitale. He touched my heart straight away because he is open, genuine and humble. I joined his mailing list. I read almost all of his books and listened to his recordings. And today he has given me the opportunity to co-author with him on this book. It is unimaginable, but true.

Several years ago I co-signed a particular legal document in order to help a good friend of mine. Even though my friend is an honest person, and had never let me down before, that document eventually came back to haunt me. I started receiving threatening letters all the time. I tried to get help or advice from friends and relatives, but they all blamed me and asked the same question; why did you sign? None of them were willing to understand or even give me moral support. I proceeded to meet with some experts, but they said prepare for the worst, and advised me to find an alternate arrangement if I lost my home, which was now more likely.

I know very well the greatest truth in life. We did not bring anything with us when we were born, and we don't take anything back with us when we leave this material world. Whatever we accumulate during our life time is left behind for someone else. Things are only transferable.

I felt that I didn't have anybody, and I was left alone in the middle of a jungle, completely on my own on this planet, lost. Darkness everywhere. I could only hear the wolves howling in the distance. I cried in secret. I started to feel low and I plummeted as the pressure started to mount. Is it the end of my life? No. Not at all. I should not allow it to destroy the future of my innocent wife and children, because it happened when I was a bachelor and they had nothing to do with it. It is more than just losing my property. The fundamental principle of law is that the "innocent shouldn't be punished." That kept ringing in my ears.

So I turned to myself. I started to talk to my heart. Only the higher power can help me now. So I started to write prayer and affirmations to God or Universe. "God I did not make any mistakes in this matter. I only helped a friend of mine who was in trouble and asked me for help. Please do not punish me for helping someone in need." I kept repeating it to myself every time I thought about it. It went on for couple of years, and the more it took hold, the better I felt.

Deep in my heart I started to believe that I wouldn't lose my home. It is my home and I love to live in there.

One day all of a sudden out of the blue, a case similar to mine happened to someone else, became the headline story on all the news channels and in the national newspapers. It brought huge publicity and sympathy, and the public wanted to change the law in matters like this. I started to see the sun rising above the horizon. My trouble disappeared without a trace. I still live in the same house with my beautiful family. Home sweet home.

Even though everyone advised me to plan for the possibility of becoming homeless, I did not even think of it.

My persistence with the power of thought and unshakable faith in truth in the Universe paid off in the end. You can enjoy the same expereince. Persistence with the power of thought will change your life.

Kandasamy Thaninathan, an Electronic Engineer by profession, is married with two children and currently lives in the UK. From childhood he has had a passion to help the people in need and suffering from illness. He also volunteers as a coach of young children, helping them succeed in their life and on their exams. He enjoys reading and writing, and wants to help introduce the LOA and improve the lives of the people who are still in the dark. You can reach him at kanda57samy@gmail.com.

Wishing everyone a "Happy and Prosperous Life."

From Rags to Pitches ... an Epic Journey

by Nicole M. Whitney

The Rags:

In the beginning... I was abandoned at birth, in a string of eight foster homes in my first three years, adopted out as an only child to a couple who were physically, emotionally and mentally abusive toward me throughout my entire childhood. Homeless by the age of 15 and on permanent physical disability by the age of 30 with three incurable diseases, raising two young children, then aged one and eight, totally alone with no family, no money, no resources, and no hope.

And things actually got worse from there.

Then something amazing happened.

A voice spoke to me in my living room. It told me to build a positive news newspaper... and to do it NOW. I had been a newspaper reporter for a few years by then, now working from home as a 'stringer' or freelancer and newspaper columnist as my health would allow.

The 'voice' incident happened just after my first visit to a science of mind 'church service' and, simultaneously, my first ever meditation experience. I remember it was New Year's 1997, and the meditation was held at 4am with others around the world, with the intention of creating world peace.

I was really freaked out that something was 'talking' to me. It was kind of like a 'build the ark' moment, though. It felt important. Begrudgingly, I moved forward, although I thought it was an absolutely terrible idea. I was very ill and unable to work. I had no money, resources or how-to-make-a-newspaper knowledge. It was ridiculous. This was not a dream or goal. It was literally a calling. And I flatly informed 'the voice' of my feelings on the matter, but did it anyway. The alternative – do nothing and continue suffering – sucked. So I did it. Being that I was coming from the very bottom, I quite frankly did not have much to lose.

I started by doing what I could with what I had, in the consciousness level I was in at the time. Every limiting belief you could cram in their from a life time of negative experiences; that's where I began.

I don't want to misrepresent this process in the early years as some kind of new age bliss trip because, for me, it was not. It was learning, growth, stretching, clearing, reaching, groping, crying, yelling and then surrounding and then succeeding and then starting over at the next level and so on, slowly finding my way. In the surrender times, or the times I was most out of the way, I could hear the voice. Those were the best times. Miraculous times. That guidance and doing what I could to connect with the perfect teachers and associates along the way made all the difference in the world.

And it was magical. Discovering that none of us are alone in the awakening on the planet and we all matter and we can all find our place and we all can make a difference. And we can all take our power back. Yay to that, is what I say.

Most importantly it was, and still is today, a "spirit-driven" event.

The "voice" is coming from a good place and seems to know what it's talking about …. so I listen.

Thus the epic journey began, and continues today.

The Pitches:

In April 2015, I received an email from a company hosting a motivational business seminar I was attending.

It presented an opportunity for ONLY five attendees of the very large weekend conference to tag along on a high end private catered affair with some of the events presenters. For a mere thousand dollars, we could hop into a limo along with the likes of Michael Jackson and Quincy Jones's music producer Thomas Bahler, Croix Sather, the man who ran across America, Oprah's Coach Marcia Weider, Passion princess Janet Attwood, the Branding Guru Gerry Foster and the original 'shark' on Shark Tank - Kevin Harrington.

My original 'default setting response' was "oh my how interesting, but of course I can't do that". It was an instant pre-conditioned knee-jerk 'no' response. And then I caught myself.

I was like hey! Why the hell not?!

Having caught the negative program red-handed, I signed up immediately. I said yes.

So it was my first limo ride …. ever. My focus has always been to priorize reinvesting back in to News for the Soul to create sustainability for the long term, which I have as we begin our 19th year in broadcasting in 2016. I'm not one to be out faffing around on the town in a limo throwing thousand dollar bills around. Not ever. But I said yes.

So we're in the limo. I sat squished in sideways beside Croix and Gerry Foster. Another attendee was on my left and Thomas Bahler was in the back with some other event staffers.

It had been a long day at the conference. We started early and I had to do a remote radio show on the lunch break, so I'd gone all day with only a protein bar to eat.

I was ready to eat my own arm. But my focus stayed locked on to the YES energy. I didn't go back into "look how much money I just spent" and "what am I doing". I just stayed in the excitement.

The magic that is possible when we counter act our programming, stay in the yes, and follow through is nothing less than paradigm shattering sometimes. And this was about to be one of those times.

After about 30 minutes in a limo we arrive at the BBQ. And there was wine.

Normally I would have been more nervous socializing with a group of strangers, especially ones I did not want to say something dumb in front of, so normally I would have been much more reserved. But there was wine.

And as the food prep was taking forever and we were left to roam and chat.

So Kevin Harrington was standing all alone and fancy-free me decided to strike up a conversation.

Fast forward to noon the following day. A different five of us were being speedily ushered into a room of a 1000 attendees, all watching as we took our places in special chairs lined across the front of the room. We sat facing the stage, eyeball to eyeball with the official "Pitch Tank" panel led by Kevin.

Our five product ideas had been picked as the best five potentials that people on the panel would like to back for real and we had two minutes to officially pitch the panel and the room.

And through out the lunch break prior to this moment, I had the opportunity 'practice pitch' Kevin directly. He'd already told me his new Star Shop network wanted to pick my product up.

Say yes! Keep saying yes. And see what happens...

There is much more to this world than we know. Be open and just try not to freak out.

Prosperity Stuff that worked for me:

The following are some of the highlights of a Prosperity Kit I created on News for the Soul about a decade ago. It's a collection of the tools and techniques that I used to become unstuck and move forward to growth and expansion. It's particularly great for those who are at the very beginning as those first few steps are the most challenging. But there's not far to fall back down, so take them!

And there is no arrival point. I find every time you level up, there's new work to be done, more limitations and

unsupportive beliefs to clear. On that note I'm launching a
level two Prosperity Kit in 2016 at www.Prosperity-Kit.com

*None of these are necessarily ground breaking ideas. But
the difference between reading about them and doing them are
colossal. The key for me was doing them. Everyday.*

STEP ONE – Feeling Good Right Now - For Real - whatever that may mean.

As we know, through our knowledge of the Law of
Attraction, we attract to us whatever we are in frequency
resonation with. If we are freaking out about bills and debt,
then we feel that fear in our cells, and that is what we are
broadcasting out to the universe. And when you are broadcasting from that station, piles more debt, worry, fear, anxiety and lack are blasted your way.

But what do we do about it?

I would find the best feeling thought I had real access to
in the moment. That's it.

When I discovered the Abraham Hicks Emotional Guidance Scale, I realized that's what I'd be doing - working my way
back up the scale. If you haven't seen the scale, Google it as it's
worth a look. It shows you where you are at and where you
can go from there… in stages. So if you are at despair, you're
happily looking forward to getting up to anger and rage.

Ask yourself what feeling do you have authentic access
to right now? Settle in and move up.

STEP TWO – Relaxing for real.

Step One becomes the foundation to stand upon. I
scheduled 11 minute time periods in which we relax on the
authentic platform, sinking fully into one level, so I could

access another higher level next. They sink into that one, reach for the next one and so on.

For now just know that altered states are key in functions of the mind and our super conscious mind. It gives us access to more of our power in impressive ways.

STEP THREE - Step into the crap, face the crap and clear the crap.

Many spiritual traditions focus a great deal on the clearing of subconscious negativity

When I first discovered Brad Yates and EFT I was absolutely blown away. In my experience it's quick, easy and provides results, sometimes practically immediately!

I also love Ho-oponopono! Dr Hew Len and Dr Joe Vitale joined me on NFTS for an amazing discussing on the 'cleaning' and healing nature of this amazing technique which I highly recommend as well.

There are many other clearing methods out there and different ones will resonate with different people so find what works for you.

STEP FOUR - It's all an illusion.

"Infinite Love is the only truth – everything else is illusion."

~ David Icke

Conscious awakening was the ultimate theme of the last two decades for me and I've had the privilege of connecting with some of the brightest lights on the forefront of the awakening movement.

It's like David Icke always says. Take a breath. Take a

step back. Look at it again from a different perspective. We are creating our reality.

Wake up.

STEP FIVE - Consciously counting our blessings.

The power and concept of gratitude is nothing new. But putting it into play from a conscious, AUTHENTIC FEELING place turbo charges the results. A lot of people go through the motions of gratitude journaling, merely listing stuff without consciously feeling the feelings in the moment.

STEP SIX - Pure possibility thinking.

As we perch on our authentic thought of the day, we need to reach upward and return to our true natural place of infinite possibilities – true possibility thinking. The trick here is to not let your smaller, earth bound self to get in the way of the process by trying to limit the vision or figure out how it is to happen.

STEP SEVEN - Conscious visioning.

Again, the idea of vision board and goal setting is absolutely nothing new. However, done in conjunction with the Spoonbending intention technology, [the product Kevin Harrington is excited about: www.SpoonbendingKit.com] from a place of authentic frequency resonation, that will add rocket fuel to your fire and miracles will happen.

It's a process where you not just imagine having it, you feel your mind power DOING it. It's like having a jet pack up your butt; quite remarkable.

STEP EIGHT – Spoonbending.

In short, this step goes more in-depth into goes more into the technology mentioned above. You can find out more at www.SpoonbendingKit.com.

STEP NINE - Surrender?

This can feel the most challenging in the moment when things are not in the flow and a deadline approaches. It's also a critical piece to breaking free of that fearful place. In my mind, I would constantly tell myself "it's coming" and to not attach to any one person, place or activity as the source of the prosperity I needed at the time. Source is 'the voice' or our 'upstairs team.'

STEP TEN - See with different eyes

I have an important story for this one.

Shortly and somehow after 9/11, 'the voice' or my 'upstairs team' as I sometimes call them, steered me straight into full on terrestrial radio. CFUN, a major province-wide (BC Canada) radio station, was a talk radio network in 2001. They used to air Art Bell at 10pm PST on Saturday nights, one of the most popular syndicated talk shows in North America at the time.

A weird synchronistic series of events led me to their door, one Dannion Brinkley in tow, to 'buy' air time and take over the Art Bell time slot.

The important moment came once I'd signed and committed to the contract.

One night at three in the morning I woke up in a cold sweat, feeling like I did not have things covered - there was something wrong! I was doing the math in my head and I was in serious trouble. Adding up what I owed, it just didn't work out.

Much to my complete shock, re-calculating that way showed me I had everything totally covered and everything was fine. Just new. Just different.

I calmed down, went to bed, and launched a 20+ career in radio that continues today.

Wake up and see with those new eyes.

STEP ELEVEN - Stay in the Moment

We've heard it a million times, but once we start growing in leaps and bounds it can be a critical element to staying on track.

The reason we begin there is this. As we grow more and receive more – way more than we are used to – it brings with it brand new opportunities for growth. Yay!

I find that for me, if I don't stay in the moment inside my head through it all, the overwhelm can take me right out like a knee buckling kick.

What I tell myself is "breathe…let it in…stay focused in NOW…everything is perfectly okay."

So in summary, feel better, wake up, see with new eyes, stay in the moment, keep breathing, remember that you are actually awesome and don't freak out.

About:

NICOLE MARIE WHITNEY, NEWS FOR THE SOUL FOUNDER, PRODUCER & HEAD HOSTESS – Nicole Marie Whitney is the only Spirit Driven Broadcaster who uses her own innovation at overcoming adversity to inspire, motivate, educate and connect people in all walks of life around the world who want to step into their full power, purpose and potential in a world inundated with negativity, limitation, overwhelm, anxiety and fear in the mainstream news. It's free to tune in 7 days a week: www.NewsfortheSoul.com

and in 2016:
www.Prosperity-Kit.com

To our empowerment...

Overcoming Adversity

by Roland Byrd

"Sweet are the uses of adversity…"
—*Shakespeare*

If you don't understand how to overcome adversity, it can easily destroy your dreams, sometimes your life. But when you understand how to survive adversity, to harness it, use it to your advantage, and even thrive from it; that's when you become truly prosperous in all areas of life!

There's a secret to harnessing adversity, a simple and powerful trick that turns trials into blessings.

Want to know what it is?

Great!

Discover adversity's lessons; use them to grow, to help yourself *and* others.

I know, it sounds so simple. You might wonder, "How does that help me overcome adversity?" and "Just how do I discover lessons in it?"

To start, make a shift and *ask better questions;* ones that empower you.

When life throws curveballs, when something happens that really hurts or knocks us down, we've a tendency to ask questions like, "Why me?" or feel like things are stacked against us. We often focus on the unfortunate parts of the event. The problem is, that puts us in a victim mentality, a place where we give up our power to act because we're too busy focusing on what life is doing to us. In short, we forget how powerful we truly are.

When you ask empowering questions, you'll discover lessons in adversity. You'll reframe adversity because you're seeking a way to use it—to help yourself and others. *Then you're in a place of power.* You're accepting accountability for your life *and* you're taking action on life, instead of letting life act on you.

Here are a few questions I've found very helpful when I experience adversity:

- "What good can come from this?"

- "What lessons are in this for me?"

- "How can I use this to help others?"

These questions help both when adversity happens and with past tribulations. Asking empowering questions when adversity happens helps you pass through it and grow, instead of getting stuck in the moment. Asking empowering questions about past adversity allows you to find new meaning, to take painful or damaging experiences and discover ways to use them for good.

Here's an example of empowering questions used when adversity happens:

Not Today!

That's what I thought as the minivan pulled in front of me and slammed on its brakes. Cars on my left, dirt shoulder on my right—motorcycle too heavy for the soft dirt...not at freeway speeds. I'd nowhere to go. *I'm not ready to die!* Flashed through my mind.

But I didn't panic.

Instinctively I tried to lay down my bike—to slide it out. Not enough time! I squeezed both brakes, leaned hard. I was sliding sideways. Almost down, but not close enough. Moving too fast, ground blurring past.

Impact!

Airborne! Flying over asphalt at 55 mph! That's when over 15 years of martial arts training paid off. I tucked and rolled, tumbling down the freeway like a bizarre armadillo, helmet slamming into the ground every rotation. WHAM! Thump. Thump. WHAM! Thump. Thump. WHAM!

I finally hit a road marker. It dug into my lower back, stopped me.

Bruised, beaten, battered, I laid there; looking at the sky, marveling that I was alive, filled with gratitude. I'd see my wife and children again. I was being given yet another chance.

That's when I asked the first question, "I wonder

what the lesson in this is and who it's for?" I remember it clearly, always will. That question set the stage for healing and forgiveness. It opened me to the possibility that the accident might serve a greater good. People who'd witnessed the accident were helping too. At the least, this was an opportunity for them to give service.

The paramedics and doctors were astonished that I'd come through the accident with few injuries—bumps, bruises, a broken wrist, and messed up shoulder…but otherwise okay. The paramedics asked permission to take pictures of my helmet, to show school kids that *helmets do save lives*. I said, "Sure!"

I could walk, my head was intact, I was able to help others, and I got to see my family again. That made it a good day!

I might have cursed my luck or the other driver. I might have felt angry that it happened, that my motorcycle was totaled and that I was beat up physically. But *what would that have accomplished?* It would have only created misery and anger, poisons I'd have to purge if I let them in. But actively seeking the good in the situation, and asking better questions, reframed the event into something that's helped others and me.

Asking how we can use our misfortunes to help others is a very powerful healing tool. It forces us to dig deep, to find good in situations that might otherwise hurt like crazy. And it helps us get out of our own ego—where we take things personally—and view our trials as lessons that allow us to improve our lives and the lives of others.

Remember:

- Adversity happens. Whether it helps us or hurts us is our choice.

- Overcoming adversity is critical to having prosperity in all areas of life.

- Empowering questions allow you to learn from and overcome adversity.

- Asking, "How can I use this to help others?" and then doing it is powerful! It helps you heal, improves others' lives, and helps you overcome adversity.

If you struggle with past experiences that still bring you pain, use the following link to download a special PDF I created to help you use empowering questions to discover the good in hardship, reframe misfortune, and heal.

http://bit.ly/DiscoverTheGood

Crap happens. We can't control others. Sometimes people make choices that hurt us and those we love. Sometimes nature wreaks havoc on our lives or freak accidents occur. Instead of living in fear of these things, *make the decision* now to ask empowering questions and *focus on* the *good* in life. Remember, what you focus on grows. As you focus on good, positive, or helpful things, even in adversity, you discover more and more good things in life.

That's True Prosperity!

And I promise, the more you *do this,* the easier it gets.

Roland

Emotionally neglected as a child and physically and sexually abused, author Roland Byrd grew up with flawed beliefs about life and himself. At 35 he nearly destroyed his family and himself when these beliefs manifested in a storm of narcissistic and hyper-vigilant behavior. But in the midst of the chaos he had an awakening. He discovered he could choose his own new path. Since transforming himself from the inside, Roland has dedicated himself to becoming the man his family needed, the person he always wanted to be, and to helping others transform their lives. http://www.RolandByrd.co/

Golden Age

by Lev Kozakov

O ur planet is approaching a period in time that ancients used to refer to as the Golden Age. Different calculations indicate dates ranging from 2025 to 2085 (or sometimes further), but most agree that the shift from the period of darkness is happening NOW. In terms of scientific successes, quality and comfort of life we are well in the Golden Age already. Now its time to make the "quantum jump" in the sphere of consciousness.

Many religious and ethnographic sources, myth from different parts of the world and periods of history, be it the Ancient Egypt story of conflict between Seth and Osiris, less known Scandinavian or Central American myths or Biblical Cain and the Abel, describe the conflict between brothers when one of them, led by negative emotions killed another one, being the first person in history who decided that he is better than his peer.

That's how our ancestors passed the knowledge to us – through myths and fairytales, but the concept when one person decides that he is better than the other one is still alive and the lesson of our forefathers is still not learned. The lesson is simple: we are solely responsible for everything that happens with us in our lives but all Mankind is a whole and a misery or a happiness of a "brother" will affect everyone.

Being aware of that we have a choice: either to follow the Cain pattern and to manifest dissatisfaction, jealousy and greed, or "love thy neighbor as thyself". And the funny thing is that most of the people would never admit to themselves that they have been often doing the "wrong" choice. Most would not found any basic similarity between for example judging others in one's mind or greedily abusing the Earth and behavior of Cain.

Many people worldwide are unsatisfied and unhappy. Even in the prosperous USA most people – 80% according to Deloitte's Shift Index survey – are dissatisfied with their jobs. 52.9% of marriages end in divorce. In 2013, the U.S. suicide rate hits the highest rate in last 25 years.

It's a clear sign that dissatisfaction – and therefore hatred – is growing that's why so many choose the Cain path of destruction.

Currently Humanity is destroying the planet where it lives: experts predict that fresh water will soon be unavailable for the two-third of the world population due to water pollution, each year forests area sized as big as the whole country of Panama disappears, seawater fish might disappear from the oceans by 2048, etc.

I believe it is obvious that now it's high time to stop the cycle of wrong destructive choices!

We are on a crossroad before the new era: either to follow the well beaten track of Cain which is broad because it is very popular or to choose a much narrower road of Love, Responsibility and Creativity to the "Golden Age" gate.

It's our personal choice and is similar to the one people faced always, for many many centuries, millions of days and billions of times. The choice is either to be led by Love or by hatred, by Responsibility or by reflex, by Creativity or stereotypes.

Previous Ages brought up people with high level of responsibility in front of what is viewed as "authority". The current era will favor the ones who will act responsibly in front of themselves, which is a "quantum jump" in Responsibility.

Previous Ages brought up people with high demands to life standards, huge consumption and borderless desires. Such approach will be transformed into respect of every form of life and conscious approach to the Nature, which is a "quantum jump" in Understanding and Creativity.

Previous Ages in the majority countries in the world were influenced by some kind of ideology that divided the society and the world into "us" and "them": rich and poor, communists and capitalists, castes, etc. Nowadays the ideology of the humanism and individuality is spreading, leading the Mankind to the "quantum jump" in Consciousness.

I was born in the Soviet Union, and each time I encounter people whose upbringing happened in a democratic society, I can feel how deep the impact of ideology is on the human mind and behavior, and how important it is to allow each new generation to freely form its point of view without any force. In Communist times we were all suppressed with what and how we should think, what to dress and behave. It may seem unbelievable now, but wearing bright colors was considered very rude and in anecdotes jeanswear was referred to as "a garment of the most probable enemy" (USA was implied by that).

Suppressive and divisive ideologies undermine individual self-esteem, and low self-esteem gives birth to fears. Fears create hatred and greed, greed creates poverty. People who grew up with low self-esteem and in a fearful environment pass that world outlook to their kids and the cycle goes on.

Luckily the ideologies and governments that go against human individuality and freedoms are doomed to fail, this has happened time and time again throughout history, and it's a good lesson to remember for everyone. It's because Individuality is much stronger than any ideology for a very simple reason: Individuality is alive by its own virtue while any ideology is alive only as long as its supported by the majority of Individuals.

The new coming Golden Age is an era of Creative, Loving and Responsible Individuals who literally create this era, live in harmony with each other and the Nature. Such individuals are the Prosperity Factors. Each of us is a Prosperity Factor, but to take a "red pill" and start this era for oneself right now and speed up the time of abundance for mankind, or a "blue pill" and just follow the flow, is a conscious decision. This must be the conscious decision of a person to be an Individual, to be Loving and not hateful, Creative and not destructive, Responsible and not stereotypical in every moment of one's life. No government, religion, ideology or any other external power can force people to make the conscious choice, in fact historically they have played a negative role in that.

Yet to come to this stage of consciousness we needed to experience authoritarian and repressive regimes in the world's history. As we can see, this period is coming to an end; political analysts are talking of already fourth wave of democracy that's happening right now, involving more commitment to individual freedom. I believe that the evolution of mankind, as well as (on a micro-scale) the evolution of each single individual, however controversial it may seem, has been a good training for us as a whole, because we obviously constitute a Whole, as well as for each of us in particular. Evolution is comprised of numerous decisions and deeds, and through this process people and society learn. We learn from both successes and mistakes; they are equal forces of the evolution. To facilitate further evolution (as well as to make it more pleasant) we could add a conscious approach to all the decisions and deeds of both individuals and society. Such an approach would generate more successes and joy, and the force of joy generated by conscious thinking and doing would lead each Individual and Mankind to Prosperity.

With all the accumulated knowledge and experience, Individual can now concentrate on the happiness and will easily discover that happiness is in one's own hands and minds. Prominent philosophers came to the conclusion that